King John

King John
THE AUTOBIOGRAPHY

John Charles

with Bob Harris

headline

First published in 2003
by HEADLINE BOOK PUBLISHING

10 9 8 7 6 5 4 3 2 1

Cataloguing in Publication Data is available from the British Library

ISBN 0 7553 1208 2

Typeset in Garamond by Avon DataSet Ltd,
Bidford-on-Avon, Warwickshire

Career statistics supplied by Jack Rollin

Printed and bound in Great Britain by
Mackays of Chatham plc, Chatham, Kent

HEADLINE BOOK PUBLISHING
A division of Hodder Headline
338 Euston Road
London NW1 3BH

www.headline.co.uk
www.hodderheadline.com

Contents

Foreword
by Sir Bobby Robson

When a footballer is world class as a centre-half and can play equally well at centre-forward you have found some player. That player was the incomparable John Charles.

The roles are completely different but he was world class in both. I have no doubt that being a defender you learn what thoughts and movements go into the opponents playing against you but to then put it into practice is a totally different thing. Yet he could move seamlessly from one to the other. A staggering talent.

Not only could he play, he was masterful in both positions but probably his best position was centre-half because nobody could get past him. He was a big fellow, wonderful in the air and read the game very well. It was like playing against two centre-halves because wherever you tried to penetrate, John would be there blotting out the horizon, never mind the path to goal.

The most difficult thing in football is to score goals rather than stop them and he had so much talent, everyone wanted John to play at centre-forward whether it was for Leeds United, Juventus or Wales. He could not stop scoring. That is the beautiful part of the game and is what excites the public. So he played centre-forward for much of his life when I am sure he would have preferred to play at the back.

I played against him for England at Wembley and many years later I had a youngster at Ipswich, Kevin Beattie, who reminded me of John Charles. He never had to foul anyone to stop them whereas Allan Hunter, who went before him, knocked people over all the time. Neither Beattie nor Charles needed to foul opponents to win the ball.

When John jumped for the ball he was the cleanest jumper I have ever seen because he would win a ball without even touching the guy jumping against him. His timing was spot on and he could jump higher than anyone else. It was as if he was able to hang in the air.

When he defended you could never see the ball when he had his back to you, as he was so big and muscular. He could turn you; he used his body to lean on you, turn and go forward and when he went what a mover he was, he really could chug along. He was also a great hold up guy, big and strong and because he was so quick, difficult to match on his runs.

But it was in the box where he was really lethal. He could pivot and hit them on the turn with either left or right foot. Imagine trying to mark a guy like that in the box, he just knocked you over.

Yet John had such a delicate touch for such a big man. You get that sometimes with big players like Duncan Edwards and Kevin Beattie – but they are few and far between.

I played against him at Wembley and he was awesome.

Where was he in the world's pecking order? He was right up there with the very, very best, Pele, Maradona, Cruyff, Law, Di Stefano,

Best, Puskas . . . you had to put John Charles in the same category, very high up indeed. He was in the same class but how many of them were world class in two such different positions. The answer to that is easy. None of them!

It was sad from a British point of view his five best years were abroad with Juventus and with no television we could only watch him at internationals and on his rare trips home.

You don't go abroad and get called King John for nothing; you have to earn that one. No one is going to call you a name like that unless you deserve it and when you think of all those great players who performed in Italy, it is a measure of the man that he is still recognised and still rated up there with the very best in the history of their game.

He and Sivori were lethal together for Juventus and very hard to mark the pair of them. I played against Sivori and admired him at first hand but he was wild and spat at me in Turin when I played against the Italian League for the Football League. I was right-half and he was inside-left and I saw at close hand how good he was. He was some player but with a nasty temper. He was the perfect foil for John who was always so calm and unruffled.

On top of everything else John was and still is a lovely man. We should all kneel at the feet of King John, the Gentle Giant.

Introduction

John Charles is universally known as the Gentle Giant, but in Italy these days he is quite simply Il Re – The King. It is hard to imagine just how popular he remains in a country where he played for just five seasons, and that a long, long time ago, but the passing years have not diminished his fame in any way. As we walked down the streets of the little town of Biella, nestling at the foot of the Alps, an hour away from Milan and Turin where he played with such distinction for a Juventus side in their absolute pomp, children and adults alike ran up to him to say hello.

Admittedly, Big John still cut an awesome and easily recognisable figure – tall, white hair swept back, broad shoulders and enchanting smile lighting up a face with the strongest of features – but it still came as a surprise as local inhabitants almost exploded with joy at seeing him again. There were cries of 'Il Re! Il Re!' as they jumped up from their seats in the street cafés, where they were enjoying the autumn sun before the snow came.

What was truly amazing was the age range of those who leapt to their feet to pat him on the back or shake his hand. From callow youth to grizzled veteran, they all knew and respected this hero of the past. No reminders were required. They knew that here was someone special.

During this visit to Italy, John's former Juventus team-mates were eager to see him again, too, and to let him know there is a permanent place waiting for him if ever he decides to see out his remaining years in Italy instead of watching his equally beloved Leeds United at Elland Road.

Former defender Benito Boldi was always on hand to guide John and his wife Glenda around the city, taking them for dinner, to meet old friends and generally looking after them. Why not? Boldi broke his leg as a player with Juventus at a time when that sort of injury more often than not meant the end of a career. It did in his case. John helped Benito set up what is now a successful business in Italy and Boldi never tires of saying thank you in the most practical of ways.

Bruno Garzena, another of the brilliant Juve team that won three Italian titles, insisted on entertaining John and everyone in his party to lunch in Turin. He told me, 'My memories of John are of a friend. He was very special for us. Our team was built on friendship and we were able to talk openly to one another, and to shout at each other – but we were friends.

'John was born to play football for all of his life, so it is easy to come up with memories. I remember when we won the first championship in John's first year with Juventus. It was an extra-ordinary year. I have seen many other players in the years that followed – Platini, Maradona, Altafini and the rest – but I still think no one has ever equalled what John did in the first season. No one.

'We were team-mates and we were so happy and everyone loved John because he was helping us to win, but for me it was different. I became closer to John after I finished playing football. I remember for twenty years after I finished playing, we would call him and invite him to come and play in charity matches and he would always come. The relationship stayed strong for all those years and more.

'I was known as a strong player but when we met on the training ground, I quickly discovered how strong John was! He was a very special player, fabulous.

'Even now, Italians remember him as a legend. They admired his football skill and loved him as a person. The first thing they saw about him was his size but he was soon seen to be a gentle giant. It contributed to their good memories of John. He knew how to make himself loved. Every time I see him, I see part of my youth because the only time I talk about football and my youth is when John comes to Italy.

'Comparing him to modern footballers makes John even more special because modern football is empty and sad with no strong friendships. Players are now like work colleagues, and that is not the same as being real friends.

'King John is a good name for him because he not only looked like a king, played like a king and was thought of by his admirers as a king, but just like a king, he never bothered to carry any money in his pocket! Unlike most of us, money was not his top priority. He was different. He was genuine and honest – always, not just when it was convenient.

'This is why we all remember him with such affection, even Sivori. John belonged to another league; he was extraordinary, in a different dimension. That's all. That is the only thing I could say.

'Even when we played away from Turin, John was well received by all the fans – even when it was a long way away like Sicily. In

Florence, he ran into the goalpost. The entire goal frame rattled. John collapsed to the ground and lay still, like he was dead. The whole stadium was silent. There was nothing, no noise, everyone held their breath. They thought John was dead.

'After a few moments the trainer ran on with the water and threw it in his face. John slowly got to his feet and the entire crowd stood up and cheered, everyone, even the Fiorentina supporters who do not love Juventus at all. The end of the story is that they had to repair the goalposts and John was fine. But I will never forget the silence.

'When we were in Rome recently, everyone knew John. Like Ulysses, he is mythological.

'Today he is just like the man I knew forty years ago. He hasn't changed. He will never grow up – I mean that in the nicest way, of course. He will always be the same. When I see him and when we talk, I start talking the way we used to talk, like players, which I find really odd.

'To be honest, there is not much to hide. I should talk philosophically about him, his life, and his drive to do things without having any particular target. He was like that as a player. He'd just go out and play. Very clean, very honest.

'I am delighted that he was so lucky as to meet Glenda. John? He expected to meet a lady like that; he took it for granted, as he did most things. It was natural. It had to happen to him. It changed his life.

'What else is there to say other than the fact that every footballer, every postman, every person in Italy who likes football will love the man forever! First the man. After, the player.'

Up in the lush green hills overlooking Turin, we came to the spectacular home of the great Giampiero Boniperti, a footballing god of one half of Turin (the Juventus half, of course). He opened the security gates himself to welcome John with open arms rather than meet him in the club offices down in the town.

It is with Boniperti and Sivori, the Argentinian-Italian, that the Charles name will be forever linked, for these are the 'Three Kings' who served the 'Old Lady of Juventus' with such stunning distinction. It was Boniperti who dropped back from his striker's role to allow the Gentle Giant to take his place as centre-forward, and it was Boniperti who made sure no opponent was daft enough to take advantage of his team-mate's reluctance to meet physical violence with physical violence.

Throughout his entire career, whether playing at centre-half or centre-forward, John Charles was not only never sent off but he was never even cautioned, and the Italian League was not exactly known in those days for its gentle approach to the art of football – just ask Joe Baker, Denis Law, Gerry Hitchens or Jimmy Greaves what they thought about the darker side of Serie A. Boniperti took it upon himself to protect John and protect him he did. You don't forget a relationship like that.

Boniperti said, 'Here, without doubt, is a very great man, a footballer up with the other gods – Pele, Di Stefano, Puskas, Maradona, Eusebio, Best – but one who, because of limited international exposure with Wales, does not dominate the spotlight at home in Great Britain. But in Italy – ah! That's a different matter.'

After a pause, he added, 'If there is another John Charles anywhere in the world today, I would carry him on my shoulders all the way back to Juventus.'

But much as the Italians would love to claim him as their own, they cannot. Wales want him, with Swansea, the place of his birth, and Cardiff, where he lived and played, battling for the honour with Hereford and Merthyr Tydfil, where he graced the grounds and doubled the gates.

Leeds, too, want their share because they nurtured him, brought him on and even tried to bring him back to rekindle the old glory days. Jack Charlton was at Leeds and saw the man up close. He is unequivocal in his opinion, saying, 'Whenever people talk of the most effective British player of all time they think of George Best or Our Kid. They forget John Charles. While everybody else just played the game, he went out and won matches on his own. He was the best.'

Ace goalscorer Jimmy Greaves said, 'If I were picking my all-time great British team, or even a world eleven, John Charles would be in it.'

Praise like this is met with a shrug by the legend himself, and prising the words out of him for this book was no mean feat, not because of his Alzheimer's but because of his incredible humility. He simply says, 'Only grandfathers remember me now.' Modesty becomes him and he would never acknowledge that those grandfathers have passed on the legend to their children and their children's children.

This, however, is the true story of the living legend, the Gentle Giant, warts and all. All rise for the King!

Bob Harris, May 2003

CHAPTER ONE

Swansea born and bred

My life began in Swansea. It was there that I was born, brought up, schooled and, at fourteen, joined Swansea football club where I hoped, rather than expected, to play my football. Strange then to realise that I never played a single senior game for the club.

When I daydreamed about football and footballers, I focused on the local Vetch Field and Swansea, or sometimes Wales at Ninian Park, or, more exotically, the World Cup. It was natural in those days. You supported, and hoped to play for, your local team. There was no television and little radio to seduce a football-mad youngster away to one of the great English teams or, even more perverse, a team abroad. Juventus? Real Madrid? Hungary? Brazil? No. My world was Swansea and Wales.

It was all inevitable. I arrived on 27 December 1931, the first son and second child of Ned and Lily Charles. I was christened William

John Charles and joined my sister Maureen in our little house in Alice Street, in the hills of Cwmbwrla, overlooking the seaport of Swansea in South Wales.

I was christened William but for as long as I can remember, I was called John. Brother Melvyn, who also went on to play for Wales, followed me on 14 May 1935, then sister Avril, and, finally, little brother Malcolm was born considerably later, in 1945.

Malcolm had great potential as a footballer, but didn't make it. I don't know why; it was just one of those things. Mel and I had the breaks but he didn't. I wasn't around a lot to find out why because I was in Leeds when he was coming through as a young footballer, but enough people told me how talented he was and that he would be the third Charles to become a professional footballer.

As children, Mel and I were close. He would follow me everywhere and would do what I did, whether it was a paper round or joining the army cadets at Manselton Senior School. But, like all brothers, we also used to fight, particularly as we got older. I would boss Mel around and sometimes I probably carried it too far, especially when I tried to steal his rabbit after mine had died.

We would always play football together, especially during school holidays. It didn't matter if it was on the street with an old tennis ball or in the park in Pentregethin Road. When we started there'd just be a couple of us, but we'd often finish with dozens playing. That was all we did from dawn to dusk: play football. But at least Mam and Dad knew where we were and that we were safe.

I wasn't really surprised that Mel followed me into football, but I saw little of him once I had moved up to Leeds – although there was a time when I thought he might join me there. Needless to say, when I went to Italy I hardly saw him at all, other than when we played together for Wales. While I was out in Italy, he got his big break at Arsenal, and he was a star in the 1958 World Cup. It was only when I joined Cardiff City from Roma that we played in the same side together on a regular basis. Throughout it all, he was a good brother and we got on well.

That was the Charles family, a cosy happy little group. Like all the families around us, we scarcely set foot outside our local environment. There were virtually no cars, just the occasional bus, the odd bicycle and horse and cart. If my parents travelled ten miles that was considered a long journey on the bus. They didn't have bicycles and the local area was our world. It was always a privilege to go into Swansea from where we lived. We were always hoping that our mother would take one of us with her when she went shopping. If she did it was wonderful – a walk around town. We lived about ten minutes on the bus from the city, which doesn't sound a lot now, but then it was one helluva long way.

All I wanted to do from the moment I could walk and talk was to be a footballer. I felt that I was born to play football, but then I suppose most youngsters did at that time. I played football right from when I can remember, whenever and wherever I could. It was not surprising because the game was big in Swansea in those days, every bit as big, if not bigger, than rugby. Swansea produced Welsh international footballers off a conveyor belt.

With no television, computer games or anything remotely similar, sport dominated every boy's life, and when we weren't kicking a ball on the local playing field, Cwmbwrla Park, or at school, we were kicking a rolled-up ball of rags in the street, wrecking our shoes in the process. Cinema was an expensive alternative because if Mam and Dad allowed one of us to go, they would have to let everyone go, and the money did not run that far.

It was nice to have a birthday around Christmas when we were on school holidays but not so good in terms of presents with the football boots or the football being for both celebrations rather than just for one. On the other hand, if someone was given a football, he was suddenly the most popular boy in the district. He would decide where and when we played, who was in his side and what time he called an end to the game and went home for his supper. You were never without a friend in Swansea in those days if you had a football.

Any item of sports equipment was treasured. Cricket bats were a luxury and, just like the boy with a football, the owner would have more friends than most. Even a tennis ball was sought after because it could be turned into a football for two- or three-a-side matches, or used for cricket.

I suppose life was tough but we didn't realise it. What did we have to compare it with? It was far tougher for the parents who had to provide us with the basic necessities of life. Dad was a miner and did not earn a great deal, but also the war was a great intrusion. Even if you'd had the money, there would not have been a lot to spend it on. Having sons like us can't have helped. Once when Mel and I went off to the park for our usual game of shooting-in, we used a pair of new shoes as goalposts, forgetting to pick them up as we ran off home in the gathering gloom. Dad had to go back in the dark to search for them and, not surprisingly, they were nowhere to be seen. A new pair of shoes in those days was a rich prize indeed, whether or not they fitted the lucky recipient.

I had a Sunday morning paper round. In Alice Street, we had a paper shop opposite us and I was paid a couple of pennies a week. It used to be a two-mile stretch with a big heavy bag, and a much easier walk back with the empty bag. Having a bike, like a football, put you in a different stratum from the rest. There was no chance of me having a bike. I was allowed to keep the money I earned from the paper round in lieu of pocket money. Put simply, my parents could not afford to give us pocket money and anything we had was earned – digging gardens for a shilling, things like that.

Junior school at Cwmdu came and went in the usual humdrum way. I was never clever at school, spending far too much time reading sports books hidden inside textbooks, or simply staring out of the window dreaming of the next kickabout. It was not until I moved to Manselton Senior School, aged eleven, that at last I began playing organised football. That was one of those daydreams fulfilled.

School livened up immediately the bell sounded for the breaks and for lunch when we all piled out and argued about who would play in which sides in our daily games in the school playground. It was all great fun, even if the lessons did interrupt the games. I enjoyed the gardening lessons, but quickly lost interest once I left school. One thing I was disappointed about later was that while at school, I did not learn my native language. We had one lesson a week and that was simply not enough. Perhaps I am being unfair; the interruption of the war has to be taken into account, but it explains why, for many years, Welsh was scarcely spoken by so many youngsters.

Everything we did as schoolchildren seemed to revolve around football. In the playground, the local field, or even walking down the street, we would be kicking a ball, a stone or whatever else presented itself. It was so obvious that a local schoolteacher, Mr Beynon, who used to play football with my dad, invited us to go round to his school after hours for special practice. This was exciting as Mr Beynon was in charge of the Swansea Boys' team.

We would rush through our homework in the lunch hour and, as soon as the school bell rang in the afternoon, we would race off to St Helens for our special training. Afterwards, we'd go over to Cwmbwrla Park to try out our new tricks until the light gave out completely.

Dad must have wished I had stayed in the park instead of playing in Alice Street when the window shattered as he was reading his evening paper. He rushed out and found me standing open-mouthed in front of the damage – wearing just my left shoe. It wasn't the football that had gone through the sitting-room window but my right shoe because I didn't have the laces to keep them on. It wouldn't have been so bad but a few days earlier I had been playing with a spinning top when I whipped it so hard that the top took off and crashed through a neighbour's fanlight.

The funny thing was that I was small for my age. It wasn't until I was fifteen or so that I really started to grow. It was an oddity because, a while later, Mel did exactly the same thing, growing a staggering five inches in a single year. It was no huge surprise at home because both of my grandmothers were over 6ft tall, one of them standing 6ft 5in in her slippers.

When Dad first took me to Manselton, he told them I could be a naughty lad at times, and to let him know if I strayed. I didn't play up, not because I was frightened of Dad, but because I would not do anything that might interfere with my chances of playing football, or cricket, but that does not mean I had no adventures.

The very first time I missed a football match through injury was after I had been given some money to buy myself a bag of sweets after doing some chore or another for my dad. To reach the shop I had to pass a house where there was an old dog. He was a terrier and almost blind. He and I were pals and I always used to stop to pat him and speak but on this occasion he must have thought I was going to tread on him and he turned on me, bit me and left me with a nine-inch gash on my shin.

I ran back home where my worried mam bandaged me up and called for a neighbour to drive me to the local hospital in his car, and there I stayed, missing two school matches. But for those games, I was more worried about my old friend than I was about the cut on my leg.

Another time, Mel and I were playing on a building site on a new housing estate. We decided to move a large paving stone because it was in our way. It was a struggle as we hefted it up off the ground until Mel lost his grip and the heavy stone fell on my foot from a height of about twelve inches. I was wearing those old-fashioned canvas gym shoes at the time, and it was agony. It was a day or two before I could put my shoe back on, never mind kick a football.

I must have been a bit of a jinx because there was another incident in Cwmbwrla Park just before my first representative appearance for Swansea Schoolboys. The lace in the old ball had come undone and worked itself loose, so that it was flapping about dangerously. It was decided that we should cut it off and I held the ball while a friend sawed at the leather lace, only for the knife to slip, slitting open my arm in the process.

Again, I ran off home with blood dripping from the wound. I imagined I was bleeding to death and my dad rushed me round to Dr Anderson who, by coincidence, was a former Scottish amateur international footballer. He seemed more interested in the upcoming game on the Saturday than my arm, and chatted away about it while he bound up the wound, assuring me that a little cut like that was not going to stop me playing.

Life was full of little disasters as I discovered again when, on the bus home, I put my bundle containing my boots in the luggage rack downstairs while I went upstairs with the other lads, fooling around until it was my stop. I rushed downstairs, grabbed my boots and ran home to Alice Street. There, to my horror, I discovered I had picked up the wrong parcel and had a bundle of old clothes. Desperately upset, I rushed around to the police station, and there were my boots. Boy, was I relieved, but not half as relieved as the lady from the second-hand clothes shop whose bundle of merchandise I had taken home.

These days I suppose I would be branded a young hooligan and, indeed, it all makes me sound like a right villain, but I was not. The only time I really let myself slip was when I had a bust-up with Mel over the arrangements for splitting the proceeds from our penny-for-the-guy efforts. It was no holds barred until we sorted that little problem out.

More often than not it was me who came back battered and bruised, with the occasional black eye, because I would rather walk away than fight with the other lads. I didn't want to fight – I wanted to play football; I wanted to master all the tricks I could with the ball, any ball I could get my hands on. My attitude to football was formed during my time at secondary school. I was very much a team player and was usually the peacemaker rather than the aggressor.

It did not matter what the weather was like. Rain, snow or shine, I would be out there in the park with the ball, juggling, shooting and heading until it got too dark to see and then I would return home, caked in mud, looking as though I had just got back from a hard day at the pit face.

I even managed to suffer an accident after one of my solo training sessions when I discovered a short cut from the park home that entailed climbing over a farmer's sheds. Unfortunately, the roof collapsed and I fell on, and killed, a dozen chicks. Another time, I climbed through some barbed wire and sliced open my leg, needing six stitches. Even then I hadn't learned my lesson and was cut up again when I laced the ball incorrectly and gashed my head heading it, requiring another half dozen stitches in a gaping wound the day before I was due to play for Swansea Schoolboys. I was fretting whether or not I would be able to play and my dad told me I could, but to be careful. I was lucky. I played a blinder and, at the same time, learned how to lace a football properly.

Dad was a good man to go to for advice because, in his day, he was reckoned to be one of the best amateurs in Wales, playing for

Llandrindod Wells and Swansea Alexandria. He had amateur inter-national trials for his country and also made the odd appearance for Swansea. The life of a professional footballer was not so rewarding in those days as it is now, and Dad chose instead to stick at his arduous work in the local steelworks to feed and clothe his growing family, and a broken leg sealed it. He admitted to me later that it was a mistake because soon after I was born, he was thrown out of work, a fate he suffered more than once in his hard life in Swansea.

Dad, like me, played almost everywhere on a football pitch, and he encouraged both Mel and me to be as versatile as him because, he said, it increased your chances of getting a game. There were no substitutes in those days, and adaptable players could be selected anywhere.

When football was not on the agenda, I ran, swam and played cricket. I was quite a quick bowler and could handle the bat as well. There were two wickets in the local park, one a lump of concrete where we laid a blanket of matting, and next to it a grass strip for the big boys. The school played on the concrete, never on the grass.

Cricket was popular in Swansea and thousands came to watch the big games. There was no charge and on a nice afternoon, families would pack the grassy banks and eat their picnics while the kids played and Dad watched the match. It made the cricket more enjoyable to play with people watching. When I was a little bit older, I enjoyed watching Wilf Wooller play for Glamorgan.

I carried on playing the game until I moved to Italy. I played club cricket in Swansea and then league cricket to a high standard while I was playing football for Leeds. The seasons were clearly defined, with a proper summer gap for those who wanted to double up – and plenty did. At the time, several top footballers also played top-class cricket, including the Compton brothers, Denis and Les.

Inevitably with my size and strength, I was a fast bowler, and quite quick with it. I frightened the batsmen a bit although I was gentle with them, but I was quite capable of putting in a few lively bouncers if the batsman was sticking. I was also a big hitter, going in at five or six to have a whack and hope for a quick 30 or 40. I loved fielding, especially in the slips because I had a good eye and big hands.

I enjoyed tennis but we had to pay to play on the local courts, and to rent the old wooden rackets, so we missed out because we could not afford it. That is why we do not produce too many tennis champions in Britain – it is too expensive for the children of working-class families to play. Those who do play, and it hardly seems to have changed in all these years, are generally from middle-class, comfortably off families whose children, with few exceptions, do not have the hunger to get to the top. To them, it's a social sport. We dismissed it as a ladies' game but only because we couldn't afford to play.

We also did a bit of swimming. After school dinner at Manselton, a group of us would run off to Gors Avenue and go swimming in the local pond, called 'Coffin Pond' because it often had a dead dog or two floating in it. Goodness knows why. If it was occupied in such a way, we would simply nip off to the next one, called 'Carrot Pond'. Don't ask me because I don't know!

We never paid much attention to the war until Swansea was blitzed by the Germans for three nights in succession. I suppose it was the docks they were after and they pounded away at our city for those three unforgettable nights in a row. It was very scary. We had a shelter at our house in Alice Street – but in fact, that was a fancy name for the coalshed. All our neighbours piled in as well when the sirens sounded while Dad went off to deal with the incendiary bombs. Sometimes we dived for cover under the table in the kitchen.

It was a hearty, stout, oak table, which came to the rescue of Mel and me one day when the roof caved in around us as the bombs shook the very foundations of our row of houses.

We had begun to wonder if the bombing was ever going to end and what was going to happen to us when it stopped as suddenly as it had started, but it had made its impact. It was terrible, very frightening, and there were no objections from me when, aged nine, I was shipped off with my mates to 'somewhere safer'. In other words, we were evacuated, taken away from our homes and schools and dropped off somewhere strange – in the country.

I was a growing lad, although still the smallest and youngest in the school team, and travelling outside Swansea was a great adventure. I was sent to a little place called Nantdereidy, along with my friend Glyn Davies. It was quiet and peaceful, a really lovely little farm – but not a goalpost in sight.

It was great having Glyn there, and I thought we would be kicking about all the time. He was as keen on football as I was, and went on to play for Derby County. The only problem was that we did not have a football and were, once again, forced to use anything that was round, usually some newspapers tied up in a ball. Down that way, in north Pembroke, we were in rugby territory but there was not even a rugby ball to play with – not that I was attracted to rugby at all. I was a football man through and through.

I couldn't wait to get back home, even though Nantdereidy was a delightful place. When I look back, it brings back excellent memories, especially of the summer. It was a proper farm with cows and sheep, and I helped about the place, carrying the milk in pails and things like that. It was an unbelievable experience for a city boy like me.

I was there for about a year before I returned to Manselton School. I liked Manselton. In fact, I enjoyed myself there so much that when I won my very first Welsh cap, I took my red shirt back to the school and presented it to them to keep. As far as I know it is still there, locked away in a cupboard somewhere and brought out for show every now and again. The idea was to say thank-you for what they had done for me, and I hoped the sight of a Welsh shirt would encourage others to go on and give football a go. Mind you, it backfired on me because they persuaded me to make a speech to the boys. I did it reluctantly. I would rather have had a big centre-forward battering me than stand up in front of all those kids.

Despite being predominantly right-footed, I was playing for the school at left-half, something else that was to stand me in good stead in the years to come when being two-footed was not so much an asset as a necessity.

Herbert Morris, one of my teachers, was a great encouragement, not only to me but to Trevor Ford, Ray Daniel and Ivor Allchurch, all Welsh internationals, plus Jack Roberts (Bolton Wanderers), Ernie Jones (Spurs) and my pal Glyn Davies, all of whom passed through his more than capable hands. In fact, he always reckoned I would have been a better cricketer than footballer.

By the time I was thirteen, Glyn and I were playing in the Swansea Boys' team with our school pals Haydn Williams and Brian Sykes. In the next season, I was made captain and we won the Swansea Shield – my first real trophy. Winning that was such a proud moment. I found it hard to understand when, some years ago, certain schools up and down the country banned competitive sports on the basis that we should all be equal. Life dictates that some are more equal than others.

I was also in the team that reached the quarter-final of the English Schools' Trophy. What an adventure that was! We played our football at St Helens and it was there we beat Bristol Schools in March 1946 and were drawn to meet Leicester. The first game was at St Helens in front of a good crowd and I recall playing into a blinding sun in the first half. They were a big side but we matched them and took the lead through a boy named Spillane. Leicester hit back and before half-time they equalised through Slynn.

We pummelled them in the second half but could not get the ball past their goalkeeper Heathcote, and we eventually drew 1–1. Even afterwards it was a great occasion, with a meal laid on for both teams at the local Mackworth Hotel, and then all of us went off to the pictures.

The replay at Filbert Street was played in front of a massive crowd of 18,000 early in April. It was my first trip to England and I could not believe so many people had turned up to watch a football match. In fact, we were a little overawed and it put us on the back foot. We went on to lose 3–0. So that trophy evaded me, but not the Charles family. Mel went on to win it with Swansea a couple of years later.

I remember that Leicester were a better team than us on the day, and they all seemed to be grown-up lads, young men, while we were still boys, even though we were around the same age. We didn't have a bad side, though, with a bright young lad named Terry Medwin, who went on to play for Spurs and Wales, Bobby Hennings, Enoch Williams and, of course, my mate Glyn Davies.

The competition gave us the taste for glory and we set our sights on the Welsh Shield. We reached the semi-final in a fairly emphatic manner, beating Briton Ferry Schools 10–0 in front of 3,000. Terry Medwin scored a couple and I weighed in with one. We were drawn against Cardiff, a team we had already beaten comprehensively in an earlier group stage at the Vetch Field. This time, however, we were drawn away, and battened down the hatches for a goalless draw at Ninian Park before thrashing them 5–0 at St Helens with Hennings scoring four.

This gave us a place in the final against Aberdare. It was over two legs and we were the firm favourites with 9,000 turning up at St

Helens to watch us win the first leg 3–0. It was now a formality and we went to Aberaman Park two days later and won 6–0. The Welsh Shield was fine and I loved winning it, but the English one was far more important.

There was no question of staying on at school for further education and, at fourteen, I was on my way. It was a terrific childhood filled with good memories. It certainly helped to have a father who loved the game as much as I did, and he was as pleased as punch when I started playing organised football at left-half, which was his favoured position.

I was like any other youngster in Swansea, I suppose, getting into a gang – but they were all the lads I played football with, and I knocked around with the same boys when I left school. Because of sport, school was a happy time for me, even though I wasn't much of a student.

I was fortunate because it was realised from early on that I had some potential as a footballer, so I was looked after and seemed to play football most of the time. In those days, they didn't control the amount we played. The feeling was the more you played, the better player you became, and I wasn't about to argue with the theory. In the light of what we know now about youngsters overplaying and doing themselves permanent physical damage, I suppose it was bad news really. But when you're young, you don't worry; you just go out and play and play and play until you're kicking around under the street lamps.

One evening in August 1946, just a few days after I had left school, my friend Bryan's dad Joe Sykes came round to our house in Alice Street, wanting to speak to Mam and Dad. I was terrified that I had done something wrong until Dad called me in and told me that Mr Sykes had asked if I could join Swansea. Dad said that I could if I wanted, and it didn't need any thought from me. Playing football certainly beat going down the mines or to the steelworks. The weekly wage was £1 and it went straight to my mam to help with the housekeeping. I didn't mind because I had the chance to do what I most wanted to do – play football with Swansea Town.

CHAPTER TWO

The Swans

The Vetch Field was hardly strange. I knew the place because I used to go there when I could. Swansea had kept an eye on my progress through school and they sometimes let me in in return for putting up the half-time scores. It was quite entrepreneurial. I used to take Dad's ladder and hook the numbers against the letters in the programme. Apart from that, one way or another we would watch the Swans. We had all sorts of ways of getting in. We couldn't afford the entrance fee but there was always some sympathetic adult willing to lift you over the turnstile if no one was looking; or we would go through two at a time, that sort of thing.

I knew all the players by sight. Trevor Ford was my hero. Some may find that a little difficult to believe because as a couple of centre-forwards we could not have been more different. I went through my career without a booking or a sending-off while Trevor used to collect them like autographs. He was all elbows, knees and bustle – but he could shoot. When I went to watch Swansea, I really went to watch Trevor Ford. He knew where the goal was and boy, could he shoot – from anywhere and everywhere, even though his left foot was a bit of a swinger. And was he single-minded! He would run over anyone in his way. I loved it. That was the excitement of going to the Vetch Field – watching Trevor knock people about and score goals. He was wonderful and he was one of the main reasons I wanted to join the club.

I was due to start at nine o'clock on the Monday morning following Mr Sykes' visit, and I was early. The new boys – and there was a group of us – were introduced to groundsman Jimmy Fairweather who showed us round and then gave each of us a little fork and a bucket for our first job – weeding the pitch on our hands and knees.

In the days that followed, we cleaned the boots, swept the terraces, cleaned the stands, tidied the dressing rooms, weeded, painted; in fact, we did everything except play football. I wondered whether they were training me to become an odd-job man. The only job I really enjoyed was cleaning out the dressing rooms. I suppose it was the smell of the liniment and the closeness to the pitch. I could almost imagine myself getting ready to go out and play. That and listening to the professionals talk football made it special. These players were all my heroes, worshipped from the terraces, and now here they were sitting and chatting to each other in front of me as if I was part of the furniture.

There were some decent players in the first team, not just Trevor Ford. One of the jewels in the crown, Roy Paul, went on to captain Manchester City when they beat Birmingham in the 1956 FA Cup final. He and Trevor, who went on to play for Aston Villa, were my heroes long before I took my broom into that dressing room, and what's more, they were nice guys and had time for us young lads.

I may have made a hero out of Trevor Ford but it did not mean I had to play like him. When I was young it was my nature to play football and not to run around kicking people. It was the way I was brought up. My father used to say to me, 'Don't kick 'em, just play football.' My attitude was that if I had to knock opponents down in order to play well, I didn't want to play the game. The public do not pay good money to see pettiness and childishness. Usually, when you have a hero as a youngster, you model yourself on him, but that was not the way I had been brought up to play football, either by my dad or my schoolteachers. It didn't stop me admiring him. In the dressing room I was in awe, and when I got to play with him for Wales, that was unbelievable. When he was trampling on people, though, I never thought maybe that's what I should do. Eventually, I grew to be a big guy and I could, I suppose, have imposed myself on other players, but I preferred to do it with my football.

Of course, once I was on the groundstaff, I could go to all the games. The only thing that bothered me was that I couldn't get a game myself. They did not run enough teams, and those they did run I couldn't get in. I don't know why it was. They must have thought I wasn't good enough. One of the problems was that I was still not very tall, about 5ft 6in. Not only that, I was fairly skinny too. But despite not playing, they fed me well. I had the odd steak and even the occasional glass of Guinness – medicinal, of course.

They kept us so busy, we used to have to train in our own time, usually in the evenings. They brought in lads from outside to have a look at them on Tuesdays and Wednesdays and we had to muck in with them. It would have made more sense to play practice matches, which would have helped everyone, the groundstaff boys, the triallists and the management. In fact, it baffled me that we never joined in any practice games. It meant the club never had a chance to judge our ability. Being charitable, I can only assume that the manager Haydn Green – small, slim, built like a greyhound – did not want to overplay us.

It was no way to run a club and you could see the confidence draining out of the youngsters who had thought they were being given the chance to play football. Even being around the first-team players began to wear thin when you couldn't play in a competitive match.

Mam and Dad weren't sure what was going on. They had their misgivings about me going to the Vetch in the first place. Dad wondered out loud whether football would turn out to be a disappointing blind alley for me with nothing at the end. You could understand why he felt that way. I was eating for two at the time and the £1 I was earning was scarcely enough to keep me fed and watered. Dad wanted me to have a trade and said he could get me into electrical work, but I pleaded with him until he and Mam didn't have the heart to refuse to give me my chance.

To make ends meet, Mam started going out to work. That may be common enough now but it wasn't then. The woman of the house was expected to stay at home to cook, mend and clean, especially with a family as big as ours. When my wages increased to 25 shillings it was a sign that I was, at least, heading in the right direction although it didn't exactly ease the financial worries for my parents.

I would go into the club with a huge bag of sandwiches to feed my ever-growing appetite in between my tasks. On a normal training day, we had to be at the ground at least an hour before the senior players arrived so that we could set out their training gear and make sure the dressing room was clear before going outside for our other duties. We would linger around the dressing rooms until the players began arriving but, for the most part, they either ignored us or simply did not notice we were there.

Not surprisingly, it was the stars who were the exceptions. Trevor Ford, Roy Paul, Jack Parry and Frank Squires took the time and trouble to chat to us young lads, with Roy Paul going even further by passing on hints about the game. As a result, I idolised him.

I was determined that nothing was going to stop me making the grade and I watched my manners, was respectful to my elders and got on with what I was told to do. One of the jobs I did with the other kids was to set concrete blocks under the stanchion supports of the main stand. As the concrete was setting, we prodded and poked about in the muck with our fingers, eventually signing our names. I was mortified when I discovered I had left the 'r' out of Charles. There it stayed for years as a reminder, long after I had gone. Instead of signing my name in concrete, maybe they should have had it on a piece of paper.

We were so fed up with not playing proper games that, in the end, we organised our own team from among our old school friends. We used to play on a Saturday morning and we were good, winning everything that was on offer to us. We were still classed as amateurs, even though we were being paid, and so we were also allowed to play for the Swansea Youth team run by schoolmaster George Hughes and trained by Pop Hopkins. The best times were when Joe Sykes put us through our paces. Bryan's father kept an eye on Bryan and me together with Terry Medwin, Bobby Hennings and Harry Griffiths. Pop Hopkins looked after us at the local youth club, where we also played. Had Swansea sent out a colts team, I would never have been involved with these other teams.

Playing for the Swansea Youth team gave me the opportunity to travel around, and I was grateful for my wages when I saw the number of men, including my own father, who were out of work and on the dole. It was even worse in Ireland. When I travelled there for a youth game, I saw huge groups of men standing around outside the employment office, waiting in the hope of a job turning up. There must have been fifty or sixty of them.

By now, I had begun to shoot up at an alarming rate, and quickly grew out of my one and only suit. Mam had to cut down one of my father's for me to travel in.

It was almost the end of my first season at the club before I actually played a match at the Vetch Field – left-half for the Under-17 team against Liverpool. All my mates were there to keep me company – Glyn Davies, Bobby Hennings, Harry Griffiths, Bryan Sykes, Terry Jones and Len Walker. It was the first time most of the officials at the club had seen any of us play.

I must have impressed someone because I was selected to play in a Welsh amateur international trial at Haverfordwest. Naturally, there was a huge representation from Swansea; in fact, there were so many of us that they hired a bus to take us there. After the game an official came in and told us that if we were wanted again, we would be notified. As it happened, I was called up for another trial at Caerau. This time there was just me from Swansea, and the club provided me with a railway warrant. Mam gave me a huge pack of sandwiches to eat on the way.

I caught the bus to the ground, asking the conductor to put me off at the designated stop. I hadn't a clue where I was going. As the friendly conductor showed me the way, he told me there would not be many to watch in the heavy rain. How right he was. It was so depressing, incessant rain, a heavy pitch and, to make it worse, I had a stinker. That was the last I heard from the Welsh amateurs. I never did play for them again.

That summer I spent playing cricket for Highbury Stepney and was delighted when one of Wales' top players, Gilbert Parkhouse, was whisked away to play county cricket for Glamorgan. I enjoyed cricket but I lived for football, and I was disappointed when the youth club closed down. That was when I joined up with Gendros. Little did I realise that my destiny was being shaped.

My development as a player was helped enormously by Gendros Youth Club on the Fforest-fach, high above Swansea, where we played under the eagle eye of former Welsh international centre-half Harry Hanford, who was ready to satisfy our thirst for football knowledge. He could not have had a more willing or eager group than we were. He had played for Swansea and Sheffield Wednesday and was a great believer in accurate passing from defence, as well as from midfield and up front. He would line up a series of skittles and have us knock them over one after another.

We were so enthusiastic at Gendros that we raised the money to buy our own set of green shirts and, on top of that, we had to pay sixpence subs per week. It was worth it for a game of football. There was no such thing as a team bus and often we would walk up to five miles to play our games, changing in the open air and playing on a glue pot. We'd put our clothes back on over the dirty ones and walk the five miles back home, often with Mel plodding along because I had to look after him.

David Evans, who ran the team, made me captain after a while, I suppose because of my even temperament and the fact that I did not get involved on the pitch or with the referee. We were so keen that we would go off on six-mile training runs with poor Mr Evans cycling alongside us. On one occasion, his chain broke so we tied a rope to his bike, hitched it around our waists and pulled him the two miles or so left of the run.

This is when I began to develop different facets of my game, such as the long throw-in and shooting from a distance although that got me into trouble one day when we were playing a game on the fog-shrouded Town Hill ground. The vicar, who was also secretary of our local league, saw that play had moved to the other end, and made his way across the penalty area, huddled behind his umbrella. Suddenly we broke quickly out of defence and I hammered in a shot from near the halfway line, literally taking the umbrella out of the vicar's hand. I have never seen anyone run so fast as he did.

But our enthusiasm paid off handsomely and in our very first season we reached the Under-18 Youth Cup final, beating the local favourites on the way – their first defeat in three years.

There was also a change at the Vetch with Haydn Green giving way to Billy McCandless. Before Haydn went, he put all of our crowd into the A team. When we saw the teamsheet a great cheer went up because, for most of us, it was going to be the first time in sixteen months or more with the club that we had been able to wear a Swansea Town shirt.

In the first match, at Pembroke, I played centre-half and marked an old friend of mine, Billy Wilkins. We drew and as Billy failed to find the net, I left the game quite satisfied. I must have done all right because I was picked again to face Barry Town in Swansea and although we lost 3–1, I kept my place against Gwayvy for a third successive game.

Now there was a ground! It was situated at the top of a big hill and we had to walk up on foot, carrying our kit. By the time we reached the summit, the weather had changed. The fog came in, the game was called off and we had to walk all the way down again.

The game was replayed the next week and we lost 2–1 and with it went my place. In fact, that was the last time I played for Swansea in any sort of game. I saw out the season doing what I had done before, playing sweeper – with a broom! I did not even make the reserves. When the next season began in the same fashion, I began to wonder whether there was any future for me in the game, especially as I had reached the landmark age of sixteen.

It was playing for Gendros that brought the change of fortune and set my feet firmly on the bottom rung of the ladder. There was always a handful of people watching our games and among them was a regular whom I thought must be related to one of the boys until one day he came across to Bobby Hennings, Harry Griffiths and me and introduced himself as 'Mr Pickard – a scout for Leeds United'. His son, Charlie Pickard, was the key. He used to tell his dad whom he'd seen and who to go and look at. That's the way they worked. Mr Pickard asked the three of us if we would like to go to Elland Road for a trial. We looked at each other and, in unison, said a very firm, 'Yes.' Nowadays, of course, that would be considered an illegal approach, but not then because we had signed nothing. All it needed was for Mr Pickard to ask our parents' permission. In fact, he not only discovered me and my brother Mel, but also Welsh international goalkeeper Gary Sprake, midfielder Terry Yorath and Carl Harris.

That was an epic moment. My dear old mother, who had never been out of Swansea, never mind Wales, said to Mr Pickard I couldn't go. Taken aback, he asked her why and she answered, with a twinkle in her eye, I couldn't go to Leeds because I didn't have a passport. I have dined out on that story. I love it.

Dad, being a football man, knew of Leeds United and the reputation of their manager Major Frank Buckley, and he was happy for me to go north, but Mam was genuinely worried, and not just about me not having a passport!

It was arranged for us to travel to Leeds the following week and on the Friday morning we caught the 07.55 train from Swansea. Not one of us had breathed a word to anyone at the club and we had even left our boots at the ground so as not to raise suspicion. The only other people who knew were our families. Mine saw me off at the station to wish me luck. As he shook my hand, Dad said quietly, 'This is a chance I never had. Good luck.'

He would have loved to have played the professional game but he was never given the opportunity. At that precise moment, I was aware of how much my parents had sacrificed to give me this chance. I was determined not to let them down.

CHAPTER THREE

Dirty old town and the Major

L eeds United invited me for a month's trial in September 1948. It was an adventure going to live so far away from home in a big industrial city, even for a short while. Leeds had taken quite a battering from the Germans and was in a state of some disrepair when we arrived. In fact, my first impression from the window of the train was what a dirty old place it was. Even the Elland Road ground, which we passed on the way in, did not live up to our expectations. It was not nearly so grand as we had anticipated. Funny isn't it that after all these years and all the fine places I could have ended up, I still live just outside Leeds, within easy distance of the ground.

Back then, it was something of a let-down after the excitement of the trip and being seen off by Mr Pickard, who not only settled Bobby Hennings, Harry Griffiths and me into our seats but also provided magazines and newspapers to help us pass the time.

As the steam train puffed its way into the station, there was the club secretary, Mr Crowther, waiting to meet us. He piled us into his car and took us on a tour of inspection. We were most impressed when he gave us some pocket money and then drove us to our digs. The landlady looked after all the young Leeds triallists and she knew exactly what she should do for her part, which made her, at that stage, as important as anyone else in the entire club. She immediately settled us in and made us feel at home.

Daisy was her name and she was in charge, no mistake. She had her instructions from the club and bedtime for all of us youngsters was ten o'clock and that was it, no argument. She was also obviously told to feed us up, and we had big meals, especially breakfasts with bacon, eggs, sausages, black pudding, baked beans, the lot. She was a wonderful lady.

The other advantage was that the digs were close to the ground. We had only to walk down the hill and we were there. We didn't even have to walk down the street because there was a path that went down the hill, right down to Elland Road. So I didn't have to get up too early in the mornings.

When we got to the ground the next morning, I discovered I had been picked to play right-back for the A team at Harrogate. That produced my first problem – no boots! It was a surprise to be picked so quickly but our furtive departure from Swansea meant that we weren't kitted out to do what we had come for, to play football. One of the officials scurried about and came back with an old pair of boots, and handed them to me. They were beautiful, a perfect fit and well broken in by their former owner. They fitted like carpet slippers.

It felt a little strange having to play in a new position, and took me a while to adjust as I had a very speedy winger against me, but at the end of ninety minutes I felt as though I had done myself justice.

Harry Griffiths didn't get a game that first week, and when they found him a pair of boots they were so tight they took the skin off his feet. He was in agony and could not concentrate on the game, kicking the ball away whenever it came near him. Needless to say, Leeds were not impressed and he was eventually sent home. It could so easily have been me in the wrong sized boots, and it made me realise how lucky I was.

Bobby Hennings also failed to make the grade, but in the end, whose loss was it? Had Leeds found Harry a decent pair of boots or, indeed, had he taken his own, they would have had a Welsh international on their staff for he went on to play for his country with some distinction. Bobby went on to play for Swansea.

Mr Crowther called us into his office after a few days, and any fears we had were quickly dispelled when he gave us some more pocket money – much needed since we'd been to the local cinemas three times since we arrived. It was while we were in the office that the door burst open and we had our first meeting with the Major. He was tall, had a fresh complexion, was wearing plus fours and had a terrier dog at his heels. The dog, we learned, was called Bryn Jones. The Major was sixty-three years old and had seen action in both the Boer War and the First World War.

Major Buckley looked us up and down and said, 'So you fellows want to be footballers, do you?' He looked at me and added, 'I like 'em big, but if you want to come to Leeds, you will have to work hard and do as you're told.' With that he turned on his heel, gave a tug on the dog leash and was gone.

The Major liked people who were tall, so you can imagine how delighted I was to be growing so fast. He liked big footballers. It's the old thing from school days, isn't it? If you had a good big 'un, he was better than a good small 'un. I did do as I was told and trained hard throughout the week. On Friday, up went the teamsheet and this time I was picked at left-back. I told Mr Crowther I had never played there either, but he looked me up and down and said, 'You're picked there – so you will play there!' End of conversation. I thought about making a protest but remembered what Dad had told me before I left, 'Do as you're told.' Hadn't Major Buckley said the self same thing?

Major Buckley would say, 'They must be strong. They must love the game. They must realise they have two feet. They must have guts. Then, and only then, can they be taught to become footballers.' I was frightened to death of him at first.

I have to admit that I was a little envious of Bobby Hennings who, in his two matches, had played in his chosen position while I was being juggled around. But I survived and, in fact, had a decent game. Even so, it was a surprise when Mr Crowther came up to me afterwards and told me that, at the end of my trial period, I could have a job on the groundstaff and I would be paid 30 shillings a week with lodgings provided. I felt like a millionaire. It was only a five bob rise from what I'd been earning at Swansea, but they were also going to pay towards my bed and my food. What more could a young man want? I did not smoke, nor did I drink anything stronger or more expensive than shandies with just a splash of beer, and we travelled everywhere by bus.

We spent our leisure time in the conventional way for that era. There were always three or four trips to the cinema, usually the Majestic on City Square, and Saturday night was reserved for the dancehall, usually the Scala Dance Hall. Often in the afternoon, a few of us would have a game of snooker in Briggate followed by a cup of coffee in one of the local coffee shops – and all of this on about ten bob (50 pence) a week after I had sent Mam five shillings and paid my share for board and lodging. It does not sound much in these days of high inflation in football, but we were all being paid the same so no one noticed, never mind complained. The important factor as far as I was concerned was that I was playing football. That was the main thing and a great relief.

At the end of the trial period, Mr Crowther gave me my return train fare and told me he would see me on the following Friday. I was the only one of the three musketeers from Swansea to survive the trial, and it was with mixed emotions that I travelled back home on the Saturday night to be met by my dad at the station. It was the early hours of Sunday morning by the time I arrived, and the buses had long finished running, so Dad had to wait up to bring me home. For the first time in my life, I experienced the joy of a taxi ride through the silent streets of Swansea.

While we were travelling back to Alice Street, Dad told me someone from Swansea had been round to our house asking where I was. Dad saved my blushes by telling them he thought I stood a better chance of making the grade away from Swansea, and he saved me further embarrassment by going to the ground to pick up my boots and my insurance card.

I spent the week lazing in the late September sun on Mumbles beach with my mate Glyn Davies before catching the train back to Leeds and the start of my new life.

Swansea were upset that I had been whisked away from under their noses but had they been a little more considerate, maybe I would never have gone to Leeds in the first place. I had gone to the Vetch Field to play football and while I didn't mind doing the sweeping up and the rest of the chores, I wanted to play football more than anything else and they were not giving me the opportunity. I would have loved to stay with my home-town club but I knew if I was going to be a footballer I had a much better chance at Leeds United.

At Swansea, I was still registered as an amateur, so when it came to moving to Leeds, there was no problem. I suppose you have to say that Swansea were a bit silly; perhaps they were trying to be too clever. They did nothing to indicate they wanted to keep me and not only did they not give me regular football, they made no offers. They finished up getting their fingers burned because they would have got a good fee for me, even at that age. Bill McCandless took the blame for losing me although it was nothing to do with him at all. They claimed they did everything to keep me. I have to say they didn't make it blatantly evident. If they had offered me a contract, I would have stayed in my home town and played for the club I'd supported as a kid. It was only after I moved that they suddenly thought I might eventually become a player.

My decision was soon vindicated, for when I arrived back in the north, Mr Crowther handed me a card with an address and told me to go and sort out a sports jacket, trousers and an overcoat. They did not know what that meant to me. I had two suits, both shabby, worn and too small for me. I had grown five inches in a year. As for an overcoat – I had never owned one. I had already decided to save £1 a week from my wages to buy new clothes, so this was a sensational development. I even felt a lump in my throat at the generosity of the club. Mr Crowther had made me feel I was really wanted and that, in turn, gave me confidence. I knew I was going to be happy at this club, even though I was so far away from all my friends and family. I discovered later that the instruction for the new clothes had come from the manager, and he paid for them himself.

It was all so far removed from the Vetch as I was plunged into the routine. The hard work was still there. Every morning I would be set tasks, cleaning the ground and the stands, but in the afternoon, coach Willis Edwards would put me through the serious stuff, kicking the ball against the wall for an hour and a half non-stop with both feet, and then another long spell in the shooting box, hitting targets.

After that it was heading practice in the corridor under the stand. The balls were suspended by string from a girder at different heights and I had to run, jump and head them in turn, and then turn round and do the same thing coming back, but this time with the balls moving about on their strings.

I started in the Yorkshire League in what was Leeds' third team because, like Swansea, they didn't have a junior team at that time. I don't think they were invented then. The Major would come to our practice matches but leave the talking to the coaches, unless he wanted to make a specific point to you personally. He would say, 'Come here, Jack boy' – he always called me Jack – 'Come here, Jack. Jack, you're not doing this right and you're not doing that right.' That's the way he was. But they were always pertinent points, things that helped me become a better footballer.

I was a shy, quiet Welsh boy with a strong accent and I could have easily been left out of things off the pitch but some of the A team included me in their group. They took me out at weekends sometimes, which made me feel better. Of course, there were moments when I wondered what I was doing in this strange town. The worst was a few weeks before my seventeenth birthday. Leeds were looking after me very well but I was missing my family. I was lonely, a natural reaction, I guess, once the novelty had worn off.

I was eventually moved to right-back and then one day, Major Buckley told me he was moving me to centre-half. The Major regularly moved players around to see how they coped with a new position and a new set of challenges. I found myself facing Barnsley in the Yorkshire League, playing centre-half for the first time in my life. By this time, I had shot up, and from being a slip of a boy I was now topping 6ft and tipping the scales at over 13 stones; and because of the Major moving me about, I felt confident with left or right foot, I could tackle and read the game. That game against Barnsley was the turning point in my career. Not only did I please our coaching staff, but I discovered what was, without doubt, my natural position.

In early December, Leeds were due to play Cardiff at Ninian Park. The Major told me I would be travelling reserve and, after the game, I could stay in Wales and have a week's holiday. That shows what a shrewd man and a good manager he was. Although I had said nothing about my homesickness, he was still able to spot it and, more importantly, do something about it.

It was much appreciated and, while I was at home, I took the opportunity to visit my old school and the headmaster, Mr Owens, to tell him how I was getting on. He told me he was not surprised and soon, he said, I would be playing for Wales. That sounded more than a little optimistic to me, as I couldn't even get into the amateur team, but I promised him there and then that if I did play for Wales, I would give my first Welsh shirt to the school. Not that long afterwards, I was able to keep the promise, much to my own huge surprise.

But I might not have done so because I almost did not go back to Elland Road. After the game, when the other players and the officials caught the train back to Leeds, I headed down the line to Swansea, arriving home at around 9.30 p.m. I had not told anyone I was coming. Mam was the only one in and when she answered the door, she was astonished and made me tell her everything while she prepared supper. As everyone else returned home, I was forced to tell the story over again.

Next morning, we were at it again with my brothers wanting to know about the football, my sisters about the shops and Mam and Dad asking whether Leeds were looking after me. It was the start of a wonderful week, visiting school and my old friends, and by

Thursday, I was asking myself why I had ever left it behind. It must have been the first case of being homesick while at home.

Suddenly, I dreaded going back to Leeds, and sat down to talk it over with my dad. He told me that Swansea had been on to him to see whether he could persuade me to go back to them before I signed the forms for Leeds.

It certainly was a temptation, but he repeated his earlier opinion that he thought I could do better for myself away from home. I spent a restless night and come the morning, I had decided to go back to Leeds, collect my few possessions and return home. I was heading for the 7.55 and just as I was about to leave, my mam whispered to me she wished I were staying. That made me even more indecisive and I almost did not return to Leeds at all, eventually catching the train with just two minutes to spare.

I spent the entire journey mulling over what I should do, and when I saw Leeds submerged in winter gloom through the grimy train windows, I made up my mind to leave. I bought the local evening paper to read on the tram back to my digs where I was going to pack my gear before going to the ground. I glanced to see whether I was in the A team for the following day. I was not and that made me even more determined to quit. I settled back to read the rest of the sports pages and it was then I spotted I had been picked at centre-half for the reserves at Preston North End.

In that precise moment, all my resolutions collapsed and I decided that if the club were prepared to show this sort of faith in me, the least I could do was to give it a try for one more match.

I went to the pictures that night with a couple of the boys, and the next day one of them, Peter Harrison, with whom I shared a room, told me I was so excited I had kept him awake all night. Excited? I was still tossing and turning trying to decide what to do with the rest of my life!

At the ground the first person I saw was the Major. 'Jack,' he said, 'here is your chance to make a place in the second team your own.' I actually started to tell him that I was thinking of quitting and returning home, but I got no further than stuttering, 'Mr Buckley . . .' when he leaned over, patted me on the shoulder, told me to call him Major, and showed me out of his office. I wonder what would have happened if he had let me finish that sentence. We lost 2–1 at Preston and the defeat was followed by the longest week in my memory as I tried to decide what to do. Finally, I made up my mind. If they kept me in the reserves, I would stay and battle it out, but if I was dropped back down to the A team, I would go back to Swansea.

The teams were always announced on a Friday morning but as I was painting one of the stands it was lunchtime before I had the chance to look at the teamsheets and, sure enough, I was again in the Central League team. I was selected in my favourite left-half position, the same position my dad played and the same position my young brother Mel was playing back home. Somehow, I knew then that it would be a long time before I went back to Wales to live.

On my seventeenth birthday, 27 December 1948, I was called into the Major's office along with Grenville Hair to be told that he was prepared to sign us both as professionals as soon as he could get groundstaff boys to replace us. In fact, I had already spoken to the trainer, Bob Brockswell. Everyone was spelling it out to me what a great club Leeds was, the crowd, the players, the city and telling me 'you've got to try this place' and 'it's lovely, Leeds' and all that. It was overwhelming and I said I would be happy to sign if they wanted me.

I knew there were no guarantees because they took on a big group of kids from all over the country, and I understood we'd be whittled down. The club would finish up with a couple or so from the year and then they'd bring in another lot. Each time, they'd be left with just a handful. It was no problem to the club because the wages weren't very big.

A couple of weeks later, two new boys reported and we were again sent to the Major's office where he pointed to two little piles of money and told us it was our £10 signing-on fee, adding, 'Your wages go up from £4 to £6 as from today, and if you do as you're told, you'll both get on all right with me.' We signed our forms and he pushed our £10 towards us, adding with a grin, 'Don't spend it all at once.' I didn't. I ran straight round to the post office in Beeston and opened a savings account with my ten £1 notes. Not only was I now a professional footballer, I also had money in the bank.

Football, until recent years, has been considered a poorly paid job, but despite the maximum wage, the money was relatively good. In fact, it was quite well paid in the early fifties. Certainly it was good money compared with the average working man's wage. In addition, you had more free time than most, something we really appreciated.

In what other job could you amble in at ten o'clock in the morning, train until twelve according to the day of the week, and then head off home or to the snooker hall or cinema. It only changed when we had a game, and then we wouldn't do so much on Thursday or Friday as we were preparing for Saturday.

There was plenty of money about at the time, with big crowds attending most of the games as people looked for a release after the horrors of war. Football provided the perfect diversion. We regularly had over 30,000 at Elland Road, so there was good income and very little paid out in wages. The club had money to play with in the fifties and it would be interesting to know what happened to it all. Where did it all go? Certainly not on players and definitely not on ground improvements until our stand burned down. But the chairman and his directors used to drive around in nice cars and have very good dinners.

I spent the next three months with the reserves, but I had it in the back of my mind that I was in the team under sufferance because the first team's Tom Holley was injured and the reserve centre-half, Roly Depear, had stepped up to fill in for him.

Then Roly was injured as well and I found myself making my first-team debut in a friendly against Scottish side Queen of the South on 19 April 1949. I had nothing to lose in a friendly, and I didn't even stay awake thinking about it the night before. As far as I was concerned, it was a good opportunity for me to gain first-team experience without the danger of lost league points hanging over me.

It was a fiery baptism. I was up against Billy Houliston, a lively Scottish international centre-forward who was not known for taking prisoners. He was a lot quicker and cleverer than anyone I had had to mark before, and I quickly realised I was only just beginning to learn the game at this level. But I stuck at it and was reasonably pleased when the game finished in a draw. At least I had managed to keep Houliston off the scoresheet.

Houliston had made his Scotland debut the previous November and had played his second international just ten days before our friendly. That was against England at Wembley and he had terrorised the outstanding Neil Franklin. There was nothing dirty about Houliston, and after the game he said in the local press that I was the best young centre-half he had ever played against. It was some compliment and I had to tell myself not to let it go to my head as it was only a friendly and I was there because two older players, better than me, were injured. I had been plunged in at the deep end, but at the right time of the season, and Houliston was a good first test.

Then came the crunch. Holley and Depear stayed on the injured list and I found myself making my league debut a few days later on 23 April at Blackburn Rovers, in front of 18,873 spectators. I was to mark Dennis Westcott, one of the leading scorers in the Second Division. This time I did feel the butterflies before the kick-off but they quickly vanished as the game began, and I was delighted it finished in a goalless draw.

As usual, the manager had been clever. He wanted me to have the experience of playing against a seasoned centre-forward away from home. This was near the end of the season and there was no pressure from our own supporters. That was the logic and it worked.

Westcott was another big, bustling lad as most centre-forwards were at that time. I thought he was a good player but I didn't let him get the better of me. In fact, I was very happy with my performance, especially when the Major came into the dressing room and said, 'Well done, Jack.' That meant a lot; the Major didn't give away compliments easily. Even a grunted 'well played' was a rarity.

There were only two games left and I stayed in the team as we drew at home to Cardiff City and then lost at Queens Park Rangers. It was not an auspicious start with three draws and a defeat in my first four games, and I wondered what the next season would hold in store for me, especially as Leeds finished down in fifteenth place, way off the pace.

The Major must have seen it a bit differently for he called me in and told me I would draw first-team wages for the four games I had played – and for the entire close season. I had gone from £6 to £12 a week and £10 throughout the summer.

Then it was off to Holland and I was included in that, too, even though I was still only seventeen. Perhaps the Major was thinking he would be teaching me other things apart from football. While it was all very relaxed, the Major still wanted us to perform well on the pitch and win our matches. Consequently, the night before a game we would all behave ourselves, eat together and have an early night, and if anyone didn't he would be back in Leeds before his feet touched the ground. The Major was strict in that respect; when he said he wanted something doing, it was done, but when he said relax, he took the pressure right off.

On the pitch, we got the ball up into the penalty area quickly against the Dutch sides while they moved it around a lot. It was good for us because it taught us to play against different styles and to adjust our style of play accordingly.

My break into the senior side made all the difference, as did the unexpected trip to Holland. Homesick? I think not. I was so pleased with myself, after my first trip abroad that I spent the first two weeks of the close season in Leeds before heading home to Swansea, with my confidence lifted. Anyway, I was not completely alone for Leeds had signed two other young Welsh lads, Eylenn Jones and John Reynolds. We travelled back to Wales together on the sleeper, tossing a coin to see which of the three of us would have the dubious privilege of the luggage rack as a bed.

I even went round to the Vetch Field with a clear conscience to thank Joe Sykes, who had given me so much advice and help through those difficult years. The Major had replaced him in my life now. What a man he was! When he arrived at Elland Road, the club had slipped down the League and looked as though it would carry on in that direction. The Major declared he would rebuild from the bottom and set about searching the length and breadth of the country for young players of quality, watching many of the 2,000 players scouted himself. That was how I came to his attention. He had never seen me personally but apparently had good reports, and he wasn't put off by the shy sixteen year old who stood blushing before him a couple of days after arriving in Leeds.

I knew of his reputation and I was nervous. I had been told the story of how one of his players had walked into his office with a cigarette in one hand and the other in his trouser pocket. The player was kicked out and told not to return until the nicotine had been scrubbed from his fingers.

The Major's memories of that first meeting were recorded some years later when he said, 'How well I remember the day. I was confronted by an Adonis of a youth. I liked his bearing and his respectful approach. Somehow he looked like a footballer. He looked like a fine, upstanding young man but he was far too shy and modest to say too much about himself. I was convinced after Jack Pickard's glowing report that the boy would express himself far better in the familiar environment of a soccer game.'

It was after that interview that he quietly told Mr Crowther to make sure I was sent to the tailor for new clothes so I would gain in confidence from being smartly dressed. He told him to tell me the club had paid and to give the impression they did it for all the youngsters. He couldn't have had a clue whether I was going to succeed or not.

The Major was born in 1885 and had played for Derby County before the First World War, winning an England cap before going into the army, which cut short his career but earned him his rank. He demanded it be used; it was always Major and never Mister, and certainly never Frank.

After the war he went into management with Norwich City and Blackpool before joining Wolves in 1927 where he earned his reputation. He was a distinctly controversial manager for his time, making decisions that altered player's careers. He sold Bryn Jones to Arsenal for a record £14,000, discovered future England captain Billy Wright and plunged Jimmy Mullen into top-flight football at the age of sixteen. He also favoured monkey gland treatment for his players, which only added to the controversy. Monkey gland treatment enjoyed a brief spell of popularity, and the Major considered it good for forwards but not defenders. I was playing at centre-half at the time and so missed out on the treat. Only the Major knew why he used it, but it is interesting that it was deemed acceptable then, given the ongoing debate about drug-taking in sport, including football, nowadays. When I played, of course, there was no such thing as drug testing or banned substances. He moved on from Molineux to Notts County and Hull before joining Leeds United where he had such an influence on my career.

I have to admit that I was concerned about my future when he played me in positions I had never played in before, but someone on the staff told me not to worry because he had done the same thing at Wolves with Billy Wright, Billy Crook, Stan Cullis, Tom Galley and Angus McLean, so I was in good company. Before we parted company, he played me in five different positions in the first team, saying, 'A genuine footballer should be able to perform successfully in any position on the field.' Just how far ahead of his game was Major Buckley? That was the philosophy of the great Dutch side that took the world by storm with their interpretation of total football so many years later.

I discovered later another reason why he would deliberately play youngsters out of position. It was because he demanded that all players be two-footed, claiming a player with only one good foot was half a player. We all had to be able to control the ball with both feet and pass on both sides, as well as tackle off either foot. I often wondered what he would have done with the left-footed Hungarian genius Ferenc Puskas. Would the English Major have made the Galloping Major an even better player? Probably!

Certainly he took some stick for moving me around, especially when he played me briefly at centre-forward for a couple of games over Easter in 1951. The local newspapers were full of what a mistake he was making, but he ignored it and did exactly what he wanted to do, and you can hardly argue with his leap of faith in me. It certainly changed my life.

They were wonderful days under the Major. Overall, he achieved the perfect balance between being strict when he needed to be, and being able to relax and let us off the leash. He liked a drink and he smoked. When you were in his company and he was drinking, he expected you to drink with him. You did as the Major told you. If he said you were going in goal, you went in goal, and if he said to have a drink, you had a drink. But he always had your best interests at heart. He would say if we did well for him, he would look after us. I used to love the man and I would have done anything for him because he knew what he was talking about. He would not only tell you if you were doing something wrong on the field, he would show you how it should be done. Being a good coach and a good manager do not always go together, but he was both.

He treated us terrifically well in every respect; most importantly, he treated us as adults. He was also generous and if we won an important match, he'd often give you a couple of pounds extra out of his own pocket. We reached the stage when he desperately wanted to win promotion. He had us all together one day, and said, 'Right gentleman, for every point you earn you get an extra pound.' It doubled our bonus, £2 for a win plus £2 extra in the pay packet.

But if a player stepped out of line, he would be down on him like a ton of bricks. He was a hard man, and outspoken, and if you didn't do right by him he would take no messing. Do it twice and you were on your way into the reserves or even out of the club.

But I always felt that the Major liked me and I was often favoured above the other players. He even let me sleep during his team talks and rarely criticised me during practice matches.

He had his weird ways and, apart from the monkey glands, he would also have us sniffing essence of beef before games and would rub us down with whisky on very cold days. We would run out smelling as though we had come straight to the game from the pub.

There were only the two competitions in those days and once you were knocked out of the FA Cup, there was lots of free time. We trained from 10 a.m. to noon each day and I lived so close I didn't have to get out of bed until nine and, if I wanted, I could be back home by 12.30. Once a week we would play a practice match, a friendly or a charity match to keep us sharp. The Major didn't just pick a local side such as Barnsley; we would find ourselves playing against Celtic or one of the top teams from Holland, Feyenoord for instance, and then in the summer we would go to play them.

The Major would let his hair down when we went abroad on those great end-of-season trips. We used to travel by boat from Harwich and the fun started right then, with those who wanted a drink staying in the bar. This was a little bonus from the manager. There were very few restrictions and no wives allowed. We all used to come home thinking what a terrific man he was and that we would run through brick walls for him the next season. He was very clever. These days it would be called bonding. Of course, we played the matches and played them to win, and we trained, but, in between, there were great nights out. No girlfriends, no wives, no one looking over your shoulder unless one of the livelier directors came along and wanted to join in. We all developed a great love for Holland and towards the end of the season we would be asking, 'Are we going to play in Holland again this summer?'

It was not very expensive in those days and the Dutch people really loved the English because we had liberated them from the Germans, whom they hated. It was like payback time; the Dutch could not do enough for us in every respect. Holland wasn't the great holiday hub it is now, but it was good fun with the bars, late dinners and lots of ladies; there were always five or six of them with us. Unlike these days, there were no travelling supporters, no press, and only those directors who were willing to join in the fun.

The Major took us away for a bit of R and R and to make some money for the club; it certainly wasn't for football, not at the end of the season, and the Dutch were amateurs in those days. He looked after us and gave us pocket money so we were never short of a bob or two to go and enjoy a geneva (a young Dutch gin) or a beer for those who drank it. The chairman would say, 'Oh I don't think we should give . . .' but the Major would interrupt and say, 'Yes, we should give it to them for a night out, give them a few bob.' No one argued because he dominated.

There were very few clubs who went away; we went more than most, I think because the Major liked to travel. It was always Holland, never anywhere else. He loved Holland. It would've been just as easy to go to Belgium but maybe he preferred the nightlife in Holland.

He was completely the opposite pre-season, very strict and no nonsense. We always pre-seasoned in Leeds. He was also strict on food – the wrong foods as it turns out now, but the right foods as they thought then. It was steaks and green vegetables. We ate steaks on Saturday lunchtime before a match and you could feel the meat lying in your stomach as you ran around. Everyone did it then; it was steak, steak, steak. You all had steaks and that was that. There was no choice, but in those days there weren't too many vegetarians.

I believe the Major would have survived in today's game, and I had a few managers and coaches to judge him against over the years. At the time, the best thing about him as far as I could see with my limited experience was that he was very fair in what he did and said. It was so good for me, to have a man like him in charge at the start of my professional career.

CHAPTER FOUR

You're in the army now!

My call-up could have been a disaster careerwise – but it wasn't. I did my time from 1950 until 1952 in the 12th Royal Lancers, stationed first at Barnard Castle and then in Carlisle. By then, I was established in the Leeds team and during the entire time, except when I suffered with a cartilage injury, I was always available for Leeds United.

My spell in uniform certainly increased my interest in sport – take part in any sport and you were excused all sorts of other not so nice duties. I even took up boxing, which had only vaguely interested me before. One day I was working out in the gym when the sergeant major asked me if I would like to give it a try. I was in good shape, I was big and, more importantly, it would give me more time in the gym and away from those 'other duties'; so I said yes.

I was entered in the novice class and quickly racked up eight wins. It was going so well that some asked if I might consider turning professional. I wasn't interested in taking it any further, because I wanted to be a footballer and, to me, boxing was just a bit of fun. We used to go round the clubs on a Friday night and get stuck in over three rounds. I was even approached, through my dad, to go with pro fighter Dai Curvis, who later coached his two sons to professional titles, but I didn't fancy that sort of life at all. I was beginning to enjoy myself, becoming Army Champion of the Northern Command, when the Amateur Boxing Association stepped in and ruled that because I was a professional footballer, I could not be an amateur boxer. What a load of nonsense! I was a soldier, so I could not make any public comment about it. Instead, I left it to the newspapers, who had great fun with the story and jumped all over the ABA for their stupidity.

I had no ambitions as a boxer, either as an amateur or as a professional. All I was concerned about was keeping fit and joining in with my comrades, and here was the ruling body stomping all over me with their big boots and shouting their mouths off. What made it even more ridiculous was that while I couldn't box as an amateur because I was a professional footballer, I could still play football with the amateurs in the army; equally, had I been a professional rugby league player, I would still have been able to play for the army union team as an amateur. During the Second World War, many stars of England's rugby union team played rugby league, but perhaps I should be grateful; maybe the ABA saved me from a beating or two but, against that, they robbed me of a good many hours in the gym.

When I finished my national service, I must have impressed someone with my boxing, for I had a letter from the larger-than-life promoter Jack Solomons inviting me to turn professional with him. I thought about it – but only briefly. I knew how boxers finished up.

Fortunately for me, however, the main sport was football and I was lucky to be able to play while I was in the army. There was regular football with the regiment team, and once or twice a month I played for the army team in London or Paris. The army team was good, with all the professional footballers available, and we used to do quite well, whoever provided the opposition.

We weren't restricted to local games. We went to Sweden, Yugoslavia several times, and we even went to Russia. There were some fascinating trips and usually big crowds. We would say, 'Christ, are we going away again?' but in truth we were glad we were going. They were a good bunch of guys and it was wonderful to be able to say, 'I can't do any guard duties tomorrow, I'm off to France.' Now there was a place I enjoyed playing. The stadium was superb – the Stade de France, or something like that.

After my call-up, I became a bit blinkered about what was happening in the outside world, other than my games with Leeds United, so when a squadron runner appeared at my hut one day to tell me that the RSM wanted to see me, I had no idea what it was about.

I came to attention in front of the RSM and he told me that I was to report to Rhyl at once. I looked at him blankly wondering what went on at Rhyl that would interest me. He must have seen the anxiety in my eyes for he quickly added, 'You have been selected to play for Wales against Switzerland.' I didn't even know that Wales were due to play Switzerland until it dawned on me that it must be one of the Festival of Britain celebration games.

The fixture was to take place at the Racecourse Ground in Wrexham, scene of my first international against Northern Ireland a year previously, in March 1950. What a disaster that was! There I was, barely eighteen and with little experience in the game, being told that I had been picked to play for my country. I was going to wear the scarlet shirt of Wales alongside the likes of Walley Barnes, Alf Sherwood, Ronnie Burgess and my two Swansea heroes, Roy Paul and Trevor Ford. I was to play at centre-half against the experienced Aston Villa centre-forward Dave Walsh.

He must have been chuckling to himself as the press proclaimed me a world-beater, a teenaged sensation, in the team for life. Imagine a teenager with just a handful of first-team games reading that – my legs turned to jelly before the kick-off and the worry of making a mistake weighed so heavily on me it gave me a headache. I was in no shape to play and by the time we kicked off I was assailed by doubts about everything I did. I dithered and changed my mind, lost my man and was all over the place. I had an absolute nightmare and I have never been so happy to hear the final whistle in my life as I was that day.

For the record, the Welsh team was: Shortt (Plymouth), Barnes (Arsenal), Sherwood (Cardiff), Paul (Swansea), Charles (Leeds), Burgess (Spurs), Williams (Leeds), Rees (Spurs), Ford (Aston Villa), Scrine (Swansea), Clarke (Manchester City).

The other ten players had to work extra hard to cover up the mistakes of their raw, young debutant centre-half, and I think we were all pleased to get away with a goalless draw. It wasn't good enough for the press, though, and all those who had praised me and called me a world-beater were now reporting the truth, that I was a long way off international class. They slaughtered me and I felt my entire world collapse around me. I thought I had reached the end of my international career after just one match.

Major Buckley was brilliant when I went back to Leeds. He took me to one side, put his arm round my shoulder and told me not to worry. He said that many players had flopped on their first international appearance and I was no different. 'Keep playing well for Leeds,' he said, 'and your chance will come again.' He was right, but I could hardly believe the second opportunity had come so quickly.

It was an evening kick-off and the Swiss immediately confused us by playing a very unusual system. We were glad to go off at half-time a goal to the good, thanks to Ronnie Burgess. The second half was a different story with Trevor Ford taking on the former Chelsea defender Willi Steffen, a man mountain of a defender. Gaps began to appear and Trevor scored twice in a five-minute spell to put us three up.

We were coasting towards my first international victory when suddenly the Swiss counter-attacked and for twenty minutes, along with a few others in the Welsh defence, I suffered another nightmare. Bickel, their captain and centre-forward, dragged me all over the park. It was his cross from the right that opened up the way for Ballaman to score the first, and another quickly followed from Antenen. We held on grimly for the last ten minutes and were lucky to come away with a narrow 3–2 victory. But my frailties had again been put under the microscope and I found myself back in the wilderness, this time until 1953.

While I was in the army, I played a couple of games at centre-forward for Leeds, but as Trooper Charles I preferred to play at centre-half or even right-back because, to be quite honest, it was easier than playing up front and being kicked by some big squaddie. Nevertheless, I managed to rupture my left cartilages twice, inside and outside. It was quite serious in those days – cartilage injuries were known to finish careers altogether – but the surgeon told me they had taken a lot out and it wouldn't take me long to get back. He told me they had left some intact to stop the bones rubbing together, and to this day I do not know whether he was serious, but he did a fine job. The operations, however, caused me to miss a large part of the 1951–52 season – my leg was sore for a while – and I played just twenty-three games for Leeds, mostly at the back. We finished sixth, after two seasons at fifth.

I was a big man to carry the weight and I suppose something had to give. It was hardly surprising my body was objecting as I was playing football twice a week in the army and once or twice a week for Leeds. One time, I played for the army in Durham on the Friday, caught a train to Cardiff to play for Leeds on Saturday and was back in camp in Carlisle on the Sunday evening. On a really good week, I would play for the army on a Wednesday, for the regiment on a Thursday and for Leeds on a Saturday. It was wonderful – and when I wasn't playing, I worked in the sports store. I also ran for the unit and won the 100 and 200 yards, and the high and long jumps. At football, I captained my unit to the Army Cup, the first trophy I had won since I was a kid.

One day when I got back to Elland Road from camp, I was told there was someone waiting to see me. It was my brother Melvyn. He had followed the Charles path from Swansea to Leeds, also picked up by the hard-working Mr Pickard. He had been earmarked when he helped Swansea to win the English Schools' Trophy in 1950.

This time our roles were reversed – Melvyn was left kicking his heels at Leeds in much the same way as I had been at Swansea. I managed to persuade him to be patient and even moved my digs so that I could be with him when I could get away from the army. He stayed for less than a year. One day he was standing on the touchline watching, telling me he was fed up and wanted to go back to Swansea. What could I say? I knew exactly what he was going through. I told him if he wanted to go back to Wales, that's what he should do. Leeds claimed they were sorry to see him go but agreed with his decision. He signed professional forms at the Vetch Field in 1952 and stayed with Swansea for seven years, making 233 league appearances for them and scoring 69 goals.

There was a pang when I put him on the train back home, but not as great as it might have been because I had found companionship with the lady who was to become my first wife, Peggy. I had met her a few months earlier at a local dancehall. Most of the players who were single went out together, mostly to the cinema, but every Saturday night we used to go to either the Scala or the Mecca Ballroom. If we didn't like the look of the girls in one, we would move downtown to the other one.

I was really no more a dancehall fan than I was a beer drinker but I enjoyed socialising with the lads. I hadn't started smoking in those days, even though no one related it to being bad for your health. Some of the adverts claimed that smoking was good for you. I've never been a beer drinker. I preferred whisky and lemonade – a little whisky and a lot of lemonade. It served me well when I went to Italy because none of the players there drank beer; it was all wine. When I arrived in Italy, everyone offered me a beer because I was British, but I would say no, I'll have a glass of wine. I had never tasted wine before. It was a rarity in my social circles.

Beer was a natural for a Welshman but I didn't like the taste. I tried it once and that was it. If I had beer at all after that, it was just a splash with a lot of lemonade. I remember going to the pub with my dad. He put half a pint of beer in front of me and said, 'There, drink that.' I supped it but said, 'I don't like it,' and that was it; I never drank it neat any more. I was about eighteen when I started drinking alcohol at all, but it was only when I went out with the boys or to some function connected with the club. The waiter would say, 'Will you have champagne, Sir?' No, I'll have a whisky and lemonade, would be my answer.

When I met Peggy, she was no football fan. She had been to Elland Road twice, that's all, but by remarkable coincidence the first time was when I made my debut against Queen of the South.

We were engaged just after Christmas 1952, on my twenty-first birthday.

When I was called up, I had started to put on some weight but the army kept me so fit that when I came out I had shed a few pounds. One reason I came out a better player than when I went in was playing basketball. It certainly helped my heading. I knew nothing of the game before I did my national service, but when I was asked to play, it was just like boxing – if I played, it would get me off some of the more unpleasant duties. Before that, I thought it was a girls' game, but I soon changed my opinion. In half an hour of basketball I burned up as much energy as playing for ninety minutes at football. The speed, the ball movement, the end-to-end play and the need to twist, turn and leap tremendous heights were of enormous value to me as a footballer. It helped me develop my stamina and taught me to jump; so much so that afterwards I maintained that every professional club should have a basketball court.

I have no complaints about my days in the army. Barnard Castle was fine for me as it wasn't far from Leeds. It would have been less easy if I had been forced to travel miles to play, but every Wednesday and Saturday when Leeds had a game, they let me off. If the truth be known, I spent two years playing sport while still doing my normal job. I felt very privileged. It was like being in the army and then spending the entire two years on leave. I trained a lot and played more than I would have done had I stayed at Elland Road. I would go so far as to say it was memorable and I believe it improved me as a player. Others claim they lost touch with the game in their two years but how does square bashing make anyone forget how to trap the ball or pass it to someone else?

I did not even have to make up for my football breaks in the summer because I played cricket for the regiment. Mostly, I played cricket to enjoy it. I still bowled fast, but no bouncers, of course, especially not to the officers – I was too much of a gentleman for that!

CHAPTER FIVE

You're playing centre-forward

I t was while I was in the army that Major Buckley dropped his latest bombshell. I had become used to playing left-half, right-back, centre-half, but when he told me one Easter Saturday I was going to wear the No. 9 shirt you could have knocked me over.

On the Good Friday, our regular centre-forward, Len Browning, was injured at Hull. It quickly became clear that he would not be fit to play against Manchester City at Maine Road the following day, 24 March 1951. I was one of eight changes and, needless to say, the biggest surprise for our fans and the press.

When the Major pulled me to one side to tell me about it, I did not think it was worth commenting. He had made up his mind and that was that. But the shock must have shown on my face because he smiled, patted me on the shoulder and said, 'Don't worry – you'll be all right!'

In fact, I had scored before. My first league goal was in November

1949 when I scored against Plymouth Argyle at Home Park from the penalty spot; I was seventeen years old. We won 2–1 and I scored the winner in the second half.

As if to prove the Major wasn't always right, City thrashed us 4–1 that afternoon, but with Len still unfit, I was given the No. 9 shirt for the next match, against Hull on the Easter Monday. This time we won 3–0 and I scored two of the goals, prompting the Major to pat me on the shoulder again, telling me, 'I said you'd be all right.'

There was a great deal of controversy over whether I should play centre-half or centre-forward. There was history involved. Leeds' left-back Jim Milburn had been pressed into service as an auxiliary forward. It didn't work and he was moved around to different positions, didn't do well and didn't get his old place back. He was eventually sold to Bradford City. With this bitter tale in mind, a lot of people were telling the club not to move John Charles to centre-forward because if it didn't work, what would happen to him? It caused a big debate in the national as well as the local press. The only person not to become involved in the discussions was me. I did as I was told. If the Major told me I was to play centre-forward, I played centre-forward – if I had refused, I would not have played at all. The Major would not have hesitated; he would have brought in the reserve. It never crossed my mind to answer him back or say no to him.

He did not sit me down to talk about this massive change in role; he just had us playing and practising, like he always did with everyone he tried in different positions. If he thought you were going to do well, you stayed there.

However, I was brave enough to tell him I had never played up front before, not even as a schoolboy. Moving from left-half to centre-half was fine, but I was not a centre-forward. I told him I didn't know how to play it. He said, 'Jack, you just go out there and play, and that's it.' Later he told me, 'You know all the tricks the centre-forwards use against you – now you can use them yourself.'

The Major was right in the long run and I went on to score 157 goals in 327 appearances for Leeds and the supporters re-christened the club Charles United. I did not agree with that. In fact, I thought it was a bit of an insult to the club and the other players, but how could I complain? They were wonderful supporters, truly unbelievable.

Leeds were desperate for that elusive promotion to the top flight and the chairman, Mr Bolton, came up with a good scheme – good for me, that is. Mr Bolton knew I was uncertain about the major shift in position and he called me into his office shortly before the game and said, 'John, this is what I'll do. I'll give you a pound for every goal you score.' I thought it was wonderful gesture; in the end, I was scoring too many goals for the chairman's purse and he had to cut back on the deal.

Those two goals against Hull did not exactly mark the start of my career as a goalscoring centre-forward. You would have thought the manager would have been congratulating himself on his shrewd move, but this is the Major we are talking about. Nothing was ever certain when he had the teamsheet in front of him. I didn't play in the next game and was back at centre-half the following week. I was selected to lead the attack a few more times but basically, despite what he might have seen, the Major dropped the idea of me playing centre-forward. It wasn't until October 1952 that he revived it with startling success.

I responded by scoring two against Halifax Town in an experiment in the West Riding Senior Cup final. Then on 18 and 25 October, I scored in league games against Barnsley and Lincoln City. It was taking off. On 1 November I scored a hat-trick at home against Hull City and suddenly I was a centre-forward. It was the first hat-trick by a Leeds player for over two years. The last one was scored by Len Browning, who was forced to quit the game soon afterwards due to a serious illness.

This time the Major wanted me to carry on playing up front, and carry on scoring. I was fortunate enough to do exactly that and took my tally to ten in six games, including the two against Halifax. Then I scored all three in a 3–2 win against Brentford at Elland Road. My last-minute winner put me in the record books for scoring all of the last ten goals scored by the club, breaking the record set twenty-two years earlier by Charlie Keetley, who scored a sequence of seven.

Suddenly, the media were no longer complaining and even Tommy Lawton, one of my heroes who was then playing for Brentford, described me as a 'great centre-forward' and compared me with Dixie Dean. I was flattered but unimpressed because I knew I was not in that class. I never saw Dixie Dean play but I know he was a terrific player.

Tommy Lawton was also a great player, one of the best strikers I have seen, especially among British players. His greatest skill was heading the ball, and I would watch and learn from him, even when I played against him. It was his overall technique. I learned everything from him. He was friendly and very helpful and he once told me, 'John, always head it from there,' pointing to his forehead. I pointed to mine, showed him the big lump, and said, 'I know that, Tommy. You only have to look at my head to see it.'

I must confess to great satisfaction over scoring the winner against Tommy's Brentford. The surface was like an ice-skating rink and when I received the ball in my half, my only thought so late in the game was to take it out of the danger area. I managed to evade three challenges on the slippery surface and then went round the goalkeeper before beating the covering defender on the line. I went on to score over thirty goals for my club that season and was beginning to think that maybe I could play in the position after all, especially with the chairman giving me a pound a goal.

He was a generous man, was the chairman, but not always totally aware of what was going on around him. He once gave me three gallons of petrol for scoring a hat-trick, a lovely present. The only problem was that I didn't drive at the time. I only had a bike and it didn't need petrol, just leg power!

The money was now tremendous in terms of what I had been earning and I was able to move out of my digs and buy myself a little house 200 yards up the road from the ground. If I recall correctly, it cost about £600 and I was able to get a mortgage to pay for it. I told them I was earning £12 a week, but really it was £15 or £16 a week if we won and if I scored a few goals. I told them that if I had a good day and got a couple of hat-tricks, I was very rich. I didn't mention there were no bonuses of any sort in the summer. Living so close to the club meant I even saved on bus fares and if I wanted to go further afield there were always friendly people with cars who would pick me up. There was also a fish and chip shop just over the road from the ground, which often provided me with my evening meal.

During that season, I also won my place back in the Welsh side, against Northern Ireland in Belfast in April 1953, I was hoping for third time lucky. We gathered in Liverpool, caught the steamer across and were picked up by coach and driven to our training headquarters in Bangor.

I was selected at inside-right to support my old Swansea club-mate Trevor Ford in what was being described as a double battering ram. Major Buckley was very obliging and even played me at inside-right in a league match to give me the experience – hard to imagine that happening now.

I had to learn to keep going backwards and forwards instead of going out to the flanks as I did when playing centre-forward. We spent two days working on tactical moves before Ronnie Burgess suggested that Trevor Ford and I should switch places throughout the game to confuse the opposition. That was radical in those days.

Our plans almost went up in smoke when the coach broke down on the way to the ground and we eventually arrived just half an hour before the kick-off. In some ways it helped because, once we'd arrived, there was no time for nerves or second thoughts. Trevor Ford and I found an immediate understanding. I scored two in the first half, Trevor added the other and we won 3–2.

There were no blank days in the fixtures back then and we were straight back to play a league game, ironically against Swansea. Four of us – Ivor Allchurch, Harry Griffiths, Terry Medwin and me – left the rest of the Welsh squad at Liverpool and caught a train to get us into Swansea two hours before the kick-off. It was cutting it fine and the inevitable happened. Weekend rail works delayed the train and we stopped so often that we arrived in Swansea with just minutes to spare. We would not have made it at all but for the fact that the delay was known about at the Vetch and when we jumped off the train we found a taxi sent for us. By the time we reached the ground, everyone was changed, ready and waiting for the latecomers.

I expected to play at centre-forward but was told I had been switched to inside-right. I didn't ask the reason why but I quickly found out when we lined up – there was Mel, lining up at centre-half for Swansea. The manager had sensibly decided not to match us up directly.

It was the first time we had played against each other, and we carefully avoided any clashes. That was to be the pattern in future games when we met. We were never in direct opposition although, inevitably, we clashed now and again.

I was delighted to score the first goal after fifteen minutes or so when the entire Swansea team, including Mel, stopped and appealed for offside. I didn't hear a whistle and carried on to score. Mel was furious but his attitude softened a little when they finished 3–2 winners.

Next time we played against each other we were both picked at centre-forward. Mel got one up on me at Swansea by scoring almost straight from the kick-off. I equalised but we lost again. Fortunately, in the return I scored a couple and we won at Elland Road.

Whenever we played against each other we always chatted, before matches and afterwards. The only time we clashed was at corners when we would find we were up against each other. Mel was not a Gentle Giant – just a giant! He didn't mind putting an elbow or a boot in against his brother – or whoever it was. When we were in opposition, I used to call him everything. The Gentleman John bit certainly did not extend to my language. That was fairly explicit.

But we were good brothers and loved each other dearly. We were very close indeed and enjoyed playing against each other. We used to laugh about it afterwards because if we didn't, we would have fought.

That is how football should be, with no quarter asked or given on the pitch, and then a drink together in the bar afterwards. I enjoyed that and I think it's sad these days that the players' bar is going out of fashion. It would be a good place for the foreign players to relax and get to know not only their team-mates but also the opposition. It is wrong to carry your animosity away with you after a game. Players should be friends after a football match, no matter what the result is. You play to the best of your abilities, and that's it.

Raich Carter took over the team for the 1953–54 season when the Major moved to Walsall. He continued to play me up front and I rewarded him with forty-two league goals (plus one in the Cup), a club record that stands to this day. I knew it was going to be my season after scoring four goals, including a hat-trick, in a little over thirty minutes at home against Notts County in a 6–0 win. In fact,

I managed fourteen goals in the first eight games, not a pace I could maintain; neither could we hold on to our top of the table place and we eventually slipped down to tenth place.

I decided very early on that I was not going to play like my hero Trevor Ford, or Peter McParland, the tough Aston Villa forward. I decided I was going to play the game by the rules. I was fortunate that the Major was not concerned about my attitude to playing football. He never asked me to go out and kick anyone. He told me to go out and play the way I knew best.

Never in my career, at home or in Italy, did I have a manager who asked me to go out and kick anyone – and that includes Jimmy Scoular. He was a hard man in anyone's terms, even in training. When I was at Cardiff, later in my career, we would have a practice match and he would kick hell out of everyone. He may have been tough, and often dirty, but he was another I liked very much; he was very companionable. He was also a very good player, a fact sometimes overlooked because of his reputation.

My philosophy was not something I sat down and thought about. It came naturally to me. Football is football and you have to play the way you have been brought up. I was brought up as a young lad to play football and not to kick people, but I understood that you would have a hard man in the team against you. It was part of the game and not a problem – it was simply not for me.

I was never booked in my entire career, a record I am proud of. I understand that Gary Lineker holds the same untarnished record, but don't forget I played a lot of my career at centre-half where bookings are more commonplace. I suppose it was the teachers at school who helped me. I have heard of teachers telling boys to 'get stuck in', and as I got bigger, other people used to tell me to sort a few out. I never felt the need. I can honestly say that, throughout my career, I never deliberately kicked anyone, nor did I go out to hurt anyone. Sure, a few might have bounced off me and got more than they bargained for, but I never hurt them. I threatened a few. I wasn't shy about cussing and swearing and, being a pretty big guy, if I had a go, players would sometimes back away. I never used an elbow because that is the coward's way.

Mind you, not everyone thought I was an angel of virtue. Jack Charlton, an old Leeds team-mate, before and after Juventus, once observed, 'John ran with his arms and elbows high and when he went on a surge he left a trail of human devastation behind him. Bloody Gentle Giant indeed!'

When I started playing up front, I took the Major's advice and thought about the centre-forwards I had played against, such as little Charlie Wayman, who was quick, had good ball control and was able to put bigger men off balance with his twists and darts. I decided the centre-forward who caused me the biggest problems was not the direct thrustful type such as Trevor Ford, but the roving kind, who switched from wing to wing and presented the centre-half with the problem of whether to follow his man or stay put on his own in the middle.

This was how I decided to play the position. I would use my height to head the ball down to my inside-forwards and go for goal whenever the chance presented, on the floor or in the air. I was not going to become a human battering ram just because of my size and strength.

Major Buckley was obviously thinking along the same lines for he said, 'No one can take the ball from him; he is so strong and sure of himself. Yet he is absolutely unspoiled. I honestly don't think he knows how good he is. That's a fine thing – and all too rare these days.' Maybe he was trying to push up my fee.

I did not always earn total appreciation from my team-mates. There was one occasion when we were playing against Doncaster with the score deadlocked at 0–0. I raced on to a through ball, but when I realised their goalkeeper, Ken Hardwick, would reach it first, I leapt over him at the last moment to save us both from a nasty collision. I had a warm handshake from Ken at the end of the game and nice applause from the crowd, but I thought nothing of it; the reaction was instinctive and I would have done the same whenever the occasion arose, whether I was in England or Italy.

I took some terrible knocks in Italy. They certainly weren't girlish over there. They respected me for my attitude and, up to a point, they did not kick me – only when they thought they could get away with it, or to stop me scoring a goal. Perhaps they respected the fact that I wouldn't kick them, so they were different towards me.

I do not say everyone should model themselves on me. The game is what it is because there are so many different styles and different characters; it's the blend of those characters that makes our game so great. If no one kicked anyone, it could get pretty tame one way or another, and I am sure Trevor Ford would not have been such a big attraction to me when I was a kid if he had gone around saying, 'After you, Claude.' If everyone played like me, we wouldn't have a game.

You knew before you ran out who was going to try to kick you. Personally, I would keep away from them. It is a lot easier today to be my sort of player because players are so well protected by referees and the changes in the laws. There are those from my era who wouldn't have got a game if they could not tackle from behind, kick people and generally create mayhem. Most teams had at least one.

The killer was the two-footed tackle, or the stamp over the ball; we used to call it the leg breaker. I remember playing in a charity match against Celtic at Leeds United alongside my manager, Raich Carter. Great player that he was, he went over the top at someone he had a grudge against. Johnny Giles was another tough customer who worked on developing his fearsome reputation as a form of self-defence to save his career. Raich was a bugger – he even used to kick his own players in training. He used to love playing in friendlies and floodlit matches when he was manager. I loved the man but I also felt he was a bit of a big-head. He was never happier than when talking about himself and he often took the credit for others' achievements. I always felt he was in love with himself.

I was becoming increasingly impatient to try my luck in the top division against the best teams. Promotion was becoming an obsession for the entire club. Leeds had dropped out of the First Division straight after the war and had been in a constant, frustrating battle to get back to the top flight ever since. One big problem was that they were competing with Leeds' rugby league side, and the many other rugby league sides around the area, for the glory and, more importantly, for the fans.

I knew I would have no problems finding a decent First Division club because I had been 'tapped' by a few who let me know there would be a place for me with them if I became available; and so the next season, 1954–55, when things were looking particularly bleak, I asked for a transfer. In fact, I had asked for one the season before to no avail. This time I was called into a board meeting to be told that my transfer request had been turned down, and I would not be able to leave. I was not really surprised and decided to buckle down and do my best for the club. What was the point of sulking?

We had won one of our first six games and although I had scored four in that time, I was moved back to centre-half to shore up a defence that was leaking goals. We recovered quite well from our bad start and finished fourth behind Birmingham and Luton with Rotherham third. We were just a point behind the promoted teams with four points separating the top six. That's how tight it was. It was a big improvement from our middle of the table position the previous season. Despite playing at the back most of the time, I scored a dozen goals in my forty-two league and Cup appearances, including five penalties.

The following season, there was strong competition again, this time between us, Sheffield Wednesday, Liverpool, Leicester, Blackburn and Bristol Rovers. Halfway through the campaign, half the clubs in the division were still in with a chance of promotion. At the end of the season just three points separated the ten teams below the promotion places.

I started in defence but was moved forward after two heavy defeats against Sheffield Wednesday and Bristol Rovers, and we gradually improved, but by the end of March it looked as though we were out of contention. We had plodded along, lost to Cardiff in the third round of the Cup and now, with nothing else to play for, we made a late challenge in the League.

On 30 March, we came from behind to beat Fulham 2–1 at Craven Cottage. Then we hammered them 6–1 at Elland Road. I scored a hat-trick in that one and then two against Leicester in a 4–0 win. We followed that with a 2–1 win over Doncaster Rovers. Then we came back from a goal down again, this time against Bristol Rovers at home in front of 50,000.

The crunch came on 28 April when we played Hull City at Boothferry Park. Hull were already relegated and we needed to beat them to clinch promotion. A total of 31,123 people watched the match, and for us it was like a home game because 15,000 fans travelled from Leeds.

I scored the opening goal but then the nerves began to twang. It was hardly surprising as the club had been trying for promotion for so long and this seemed to be our last chance. Hull equalised before the break and we began to struggle as everyone became more and more anxious. But it settled down when I scored my second with a penalty, and we went on to add two more through Harold Brook, eventually winning 4–1.

It meant we finished second, three points behind Sheffield Wednesday on 55 with 101 goals, with Liverpool, Blackburn, Leicester and Bristol Rovers all close behind us on the same number of points. Had we failed that season, I had the feeling everything could fall apart. It was widely known that Raich Carter would have gone, for a start.

But we had done it and we were rewarded with an official bonus of £20 – no unofficial bonuses, sadly. By then, the directors must have decided we owed them and I did not even get my £1 a goal.

It was tight all season although Sheffield Wednesday always looked favourite; for the rest, it was a constant battle. The crucial games for us were those two against Fulham and Bristol Rovers when we came back to win from being a goal down. Had we lost to Fulham, we would have slipped behind, but the win gave us that extra bit of confidence; and when we did the same against Rovers, we had the feeling that luck, at last, was on our side and nothing could stop us. Confidence can achieve that in sport.

Promotion and the thought of mixing it with the big boys meant the atmosphere on our traditional end of season trip to Holland was very special. Most of the £2 per day allowance went on Dutch gin and beers as we celebrated. We even had something to eat occasionally!

CHAPTER SIX

Life in the top division

I had waited a long time to test myself against the best English football had to offer. From the moment I signed for the club in 1947, the one aim of everyone at Elland Road was to take Leeds United back to the First Division. Our failure to do so had me so concerned about my long-term future that I even asked for a transfer. Yet, after all that effort, I played for just one season in the top flight before moving on to Juventus.

But it was a year I will not forget. Manchester United, Spurs, Preston North End, Blackpool and the rest made it memorable in every way. As much as I respected the players in the lower divisions, working to better themselves, I wanted to play against Stanley Matthews at Blackpool, Tom Finney at Preston North End and Billy Wright at Wolves – not just at international level but in the bread and butter Saturday afternoon football of the First Division.

We were full of hope and expectation, especially when we beat Everton 5–1 in front of 31,379 ecstatic fans at Elland Road, but it was a tough baptism and we were wondering whether it was too much of a challenge when Spurs mauled us at White Hart Lane early on in the season. But we had a good, promising, young team who were prepared to learn, develop and fight.

We had finished the 1955–56 season as runners-up to a much more mature Sheffield Wednesday side that had scored over 100 goals and lost just eight matches compared with our 13. What a difference there was this time! As with any team gaining promotion, our collective aim was to consolidate and survive, but we finished in a very creditable eighth place with exactly the same number of defeats as the season before. The difference was that we drew 14 of our 42 games. By contrast, Wednesday struggled and finished fourteenth with 38 points, six less than us – and in those days, it was two for the win and one for the draw.

I enjoyed myself, mostly at inside-right, and was fortunate enough to score 38 goals in the league programme of 42 games, making me the division's top goalscorer – very flattering but a credit to my team-mates who helped me score those goals.

Champions for the second time were Manchester United, the famous Busby Babes. What a team that was with Duncan Edwards, Roger Byrne, Dennis Viollet, Tommy Taylor, Bobby Charlton, Jackie Blanchflower and the rest. It seems incredible now that they had to fight the Football League before gaining permission to enter the European Cup competition as a result of their 1956 title win. They promptly thrashed the seasoned Anderlecht side from Belgium 10–0, prompting their skipper Jef Mermans to comment, 'Why don't they pick the entire side for England? The best teams from Hungary have never beaten us like this.' They were beaten in the semi-final by the incredible Real Madrid. Now they had qualified for the competition again, but the campaign was to end with the catastrophic air crash in Munich in February 1958.

The Babes reached the 1957 FA Cup final against Aston Villa, losing out on the double when Peter McParland crashed into goalkeeper Ray Wood, knocking him out and fracturing his cheekbone, leaving United with ten men. Even then, they lost 2–1 only, with Jackie Blanchflower in goal.

Our Cup run ended prematurely when we were knocked out in the third round by Cardiff City, 2–1 at home for the second successive season. That was part of a hat-trick – they did it again the next year, not only by the same score but again at Elland Road. What sort of odds would you get for that sequence?

We were not a renowned Cup side; we had not won a Cup-tie since 1952, and with the exception of a defeat by Spurs, we were put out by clubs who were lower placed than we were and teams we expected to beat. But Cup-ties prove nothing in a league environment where form over the entire season counts. We were surprised, I remember, by the difference in quality between the top two divisions, not just the odd international player but generally. In fact, I found the difference huge. Football was much smarter in the top division; the higher the class you played, the quicker you had to think.

In the lower division when I played centre-half, I could go forward, confident that, if things broke down, I would be able to get back before my absence could be exploited. It was not the case at the upper level where they not only spotted the gaps in your defence but also worked the ball forward so quickly and accurately you were given no chance to get back into position.

In the Second Division, every team wants promotion, then for the honour and the glory, now for the big, big money. The result is a mad scramble for the top places. Football was undoubtedly harder in the Second Division when I played, with the ball player often submerged by tough tackling opponents. A promotion side not only had to be a good, winning side but also a very resilient one, able to take and give the knocks, but once in the top flight, they discovered the difference. There the ball players, the quality footballers and the rapid thinkers prospered, with brains punishing brawn more often than not.

I was delighted to have the chance. As an individual, I felt that not only was I tested but also the best was brought out of me, and paved the way for my transfer to Italy.

An interesting footnote to the season was the return of air travel for the bigger clubs. It was banned as a form of team travel by the League because their insurance did not cover it, but the ruling was relaxed at Easter during my one season in the First Division when Chelsea were granted permission to fly to and from Newcastle while Blackpool flew to London and back for their game against Arsenal. It was on Easter Friday and the teams had another fixture the next day, so it made sense. Motorways were not built until the next decade and most of the away travel, especially for us at Leeds, was done by train.

There was trouble during the season over illegal payments. I don't think they would have been too worried about our odd £1 here and there, but Trevor Ford mentioned something in a newspaper article and was suspended.

I was interested to observe what was going on around me. In the Second Division, everyone was fighting to prove themselves; some wanted to better themselves and others, like me, yearned for top-class football every week. But in the First Division, there were some who clearly thought they had made it and I must say that big-headedness ruined more football careers than damaged cartilages did. There were players who thought they were the world's gift, and they would sink quicker than the Bismarck.

The most dangerous time for a footballer is up to the age of twenty-one, when he can think he is better than he really is. You need a big heart, not a big head, to make it in sport. The big heads rarely made it beyond twenty-one. They would disappear. You have to have self-confidence but you have to know where to draw the line and to be able to do things properly without showing off. It wasn't up to you; it was up to other people's judgement.

Personally, I was never totally satisfied with my performances but I knew the difference between having a good game and a bad game. In those days, a player would come off and admit to having a stinker. You don't hear that so often these days.

I was always my own severest critic; it was the only way to improve. I used to go back in the afternoons to work on my weak points, such as my left foot. Major Buckley would always send a trainer out to work with me, to encourage and help me. That was how I became two-footed. The Major used to hold up his hand above his head and say, 'Jack, you only jumped that high when you should be jumping higher.' He made me jump up and head the crossbar, no ball. It was a recipe for a headache but it worked.

So I concentrated on learning my trade at a higher level and, by Easter, I was preparing myself for an even greater challenge.

CHAPTER SEVEN

Signing for Juventus

J uventus were very patient in their bid to take me from Leeds
United to Turin. Their interest began in 1955 with the visit of
their scout and my friend Gigi Peronace; it came to fruition
when I signed for the famous Italian club at Easter 1957. During
that time, there were many suggestions about where I would go,
thousands of rumours and several big, big bids.

The first time I read of any interest in me from outside was in
March 1951 when it was reported that Major Buckley had turned
down an offer from Sunderland of £15,000 plus Ivor Broadis. The
Major confirmed that he had turned down the bid, but still wanted
to buy Broadis.

A year later, I read that a world record bid of £40,000 had been
made for me by a mystery club, beating the £34,500 paid by Sheffield
Wednesday to Notts County for Jackie Sewell. The figure was
stunning – even more amazing was the fact that Major Buckley had

turned it down. Many people thought the mystery club was the then wealthy Sunderland again, but I believe that it was Arsenal. I think Tom Whittaker was the man who was prepared to break the bank for this young Welshman, who wasn't sure he was worth that sort of investment.

After the first bid/rumour there were many others and, indeed, Arsenal were back in for me in 1953 after an awful start to their season. Such was the strength of the story, the London papers were predicting that I would stay in the capital after the Saturday game at Fulham and would be playing for Arsenal against Chelsea on the Tuesday. I scored twice against Fulham in a 3–1 win and Raich Carter was as adamant as Major Buckley had been before him, saying, 'John Charles is not, I repeat not, for sale. You just cannot afford to sell players like him because money could not buy a replacement.'

Manchester United and Sunderland were reputed to have topped Arsenal's bid, lifting it to an amazing £50,000, with Lazio of Rome topping the lot when they offered £65,000.

I have to admit that I thought about what it would be like to play for Arsenal or Spurs or Manchester United, and my taste of international football with Wales only succeeded in increasing the urge to try out against the best, whether it was at centre-half or centre-forward. My ambition was to play against these great teams for Leeds but, in 1953, that looked a long way off, which was when I asked for a transfer the first time. Nothing happened despite lots of stories and rumours so, in 1954, I asked again and that really took the lid off it. Cardiff manager Cyril Spiers put in a tremendous bid of £50,000, followed, it was said, by a stream of others.

It caused a huge fuss in Leeds and there were even polls taken in the *Yorkshire Evening Post* about whether I should go or stay. It was very even, with those for me staying saying that the club should build a team round me, and those wanting me sold making the point that they could buy two top players with what I would fetch.

There was an old saying that if you stayed in the Second Division too long, you became a Second Division player and, in this respect, the finger had been pointed at my countryman Ivor Allchurch and the outstanding England and Fulham player Johnny Haynes.

The Cardiff bid was a sustained one with Sir Herbert Merrett, president of Cardiff, telling the *Western Mail* in Wales, 'You can tell the public of South Wales that if Leeds United agree to sell John Charles then Cardiff City will leave no stone unturned in order to get his services. I have been told that Arsenal are the favourites with us for his signature. All I can say to that is anything Arsenal can do, Cardiff can do.

'For a long time, I have been a keen admirer of John Charles and I am convinced he could do us a power of good. In view of that, we are prepared to go to the limit because for a long time now I have made it known that Cardiff City would always go after Welshmen of note.'

I was flattered by the interest shown by Arsenal but a move to Cardiff would have meant moving back home and that made them more interesting to me than the Gunners.

Two days later, Leeds told new Cardiff manager Trevor Morris they would not sell. They called me into the boardroom to tell me the news and then sent me out to play in a friendly against Hibernian. They even announced over the loudspeakers that I was staying and not going to Cardiff, Arsenal or Sheffield Wednesday, the other club who were offering big money for my services. There was no use moaning or throwing a tantrum. In those circumstances, you simply had to get on with the job and that's what I did. The rumour and speculation did not affect me at all. By this time, I was married to Peggy and we were settled in our house in Leeds. I decided that until I was directly involved, there was no point in worrying about where

I might be playing next week or next season. Leeds had turned down two transfer requests so I settled down, ready to see out my career with them.

I had far more problems with the description of 'the world's greatest player'. That I found really embarrassing and not worth the paper it was written on. I was part of a team, not an individual. I was only as good as those around me, particularly when I played up front and relied upon their service. Leeds were treating me well, I was happy and the only cloud on my horizon was the fact that we were still struggling to take our place in the top division. How could you call anyone the world's greatest player when he wasn't playing against the best players week in and week out?

That, however, was not the end of the matter. Over the two years he had been coming to the club, Gigi Peronace continued to watch me train and play, so I got to know him well. In those days, it was considerably easier to make contact with professional footballers than it is now, especially if you had good contacts – and Gigi had many. Finally, on 6 April 1957, when we were due to play Arsenal at Highbury, the personable Italian told me that Juventus had made up their minds to sign me at any price. He said they were not only prepared to pay Leeds a world-record fee but I would receive a huge signing-on fee, which would make me richer than any British player in history. I had known Gigi for a long time, and I was not inclined to get excited about his latest statement, interesting as it was.

The story began to take on substance four days later when it was announced that the twenty-two-year-old Signor Umberto Agnelli, the new President of Juventus and one of the bosses of the massive Fiat Motor Company, was flying to Belfast to watch me play against Northern Ireland at Windsor Park.

This seemed to take the flame to the touch paper; the very next day there were newspaper headlines to the effect that Real Madrid,

One of my favourite pictures of me with my parents, Ned and Lily.

Between 1950 and 1952 I was called up to do National Service in the 12th Royal Lancers. I'd already started playing for Leeds United by then, and was allowed back to play for them at weekends.

Cup action against Bolton Wanderers in my first full season at Leeds in the winter of 1949–50.

COLORSPORT

EMPICS

I may have scored in this October 1953 game against Brentford (and went on to score a record forty-two league goals in the season), but we lost the game and ended up in mid-table – the two important statistics.

Finally, after nine seasons in Division Two, we secured promotion to the top level with a 4–1 victory at Hull City in April 1956. About 15,000 Leeds fans made the journey, and they were all keen to congratulate me.

Some of the promotion-winning squad relax in a snooker hall. We are, from the left: Keith Ripley, Jack Charlton, me, Bobby Forrest, Jimmy Dunn and Harold Williams.

England keeper Ray Wood covers up as I head for goal in the Wales v England international at Wembley in November 1954. We lost 3–2, despite my two goals.

Although we never all played in the same side, around 1960 Wales had three sets of brothers to call upon: me and Mel, Ivor and Lenny Allchurch, and Bryn and Cliff Jones.

Following a fire in the main stand at Leeds, the club decided to cash in on the transfer fees being offered for me and I was sold to Juventus for £65,000 in April 1957. When I arrived in Turin, captain Giampiero Boniperti was there to measure me up for the famous black and white shirt.

In flying action in Rome in September 1957. I was to end the season as the Italian Player of the Year, the leading goalscorer in the league and, above all, part of the team that won the precious Scudetto.

Getting ready for action alongside my strike partner Omar Sivori. The Argentinian was a tough little character, but a terrific player.

The Inter Milan defenders Cardarelli and Fongaro challenge for the ball, but I still manage to get above them to score.

GETTY IMAGES

Peggy and I take our three sons, Terry, Melvyn and Peter, to the beach near our holiday villa.

The villa I bought with the money I earned at Juventus. It was the perfect getaway, just two hours from the pressures and scrutiny in Turin.

La dolce vita in Turin. At home with the family, where we were so well looked after by the club and by the fans.

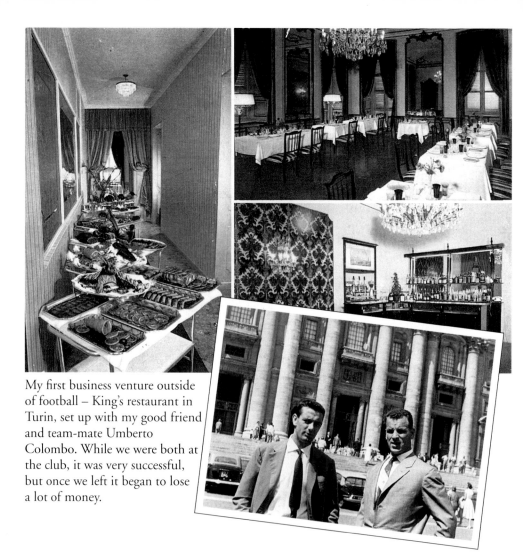

My first business venture outside of football – King's restaurant in Turin, set up with my good friend and team-mate Umberto Colombo. While we were both at the club, it was very successful, but once we left it began to lose a lot of money.

While never a full-time career, I always enjoyed singing, with songs such as 'Sixteen Tons' and 'Love in Portofino' being particular favourites. Not all the audience seem to be sharing my enthusiasm!

who had just beaten Manchester United in the semi-final of the European Cup, were also in the hunt, along with Lazio and Inter Milan from Italy, offering competition to Juventus. No one on the Leeds board was saying anything to me and, as far as I knew, it was Juventus in the chairman's office making a big money bid.

In those days, footballers were not superstars. We lived ordinary lives in ordinary houses among other ordinary people, but suddenly fans were stopping me in the street, newspapers were telephoning me at home and knocking on my door. Eventually, I went to see the chairman, Sam Bolton, and Raich Carter to ask them what was going on, and they assured me they would keep me informed. If one of these fabulous offers materialised, they would not stand in my way. They also told me they would not entertain an offer from any British club because all they could give me was exactly the same as I was earning at Elland Road.

The background to why Leeds eventually had to sell me was simple. We had started the 1956–57 season well and were chasing Manchester United at the top of the table. But on 18 September, just before we were due to play Aston Villa at Elland Road, a fire caused by an electrical fault razed the under-insured West Stand to the ground. The problem was, everything was contained in that stand: dressing rooms, offices, stores, everything and we lost all our kit and all of the physio's equipment. It was chaos. We had to change at a local sports field owned by Petty's the printers, and travel to the ground on a coach, which we used as a dressing room at half time. We had to play Villa in new boots that we hadn't had a chance to wear in and we were lucky to get away with a 1–0 win.

So the meeting took place in a temporary office. The price on my head had been going up and now Leeds decided to use the transfer fee Juventus were offering to help rebuild the ground, as the club did not have the available funds to cover the heavy costs.

It transpired that on that same day Leeds received a cable from Signor Agnelli advising them he was on his way to make them an offer for my services, but Leeds did not announce they were prepared to sell me to a foreign club until he arrived, two days later on 17 April.

Agnelli was immediately whisked into the BBC Television studios to be interviewed by Kenneth Wolstenholme for an edition of the popular midweek television programme 'Sportsview' on comparative salaries in England and Italy. I learned later from Kenneth that Agnelli had moved so quickly because he had heard that Lazio's English manager, Jesse Carver, wanted to take me to Rome. It was said that they even tabled a £50,000 bid, but Agnelli was more frightened that Real Madrid would steal me away rather than any rival Italian club.

You can imagine the build-up. It was frenzy. No previous transfer had aroused such interest in Britain. An anonymous Leeds business-man offered me £10,000 to stay at Leeds. Presumably, the figure had been reached to counterbalance any signing-on fee I may be offered by Juventus. Illegal payment? Who knows? But it was strange that the figure exactly matched the sum I was being offered as a signing-on fee. It wasn't, in any case, the sort of web to become entwined in with all the possible ramifications at a time when the Football League were investigating all sorts of illegal payments.

In the midst of all these stories, it was announced that Inter Milan were also sending a representative to Leeds.

The day Agnelli arrived, I received a cable which read, 'Am leaving London first thing in the morning with Kenneth Wolstenholme. Do nothing until we arrive.' It was signed Teddy Sommerfield.

Here was the other first. Teddy was an agent, the representative not of sportsmen and women but of broadcasters and musicians. He looked after Harry Carpenter, the boxing writer and commentator,

Eamonn Andrews, probably the best boxing commentator ever and presenter of television programmes including 'This is Your Life', and the versatile Peter West who captivated the nation on boat race day. Teddy had taken over my business affairs a couple of years earlier. Kenneth was not only a friend of his but also one of his men, and his knowledge of football was about to be put to full use.

To add to the fun, Peggy was pregnant with our third child. Journalists and photographers besieged our house but I have to say they were excellent and respected our privacy, and especially the fact that a baby was due soon.

I arranged to meet Teddy and Kenneth at Leeds railway station the next morning but, according to the press, the world and his dog were heading towards Leeds station, and while the Juventus party had left their Claridges Hotel by car – Fiat, of course – it was widely rumoured that Inter Milan and Lazio both had representatives heading north on the train.

Teddy and Kenneth were met by a porter from the adjacent hotel who immediately recognised Kenneth but thought the small dark man alongside him was an Italian. He promptly whisked them in through the back door of the hotel and up to room 222 where I was waiting. The three of us proceeded to go through everything that Teddy and Kenneth had managed to find out. We stayed in the room for around seven hours, breaking off only for dinner in the hotel's restaurant where, all through the meal, the Italian waiters tried to sell me their country, talking non-stop about the good food, the perfect climate and how lovely the people were. They did this believing that Teddy, born and bred in Warrington, was an Italian trying to sign me!

The other light moment came with the later editions of the *Yorkshire Evening Post*, announcing that 'John Charles and his friends have disappeared'. We had disappeared back to our room where we continued going through every detail, possible and impossible. Teddy was on and off the telephone to his London office where he had his lawyer and accountant working on every conceivable wrinkle, including the cost of living in Italy. We even knew what other Italian players were earning. Somehow they had got hold of an English translation of the complete rules of both the Italian Federation and the Italian League and how they affected the players, and also the standard form of contract for players there.

The two of them talked me through every angle and I doubt any player had ever gone into transfer talks better prepared. Certainly in England, with its maximum wage, it was a straight, 'Do you want to join us – yes or no?'

It has been widely reported that the two clubs were locked in talks in the same hotel – not true. The discussions were held at a factory on the outskirts of Leeds with chairman Sam Bolton, director Percy Woodward, a bluff northern businessman and a real character who lived just round the corner from me, and Raich Carter representing Leeds while Umberto Agnelli, Gigi Peronace and the general manager of Fiat in England, Gaetono Bollo, batted for Juventus. That last one I found a little strange. It was only later that talks moved to the Queens Hotel, room 233, just across the corridor from where I was meeting with Teddy and Kenneth. No one listened at the door.

It was deep into the evening when the two clubs eventually agreed on everything and I was summoned to their room; I insisted that Teddy be allowed to join me. The Italians quickly discovered why when Teddy revealed how much he knew about Italian football and their transfers. We talked for two hours and I believe we wore Agnelli down. He had had a long day of continued meetings and faced a car ride back to London overnight and a morning flight back to Turin. We suggested a break so he could have something to eat and he telephoned room service to order boiled eggs, red wine and coffee. I thought they had some strange eating habits in Italy.

There was just one stumbling block. Juventus were struggling fourth from bottom of Serie A and if they were relegated, both parties agreed the deal would be off. Clubs in the Second Division were not allowed to sign foreign players and, in any case, I would not have wanted to go to Turin in those circumstances.

The negotiations had gone on forever and it was well after midnight when Agnelli stepped outside to tell the patiently waiting newspapermen that agreement had been reached – not that it did them much good because it was Maunday Thursday and there were no newspapers on Good Friday in those days. At least they had their story for when the presses did roll again.

I left the hotel room at 1.15 in the morning, and while I returned home to bed, Kenneth and Teddy stayed, going over every detail of the contract again until after 4 a.m. It still awaited my signature.

The next day I travelled with Leeds to Sunderland. We played three games over Easter and it was not until 23 April that Peggy and I caught the sleeper to London, the BOAC flight to Rome and on to Turin. The journey was broken up when we ran into the Northern Irish team at Rome airport. They were on their way to play Italy in the Olympic Stadium two days later in a World Cup qualifying game, and we spent a couple of jolly hours with them at their hotel before catching the onward flight. When we arrived, thousands of people were waiting to greet us. I wondered what they were all doing there. Apart from the reporters, photographers and the fans, Umberto Agnelli, the manager Ljubisa Brocic, from Yugoslavia, and all the players were there. I couldn't believe it. Peggy and I were swept away with the atmosphere.

From the airport it was straight on to the Molinette Hospital where I had to take a series of medicals that still make me wince to think about. I was shattered after playing the usual three Easter games for Leeds and tired by the travelling. These days, it doesn't seem very far from Leeds to Turin, but then it was a long journey. Flights were infrequent and expensive and, after we moved there, we often made the trip by train, boat and train.

At the hospital, the doctors turned me inside out; X-rays were taken and my old cartilage scars were studied intently. I was examined by an orthopaedic expert and then by a heart specialist. At the end, I had been gone over from head to foot, literally, and I felt more like a prize racehorse than a footballer. It was a bit scary because I thought if they found anything, it could wreck the deal.

In the end, they had settled on a transfer fee of £65,000, which was only £7,000 less than the world record paid by AC Milan in 1954 for the Uruguayan Juan Schiaffino. As part of the deal, they also arranged a friendly against my old club, with the gate receipts going to Leeds.

The media dissected everything and it was worked out that Juventus had paid £375 per pound for me; at the time, gold cost £192 per pound. I was, they said, the richest footballer Britain had ever known but, of course, next to today's vast sums it was all pretty paltry, even allowing for the vast hike in the cost of living. My weekly income looks small beer next to the £40,000 plus per week of the modern superstar. Inflation hasn't gone up that much.

There were many exaggerated tales about what I was earning. There was an instant £10,000 in the bank plus £60 or £70 a week, depending on which newspaper you read, huge bonuses and everything tax-free. The truth was a bit different.

The £10,000 signing-on fee was correct but it was paid at a rate of £416 13s 4d (£416.67p) per month over the two-year duration of my contract, less Italian tax – and it was made very clear to me that if I brought any of it back to Britain it would be taxed again at home. And, contrary to what everyone seemed to think back home, there was a maximum wage in Italy. I was paid around £16 a week, which was less than the salary of a player in the Football League. One big difference between English and Italian contracts was that the wages were structured according to the size of the town the club played in, and they were paid for fifty-two weeks of the year, unlike at home where the wages were reduced in the summer when we weren't playing competitive football.

It may not sound much for beating Torino, Roma or Inter Milan, but on top of that we received big bonuses. Every player was paid the same weekly salary and the same bonus; the variations in what players received each week came from the signing-on fee, which was all-important. Despite this, there were no jealousies; if I was given a £10,000 signing-on fee, the others just said good luck to you.

The bonuses were huge by standards back home, with around £40 for an away win and £28 for a home victory, but when we won a really important game, the chairman or the directors would give us a 'little extra'. A win against Torino, for instance, or either of the Milan sides would prompt the chairman to dig deep to show his thanks. The money would be given to the captain and he would hand it out to the players. It was strictly against the regulations but who was going to blow the whistle? The amount was unpredictable because it depended on how well we did. We did well while I was there, and they were always saying thank you. At other clubs, not only would the players not be picking up bonuses, but they were being fined for all sorts of reasons, basically because they weren't winning.

The Italian clubs were also permitted to pay their players a bonus of up to £150 at the end of the season for performance and good conduct. A bad-tempered chairman whose side performed worse than he had hoped for could slash that to nothing.

So we earned money by winning, and then there were the perks. All our travel was first class, hotels were of the five-star variety and I was provided with an apartment overlooking the town rent free. They also gave me a new Fiat because Juventus is Fiat. There were no complaints from me, and Agnelli could afford it; his company was churning out a thousand cars a day in Turin. I had been driving around in a second-hand Citroen but Agnelli would never have allowed one of his star players to be seen driving around in a battered old car. It was against their family honour. So a fancy new sportscar it was, regularly replaced by a grateful president. All told, I reckon Juventus were paying £240 a month for perks outside my wages.

At the start of the season, an Italian club would nominate fifteen or sixteen first-team players for the squad and the rest would be decreed reserves. Promotion and relegation between the players could take place at any time during the season for disciplinary or performance reasons. If you reported unfit at the start of the season, the club could halve your wages, or even dissolve the contract, without any discussions with the player. The reserves didn't play in a league, just friendly matches against local sides, plus occasional run-outs in Cup games. Keeping match fit requires matches to be played, even if they are only friendlies, as Kevin Keegan discovered many years later when he tried to run Newcastle without a reserve team and found it didn't work.

There were no surprises awaiting me in terms of money or contractual conditions. I knew the score and was ready for it, but some other British players were not so well prepared when they tried their luck abroad, causing them and their families great unhappiness.

I saw the move to Juventus as a great opportunity, a whole new world opening up. The extra money was, of course, a big attraction, and the chance to improve our lifestyle and maybe even save a little. I eventually parted company with Teddy Sommerfield; he carried on with his television-based business in England. Kenneth became a good friend and visited us in Italy quite often. He knew everything, every secret, and he kept his mouth firmly shut.

CHAPTER EIGHT

Italian Footballer of the Year

The day after arriving in Italy I paid my first visit to the ground and stepped into my first row. It was suggested in the English newspapers that I had been cold-shouldered by the players and it was reported that only the goalkeeper Viola would talk to me. Nothing could have been further from the truth; all the players made me welcome and happily posed for pictures with me until it was time for training, and then skipper Giampiero Boniperti told one persistent cameraman that he would have to wait to have a picture of us taken together.

The story was written and headlined that Boniperti had refused to have his photograph taken with me. How ridiculous! I got on as well with the skipper then as I do now. When Peggy gave birth to Peter, Boniperti was the first to congratulate me; he invited me to his home and opened a couple of bottles of champagne.

In fact, when I went to the training ground on that first day, the spirit was so good I was instantly convinced that, even though they were three points off the bottom of the table, this side would not be relegated and I would be living and playing with them come June. It would have been disastrous for all concerned if they had gone down. Apart from anything else, the deal would have been off and I would have been left in limbo, presumably to go to Real Madrid or Lazio or somewhere else. This was a big, powerful club; playing their football in Serie B was not an option they would have accepted.

There was a certain style about the place. There was no scruffy, faded training gear but bright new kit, freshly laundered every morning instead of once a week. There was a wardrobe instead of a peg for every player and even wooden clogs to wear in the shower rooms. Benches? Forget it! We had easy chairs that converted into beds if you felt you needed a lie down. Potted plants abounded and the central table always had fresh flowers and a cage with a dozen budgerigars. The lockers were 6ft high and numbered, and the electric kettle was never off the boil. I was a bit shocked when I discovered the Italians didn't put sugar and milk in their tea – but slices of lemon.

They were much stricter on diet than in England, except we still had steak. We did not see chips at all; we had soup and steak before games. Perversely, they discouraged pasta at first. How that has changed! The club watched our eating and we were weighed every two days or so to ensure we weren't stuffing our faces in private. If you were a couple of pounds over, you would be back in the evening working off the flab.

A lot of the players smoked – we still weren't fully aware of the health hazards – but there was not the drink culture we had in England. The Italians liked a glass of wine but I cannot remember anyone who drank spirits or beer. It suited me and, in fact, I hardly drank at all while I was playing for Juventus.

In terms of medical treatment, we had three doctors on permanent call, three specialists in different areas. The physiotherapy was of the highest quality, not like back home in England where a former player would pass a course and then look after the best players in the land with the help of a bucket of ice-cold water and a sponge.

Off the pitch, it was totally different from anything I had come across in Britain. The clubhouse was sheer luxury with dining rooms, cocktail lounges, and dance floor, swimming pool and tennis courts. It must have cost them a fortune to maintain such luxury and pay the wages and bonuses but I learned I was helping to subsidise some of it as gates increased by a quarter in my first season – at home and away.

We were pampered and looked after totally. The club found me a beautiful place to live where I was comfortable with my family and where they could keep an eye on us. The two boys settled in at local schools and there always seemed to be someone looking after the family and me, especially when the baby arrived. I was very much a family man, and finished with a five-a-side team, including me. We had Terry, Melvyn, Peter and David, who was born when we returned to England.

The club liked to know what was happening with their players, and there would soon be someone to tell them if you were seen out drinking or went to a nightclub. I wasn't a big enough drinker for it to worry me but if one of the lads went out, the club would know exactly how much wine he had drunk over the course of the evening because someone would always tell them.

As for the people of Turin – I was feted. No sooner had I arrived than someone sent along one of the top tailors to measure me for a new suit while someone else sent me a pile of newly hand-crafted silk shirts. Restaurants and bars welcomed me with open arms and no one would let me pay for a thing. In fact, I hardly bothered carrying money around with me the whole time I was there. It was a waste of time.

Everyone was fascinated with my background and couldn't understand it when I tried to explain that I did not come from England originally, but from Wales. No one seemed to understand that Wales was a completely separate country from England.

Juve's fans were reckoned to number over 10 million in Italy alone and I was fortunate in the way they took to me wherever we went, even if their enthusiasm was slightly embarrassing. Of course, scoring goals in a league paranoid about defence helped. The supporters were fine as long as you were winning. Lose a couple and they were on your back, but they were not as bad as the directors. They were the ones to watch out for if your form slipped. The board of directors was small but very select. They were all very rich men, not just the Agnelli family, but Agnelli was the boss and everyone knew it.

There were two Agnellis, Jani and Umberto. Jani had handed control to the young Umberto shortly before I joined. Umberto had an office at the ground and was there every day, watching training and getting involved with everything to do with the club. He remained very friendly with me right the way through my career with Juventus, and afterwards.

The club, the fans and, of course, the press wanted to know everything about everything, well beyond the boundaries of the pitch and the dressing rooms, right though my own front door. It was very intrusive but it was all a part of the lifestyle and I had to accept it for the rewards it gave me. I had decided at the outset that I would take the bad with the good, and not make a fuss about the things I did not like, so much so that my team-mate Sivori once said, 'John was never a great talker, and if he had problems in Turin, it was always his way to suffer in silence.' Unlike him!

Two other British players, Tony Marchi and Eddie Firmani, were not so lucky as I was. I did not realise when I signed that Tony, bought from Spurs for £40,000, would be forced out because of the Italian rule restricting the number of foreign players in the team to two. He went to Lanerossi and just when it looked as though he would have to go back to England, Napoli stepped in to sign him. Eddie, one of the first players to move from England to Italy when he joined Sampdoria from Charlton Athletic, fared better because he had an Italian grandfather and qualified as an Italian.

It did not take me long to realise there was another side to the dolce vita of Italian football, its gifts, its lire and its promises. In my very first game, against Verona, I quickly learned this was very different from English football. Although we won 3–2, I found myself running into a brick wall with defences so packed you had to waste time searching for chinks of light. Every manager in Italy feared defeat and that became the justification for playing the closed game, catenaccio, with defensive covering pushed to absurd lengths. In England, a defeat was a defeat – in Italy it was a tragedy.

Even the fans did not make too much fuss about most teams' defensive attitude because they felt very much the same way, and would gladly suffer a goalless draw rather than a 3–2 defeat. The limitations I faced were all new to me, and the films I had watched and the reports I had read did not help very much. I had to learn from experience, and learn quickly. My mantra became: this is tough going and no joke.

The Italians looked on our attitude to football in England as a joke because games were more likely to finish with a drink in the players' bar, even with local rivals, than in bad blood. That was not possible in Italy, and especially not with Torino. Prestige was everything. Rather like Manchester United and Liverpool, Juventus and Torino were great rivals. Torino were dominant until a dreadful air crash in 1949 in which most of the team were killed. The cream of Italian football was wiped out when, returning from a European game in Portugal, the plane crashed into the hillside at Superga, within view of Turin. Eighteen players died, many of them internationals, including the captain Valentino Mazzola, plus English coach Leslie Lievesley. The death toll was thirty-one.

Torino had won four successive league titles and were four points clear at the top on the day of the crash. The Torino youth team completed the season and received the Scudetto, but suddenly Torino were playing second fiddle to Juventus, and they didn't like it. The rivalry between the two Milan clubs was almost as intense. History is everything to these people. The Torino fans, men and women, still talk about their great team and demand a return to those days. They know everything about the game. Then, as now, they supported only their team and wouldn't consider going to watch the other team in the city unless they were playing each other. I was so lucky that the Torino supporters were good to me, as were the supporters in Milan where I went quite often to enjoy dinner or a change of scenery.

Another big difference was in the training. English managers had not fared well in Italy. Bill Dodgin at Sampdoria was relieved of first-team duties after a few months and put in charge of the juniors while Alec Stock was with Roma for just a few weeks before there was a dispute over team selection. I heard that neither manager was liked by their players because of the tough training routines they tried to impose.

In England, I always felt that we did too much training – in Italy, too little. However, the thing that benefited me more than any other in Italy was the individual work. When I arrived at Juventus, I knew that I had a weakness in my left foot and so, in training, I worked hard, using only the left foot for kicking. That paid off handsomely and I was soon scoring more goals with my feet than with my head; until then, I had more confidence in scoring with my head than with either of my feet – and it was lovely to come out every day with the sun shining. That made training a lot easier, especially thinking about the rain and snow in Leeds.

One Italian player once asked me of English training, 'Are they trying to produce cross-country runners or all-in wrestlers?' The observation was made because we did so much training without the ball while the Italians were rarely without a football at their feet during their sessions.

Major Buckley at Leeds did not like us having the ball at all during the week other than for a practice match. His idea was to make us fit and make us hungry for the ball. The Italian attitude was quite the reverse and quite often I would take a ball home with me. We did the usual pre-season runs, which are probably still done in every country in the world, but once training began in earnest, there was always a football. The Italian argument was that you played football with a ball while the English reply was that you did an awful lot of running off the ball and only one player at a time has the football in his possession. Both arguments had their validity, but as far as I was concerned, the more I practised with a football, the more I became used to it, and it showed in the skills. At Leeds, and in other English clubs, we were hard running, hard working, competitive, exciting and played with a passion; Italian football was more controlled. I enjoyed the Italian attitude; we would have our hard sessions early in the week and tail off. It suited me much better than the English style and I went into matches fresher and full of running.

Pre-season was strict in Italy. They would take us away and lock us up away from our families and any other distractions but we were always taken to very nice places and we were treated exceptionally well with the right food and drink.

On this issue, Juventus paid special attention to me. I was a big man and the club were aware that any over-indulgence on my part could have led to my putting on weight. So, as with all the players, they always checked the scales and my diet very carefully and were particularly worried whenever we went home to the UK. They let us go home for special events like Christmas, but they insisted that I train on my own every morning and watched what I ate.

They would weigh me as soon as I got back to the club, because they knew I was not a good dieter. I liked my food and I basically ate what I liked: steaks and cheese and pasta and lots of sauces. I also liked fizzy drinks and after a hard workout the players would look on in amazement as I drank three or four straight off.

Like all footballers, we played cards and chatted to pass the time, which helped me understand not only the language but also the Italian way of life. The difference was that the gambling, like the heavy drinking, was not there. In Italy, they played for small insignificant sums whereas in England they played for much higher stakes. There were casinos up in the hills and by the seaside so there would be an occasional trip for a flutter. I looked forward to a game of roulette every so often but I would still kick myself when I lost a few pounds; Peggy wasn't too happy when I lost but delighted when I had a few big wins. It wasn't a disease with me the way it can become with some. It was an occasional lapse.

The biggest problem with pre-season was the boredom. After a while, I'd get sick of sitting around and, in the end, it made me nervy and jumpy. The routine consisted of getting up, training, resting, eating lunch, resting, walking, eating dinner, walking and going to bed by ten o'clock. I wasn't the only one to get bored with it; most of the others, particularly those who were married, felt the same way. But it was a ritual that had to be observed so that the trainer could watch over his charges for twenty-four hours a day, weeding out the temperamental problems that were not uncommon.

On one pre-season we went to our manager and complained that we wanted to see our wives. It was agreed they could come and visit us for one night. We were delighted but the club had the last laugh – we were billed for their visit. On another occasion, a player received a bill for a stamp he had from reception. They paid us well but charged us for everything.

During the season the routine was pretty well set in stone. We would go away after training on the Friday before the Sunday game, travelling if it was an away game or going to our retreat in the hills if it was at home. The system was called 'ritiro'. After the game, we would have a meal in the early evening and then go off to bed, and we would not talk about the game until the following day. I coped with it; I just went with the flow. It was no problem being shut away – we were up in the foothills of the Alps overlooking Turin, a magnificent place with a wonderful view. I suppose the system was effective because we won a lot. In any case, no one was going to argue. It was something of a placebo but Italian players generally liked to relax after a game. It is the culture, what you are brought up to do.

From Tuesday to Friday we trained every afternoon, reporting at 2.30 and finishing at four o'clock. We were always away by 4.30. This fitted in with the Italian tradition of eating late. It was thought silly to train in the morning because players would have gone to bed on a full stomach and consequently be good for nothing the next morning. They were quite happy for us to stay up late with our families and sleep in the next morning, although some clubs would have their players report at the ground in the morning and then go home before reporting back for training, just to check they were around and hadn't gone away somewhere the night before. Juventus was not one of those teams, thank goodness.

I would often go to the ground on Mondays, our day off, and in the mornings, to train on my own, partly out of boredom but more to improve myself. I was naturally fit and enjoyed training. If Ljubisa Brocic thought I needed some extra training, I would go and do it. An hour or so a day did not seem a lot, even in the heat. When it was very hot, we would train later in the day and always the sessions were hard, even if they were with the ball. Brocic believed in doing a hard hour, probably because it was the way he was brought up in Yugoslavia. To him, it was what worked.

The referees approached the game differently, too. Things that would earn no more than a finger wagging or a quiet word in England would bring punitive action – a booking or a sending-off – and these were written in stone. There were no appeals and you would be hit with a suspension and a fine, loss of wages and loss of bonuses. It was an expensive business for the hot-tempered player, but I decided from the start that I would not say a word to the referees, or about them, whatever the decision. With this in mind, I didn't make gestures at anyone – no appealing, no dissent, just a nod of the head. It was not an earth-shattering plan but it worked.

The Italians would say, 'We don't break legs', but they did not mind treading on your feet, pulling your hair if they couldn't get your shirt, elbowing and, worst of all, spitting. I did not mind knocking a man over to beat him to the ball, but only if it was shoulder to shoulder as the laws of the game stated. I told Agnelli when I signed that if I was kicked I would not kick back. That has been my attitude throughout my footballing life and it will always be my attitude. Agnelli, to his credit, accepted what I said and did not argue the point at all.

However, my attitude caused some complaints and moans from my team-mates. Sivori, for example, would go crazy if I kicked the ball out of play so an injured player could be treated. He said that opponents took advantage of me, and I am sure that was the case, but I did not want to take that chance if someone was injured.

I may have been big, but opponents would still have a go at me. After one game, against Lanerossi Vicenza, I finished up in hospital because of the treatment handed out to me by one of their defenders, who kept punching me from behind. There were others who were not afraid of my size, maybe because they knew I would not hit them back. It was not so bad when you could see what was coming, but it was the attack on the blind side that caused me most problems.

Most of the time I managed to hold on to my temper but at other times I would threaten the offender and more often than not that would solve the problem for a while.

In England, the football was intensely physical and every club had at least one hard man or enforcer; in Italy, the spitting and the shirt tugging would irritate English players no end while the hard tackling of the English would upset the Italians. I had to hold myself back when I was spat at but the rest I could take, and it was no surprise because I was warned. At our ground, opponents were frightened to do their worst but they would have no fears on their own ground, somewhere like Naples or Palermo.

It wasn't just on the pitch that the underhand tricks would be played. When we were trying to sleep in a hotel before an away game, we would frequently be woken up around two in the morning by loud music outside the hotel. The home fans would try to keep us awake all night, and it was no use hoping the police would intervene because they were local supporters as well and could, on occasions, make as much noise as the supporters.

I could understand the problems that Denis Law and Joe Baker had when they joined Torino a year or so later. Their problem was that history went against them. The Torino fans were used to being the best until the plane crash and hated handing over the baton to their neighbours; we were the dominant team not just in Turin but in Italy, and they hated that even more. Torino expected Denis and Joe to lift themselves and their team-mates to challenge us at the top of the League, and while both did well it was not considered good enough because we were always above them. It was the fans as much as the club who eventually drove them away.

Denis Law would have been a sensation at Juventus and would probably have still been there now had he signed for us instead of our rivals. I was disappointed when Denis and Joe said very harsh things about Italian football on their return to England. It was sad it did not work out for them but it was just one of those things. They were successful, even in their brief spells in the country. The same was true of Jimmy Greaves who hated it more and stayed for an even shorter spell than Denis. I didn't see as much of Jimmy because he was a few miles away in Milan, but I often had dinner with the other two. I was sad that Denis didn't stay on, but he didn't do too badly when he moved back to England and Manchester United, so I guess he has no regrets!

There was no point in any English defender ever thinking about making a career in Italy because they had defenders in abundance. While we enjoyed shooting at goal as kids in the park, they enjoyed defending, and consequently every team was bursting with good Italian defenders, as was their international side.

Their favourite British defender was Dave Mackay of Scotland and Spurs. They loved watching him on television, his commitment, enthusiasm, fierce tackling, leadership . . . everything except the way he joined the attack and scored goals. That, as far as the experts were concerned, ruined him for the Italian market. They liked defenders to be defenders.

Because of this emphasis placed on defence, few Italian youngsters were willing to gamble on the slim chance of scoring goals. The young strikers were soon submerged in the catenaccio defences, which suffocated them, never to appear again. It had reached the stage where Italian forwards were expert defenders and not very good goalscorers. That was why they came hunting for British strikers in the early sixties, partly due to my comparative success, and why they went out and bought Hitchens, Greaves, Law and Baker. They would have paid a king's ransom if they could have persuaded Bobby Charlton to join them while Bobby Smith, the Spurs centre-forward, was reckoned to have the strength and power to punch holes in those packed defences and score goals, maybe not as many as he scored in England but they would have been twice as valuable.

Others of that time who might have succeeded were Cliff Jones, the flying Welsh winger, and John Connelly of Burnley. They would have thrilled Italian fans with their wing play but I am not so sure that our British midfield geniuses Jimmy McIlroy, Johnny Haynes, John White and Phil Woosnam would have been as successful. The Italians liked their midfield ball players to be both excellent and fancy, and our boys would have been too utilitarian for them. A classic example is Sivori at Juventus, an incredible ball artist who would have been rapped over the knuckles by British coaches for being too clever. He overdid the trickery but the fans loved it. They would shout and scream with joy as he juggled the ball, beat three men and delayed his final pass until no one was properly placed to receive it. I slapped his face once when he lost his temper to bring him back to normality – he said thank you after the game – but I felt like doing it on several other occasions when I had run into goalscoring positions and he tried to beat just one more defender.

That is why British strikers were the ones to be lured with the lire, but to be a success you had to accept that goals would be few and far between, and life would be fine if you fancied banging your head against a brick wall while your shirt was being tugged and someone was treading on your feet so you couldn't jump. If a player could accept this, and few did, the benefits were enormous – the big signing-on fees, the huge bonuses, the fabulous houses, the number of games you were asked to play.

There is no question that the depth of football in England was much greater than anywhere in Europe and, strangely, it has remained that way. Certainly in my day, Juventus, Real Madrid, Santos, Atletico Madrid, Barcelona, Fiorentina, AC Milan, Inter Milan and Roma were the only teams that would have made an impression back home; the rest would have struggled. If the Italian Second Division teams had played in England, most of the clubs would have been in Divisions Three or Four. Although there are some problems in English football now because of the loss of the television money in the Football League and careless overspending by ambitious chairmen, the game is still strong, perhaps even stronger than before. The Conference is proving to be a well-supported and well-run fifth division. Nowhere in the world do they have a similar depth of professional football, and at a high standard, too.

The critical avoidance of defeat in Italy took away from the entertainment value and English football was, and still is, better entertainment and better to watch, as can be witnessed by the respective attendances in the two countries and the number of countries where the English game is sold for the television audience. It is easy to understand why. Whenever we played a team of lower status, there would be one man up and the rest not just in their own half but in their own penalty area. They let you attack and hoped to get a break and score a goal to win 1–0. To be fair, they broke quickly and smartly, but then again, they had had enough practice at counter-attacking to have become experts.

Juventus were the exception to all the rules because we played attacking football at home and away, which helped me to average almost a goal a match while Sivori was never that far off me. Before I arrived, Boniperti played centre-forward and he scored his share of goals, too, but when I arrived, he was moved back to midfield and he was the chief supplier to Sivori and me, a job he did without complaint.

What a character Omar Enrique Sivori was! As I've said, he loved to play to the crowd, beat defenders and show them up. It was so bad he was known as 'Cabezon' – Big Head – by his fans in Italy and South America. Small, with his backside near to the ground, like Maradona and many other players to come out of South America, he was able to humiliate and embarrass opponents in the most outrageous ways. When he scored a goal it was murder; he would be off with flips and jumps. But he was a wonderful player to play alongside. He was quick over short distances and when I look back at the goals he scored, he was unbelievable.

He cost a then world-record fee of £91,000 when he joined Juve from River Plate and scored 134 league goals in eight seasons before falling out with the coach and moving to Napoli where he forged an outstanding partnership with Jose Altafini. He played twelve times for Argentina and, as happened in those days, nine times for Italy.

Sivori had a strong temper and would react not only when he was kicked but also when I was kicked. He knew I would not retaliate and he would take it on himself to dig back for me, and if it wasn't Sivori it was Boniperti. Sivori was only small but he was a hard man who more than punched his weight. He could not only look after himself but he could also play. He and Boni would make sure the player who had fouled me knew that he had it coming. They would point to me and then back at him. That player would think twice about doing it again, and usually spent the rest of the game looking over his shoulder.

I had never heard of Sivori, but I was soon to find out all about him. I suppose the reason why we paired off so well was because we were both so different. He was an explosive little man who would flare up in an instant and was never afraid to kick a defender or two and he certainly fancied himself. He was a great player and wasn't afraid to tell anyone, on and off the pitch! There is no doubt he was a bit crackers in those days.

But we got on well together. We made and scored goals for each other and, in the early days, even stayed in the same hotel. Neither of us could speak Italian and neither of us could speak the other's language so we used to sit there just looking at each other. They would call it bonding these days.

Boniperti was the original Golden Boy of Italian football. He signed from minor club Momo in July 1946 and within a few months had established himself in the Juventus team. He was promoted to the international side and made his debut in a 5–1 win against Austria in November 1947. He won five Italian titles with Juventus, playing 444 league games and thirty-eight internationals. Sivori was a very awkward lad, but very nice. On certain days he was superb and would do anything for you but on others he wouldn't even want to talk to you. Boniperti, on the other hand, was a gentleman. He lived for Juventus, just as he does today. There was no way he could have been transferred. He was very well in with Umberto Agnelli, and Jani Agnelli liked him, too, and appreciated his loyalty. The family helped him in his business until he became president of the club, under Agnelli patronage.

Boniperti was such an intelligent player he could perform any-where. He was picked on the right wing for the Rest of Europe XI, scoring twice in a 4–4 draw with England in 1953. He could break up attacks and set them up, a middle of the field man who loved playing there. He had two great feet and made many of my goals for me. Having tasted the glory of being a goalscorer, especially in Italy, it must have been hard for him, but if it was he never showed it.

Goalscorers were the heroes in Italy. Score the goal in a 1–0 win and you would have a caravan of cars driving up to your house hooting their horns in thanks. It was bad for sleep but very good for the image. Goals were a priceless commodity, and Juventus had plenty of money and believed in attacking football. If we thought we were short of a world-class centre-half, the next day a superstar would be brought in, very much like Real Madrid and Manchester United now; but it did not matter how much they spent on a defender, it was the strikers who remained their true gods.

Everything centred on the league championship, the Scudetto. That was the ultimate prize; it meant everything. It was far, far more important than the European Cup, the World Cup or anything else in football, and clubs would not hesitate to pull players out of internationals to keep them ready for the league matches.

One of the great advantages for me was the fact that I settled so quickly in Italy. I was determined to do so. You have to acclimatise and pick up the language quickly. That was my first problem. I worked very hard at it and it took me a while but I could get by after two or three months. I had to – it would have left me in no man's land, not speaking the language, and I would soon have been on my way home. Apart from team matters, you have to go out and meet people; otherwise there would be many other problems, including homesickness, to contend with. Learning a new style of football is hard enough without adding other problems.

To start with, I relied heavily on team-mate Umberto Colombo, who became a close friend. Our families became friends, too, and we used to visit his home in Como. He could speak English and acted as my translator, especially at team-talks, although the manager, Ljubisa Brocic, also spoke good English.

I liked living in Turin. Our first home did not go down too well with Peggy, because it was a flat on the ground floor and it didn't have a proper garden for her and the children. It was about a year later that the club found us the apartment on the Cavoretto hillside, with views overlooking the city on one side and the Alps on the other. It was huge, so we were able to move in all of the furniture we shipped from Leeds – big chairs and settees, the sort we love in England, the sort you could spread yourself out on.

In 1958 we bought our own apartment on the Ligurian coast on the recommendation of the British Consulate, who always seemed eager to help us. We looked and fell in love with a place being built in Diano Marina, and it gave Peggy and the boys somewhere to go.

The club were tremendous, always checking to see if everything was all right and even Agnelli would occasionally pop round to make a personal check.

I found it much easier to settle than I expected and I had no problem switching from whisky and lemonade to red wine and from roast beef and Yorkshire pudding to spaghetti. The only thing we couldn't get over there was proper English bacon and we would ask people to bring some with them when they came to visit.

We all soon spoke Italian, even Peggy; while for the eldest two boys, Terry and Melvyn, it soon became their first language. After Peggy had Peter she learned to drive and was given her own Fiat, a gift from Umberto Agnelli who never missed a trick. The garage at our new apartment was massive, but hardly big enough for all the cars and scooters.

I have to say I had my doubts in the first pre-season as we were taken away for six weeks training, hard physical work as well as working with the ball. It was like living in a monastery and hardly what I had been used to, but I had to accept it. I was quite relieved when the season began in earnest on 8 September and, in front of 72,000 at the Stadio Comunale, I was lucky enough to score in the fifty-eighth minute. We went on to win 3–1 against Hellas Verona.

Despite the tight defences, I took to the Italian game immediately. I felt comfortable and I was playing with excellent team-mates who created chances for me. I scored my first hat-trick for the club against Atalanta in December in a 3–0 win and, having been close to relegation at one point in the previous season, the confidence of the team grew and grew. I popped in another three goals against Lazio at the start of April and when I repeated the act against Sampdoria we were on the verge of our first Scudetto since 1950, which we clinched with a draw against Fiorentina on 4 May with three matches in hand.

It sounds remarkable nowadays that Juventus could win the championship a season after just escaping relegation. But it wasn't just down to me. I was the first of three signings made by Agnelli in 1957. I was followed by the capture of Sivori from River Plate and the club also paid £85,000 to Padova for the seventeen-year-old striker Bruno Nicole. I learned that Agnelli was keen to sign me before the Sivori deal was announced, in case they had to pay more for me when the Argentinian's fee was revealed.

There were many other changes too, not least of all the arrival of the new coach Ljubisa Brocic, the Yugoslav who had coached clubs in his own country and the national sides of Egypt, Albania and Yugoslavia. Apart from the three big signings, Juventus also brought back on-loan goalkeeper Giovanni Viola and centre-half Rino Ferrario, while position changes for the great Boniperti and Colombo made it a completely different-looking side to the one that had struggled in 1957. When we got together for our pre-season tour to Sweden, everything clicked straight away.

Our success meant we were in demand for friendlies around Europe. These were not meant to keep us in shape but to keep the money coming in to pay the bonuses when the matches did matter. Friendlies were an important source of income for the club, and one of these took us to London in February of 1958 to play Arsenal at Highbury. It was November and London seemed to be filled with Italians carrying banners and bottles of Chianti. It was a festive, friendly occasion; the Metropolitan Police Band played 'Santa Lucia', 'Funiculi, Funicula' and 'Come Back to Sorrento' before the floodlit game, which Arsenal won 3–1. I forced a good save out of my Welsh team-mate Jack Kelsey when I connected with Stivanello's cross, but I played much deeper than usual and went back to help the defence for corners and dead-ball kicks. It was all very gentle with nice football, lacking the physical aspect from the English team and the usual irritating habits of the Italians.

I was delighted to win the Italian Player of the Year award as leading goalscorer, with 28 in 34 matches. Between us, Sivori and I scored 50 of Juve's 77 league goals and we won the title by eight points when it was only two points for a win. To cap a remarkable season I was voted in the top three for the 'European Player of the Year'.

I was big, fit and strong and had been made to feel really welcome. Even the press seemed to like me. On 14 April 1959, a headline in a local paper read: 'A magnificent 6ft 2in hunk of Welsh marble bestriding the pitch like a colossus in the No. 9 zebra shirt of Juventus.' And Giuseppe Melillo of Rome's sports paper *Corriere Dello Sport* likewise went over the top, describing me thus in his column:

The greatest and most irresistible soccer leader in our memory. We recall the great Swedish centre-forward Gunnar Nordahl . . . the wonderful Taylor, with his superb style . . . the genial and clever Hungarian Kocsis . . . the spectacular Brazilian centre-forward Pele . . . the fine Sindelar, of Meisl's Wunderteam . . . the fantasy of the great Argentine Alfredo Di Stefano . . . but frankly we cannot find any parallel with John Charles. The Welsh Giant is a centre-forward completely different from the others; he is a new model, unique, unmistakable.

Boniperti added, 'The diamond was John Charles. He made everyone raise their game.' It was all a little embarrassing but it came on the back of an excellent first season for Juve and for me. Praise and compliments never sat easy for this boy from Swansea but you had to accept it in the spirit it was given; in Italy, footballers were worshipped. Football is a religion to them and certain players, particularly those who scored goals, became gods.

CHAPTER NINE

Playing for Wales

When I look around now at footballers winning a hundred and more international caps, I must confess to a twinge of envy. I won only thirty-eight for Wales in my entire career. International football has to be the pinnacle for any footballer; representing the country of your birth is better than all the medals put together. Maybe the Welsh feel it a touch more than some of the others; almost from birth we are dreaming of representing our country at rugby, football or some other sport, or in some other field, to bring honour to Wales. But, as you find out, it is not just a question of making yourself available, turning up and playing.

I was picked before I was ready, brought back for one game and left out again, and then, when I had established myself as a regular in the red shirt, I found it not so easy to gain my release from Juventus to play for my country. In fact, I all but missed the 1958 World Cup finals, perhaps the best World Cup ever! I have to confess, though, that Juventus were not always to blame for my absence.

Before I went to Italy, I played in twenty-one consecutive games for Wales, regularly switching between inside-forward, centre-forward and centre-half, and sometimes playing all three in one game. In those twenty-one games, I wore the No. 8 shirt four times, the No. 9 shirt eight times and the No. 5 shirt nine times.

Times and rules have changed. Now clubs around the world are obliged to release their players for competitive internationals plus a certain number of friendlies in a calendar year, but that was not the case when I was in Italy. With many of the Italian League games being played on a Sunday, there was no way Juventus would release me for a Saturday game, even though, more often than not, I was perfectly willing to play twice in two days. They also stopped me playing in a number of midweek internationals because they were afraid that their investment might be injured.

There was a big hue and cry when Jimmy Greaves, Gerry Hitchens and Joe Baker were the subject of headline stories about being released. What a travesty! This was at a time when English clubs regularly refused to release players from Wales, Ireland and Scotland. The rule was if you played in your own country, the club was obliged to release you, but once you moved outside your country's jurisdiction, there was nothing to say you had to be released. When I was playing for Leeds United, they could refuse to release me, just as Juventus did when I was earning my living in Italy.

The situation was eased somewhat when the Football League in England allowed games to be postponed if two or more players were selected for international duties for the home countries, but the problem was not completely resolved until FIFA stepped in and made it an order for all countries; even then, there were some very suspicious short-term injuries announced, myself among them.

Playing for Wales meant a great deal to me. I played for the first time at the age of eighteen in 1950 against Northern Ireland at Wrexham in the Home International Championships, and for the second time a year later against Switzerland in a match to celebrate the Festival of Britain, again at Wrexham. Both were a nightmare. The problem was nerves. I was very young and unsure of my ability. The players helped but I still suffered. It was such a big thing to play for my country. It was the major prize and I was desperate not to let anyone down – myself, my family, my fellow players and most of all my country.

There were not that many chances with only half a dozen games a season, including the home internationals. By the time I was called up again, in 1953, I was playing centre-forward. Wales had lost 5–2 to England and there were going to be changes. I didn't think I would be picked because Ray Daniel was a fixture at centre-half and the selectors certainly weren't going to axe Trevor Ford as centre-forward. In the end, they dropped the Newcastle pair Reg Davies and Billy Foulkes, and Roy Clarke of Manchester City, bringing in Terry Medwin, Harry Griffiths and me to face Northern Ireland in Belfast on 15 April.

The oddity was that our entire forward line was born in Swansea – wingers Terry Medwin and Harry Griffiths, inside-forwards Ivor Allchurch and me, and Trevor Ford at centre-forward. I felt I was among familiar faces with my old schoolboy team-mate Terry Medwin, and Harry Griffiths who had left Swansea with me for trials in Leeds. This felt good and I was desperately hoping that it would be third time lucky as we travelled to Belfast.

This is one game I remember well for Danny Blanchflower, then playing for Aston Villa, was immaculate in midfield. He stopped us going forward time after time and when we went a goal down, I thought to myself, here we go again, we're on another hiding.

But ten minutes later I was in heaven. Harry Griffiths hooked the ball across the face of the goal and I hit a left-foot shot through a crowd of players straight into the back of the net. I could have wept. We were level and I had scored my first goal for Wales – and it was with my left foot, a rarity in those days.

It didn't end there, either. Trevor Ford and Terry Medwin worked their way down the right wing and Terry crossed perfectly for me to head home to put us 2–1 in front.

I might have had a hat-trick before half-time. Roy Paul put me through and as I steadied myself to shoot, with a 50 per cent chance of scoring, I noticed Trevor Ford clear on my right. I slipped the ball to him, confident that Trevor wouldn't miss from there. He didn't and we were 3–1 ahead.

After that 3–2 win, I felt I had repaid my debt for those awful first two appearances, and it seems the selectors agreed because suddenly I was a regular; not that it brought instant success.

That game was followed by a short tour to Europe and I was quickly brought back down to earth as Raymond Kopa and Just Fontaine, two of the world's great strikers, led the French to a 6–1 win in the Parc des Princes. This was followed by a 5–2 thrashing by Yugoslavia and we returned home a chastened bunch. The French were a very good side at the time and the Yugoslavs were always difficult to beat at home in what was a very intimidating atmosphere – police with guns and wild fans. Kevin Keegan discovered some years later just how intimidating Belgrade could be when the Yugoslav police assaulted him at the airport and he had his passport confiscated for no greater reason than sitting on the luggage carousel.

It did not become any easier the next season for first up was a game against England in Cardiff with every Englishman playing for a place in a side due to face the Rest of Europe at Wembley. The England team that day looked about as strong as it could be with Birmingham's Gil Merrick in goal; Garrett of Blackpool and Eckersley of Blackburn were the full-backs; Wright (Wolves), Johnston (Blackpool) and Dickinson (Portsmouth) were the heart of the team, and the forward line was packed with talent and goals with the incomparable Finney (Preston North End), ballet-dancing Quixall (Sheffield Wednesday), the Lion of Vienna Lofthouse (Bolton Wanderers), Wilshaw and Mullen, both of Wolves.

It looked far too strong a line-up for us: Howells (Cardiff); Barnes (Arsenal), Sherwood (Cardiff); Paul (Manchester City), Daniel (Sunderland), Burgess (Spurs); Foulkes and Davies (Newcastle), Charles (Leeds), Ivor Allchurch (Swansea), Clarke (Manchester City).

Trevor Ford had cried off with injury at the last minute, which weakened us further, but on the day, we fancied our chances and for half an hour we ran England ragged and should have been four goals ahead. Instead, we had to settle for just the one from Allchurch. The main reason for us not being able to cash in on our superiority was that the England goalkeeper, Gil Merrick, was magnificent.

Then came one of those moments when a game turns. Alf Sherwood and Tom Finney were involved in a sickening collision. Alf came off worse and was led off with concussion while Tom was nothing more than winded. There were, of course, no substitutes allowed in those days and we played on with ten men until five minutes after the break when Alf was able to rejoin us. He must have wondered if it was the same game for, by then, we had gone 4–1 down. Dennis Wilshaw had cruelly equalised a minute before the interval and then, in three crazy minutes at the start of the second half, Wilshaw scored again and Nat Lofthouse scored two.

Finney was superb, as he was more often than not. He was a great player who suffered in comparison with Stanley Matthews. For me, that was an unfair argument because the critics were not comparing like with like. They were both great players but they had different ways of playing. Tom could go to centre-forward or inside-right, or play out wide, but Stanley was a right-winger and a right-winger only. That was his position and that is where he played.

Tom, as a winger, was far more direct than Stanley, and scored goals for fun, whereas Stanley rarely scored but continually made goals for other people, as he did in that unforgettable 1953 FA Cup final when Blackpool beat Bolton Wanderers 4–3. Stanley could take people on and crossed inch perfect, but he demanded the ball to his feet and if it did not arrive spot on the target he ignored it, while Tom would work. He was two-footed and a great servant. There weren't that many two-footed players around in those days. It is a tough call to choose between the two superstars because they were different. Stanley was creator and Tom was both creator and scorer.

I thought England was wrong in considering them too similar, and both should have been in the side for every game; they certainly would be now. If you have two world-class players, you don't leave one out, especially when Finney was so versatile and capable of scoring goals as well as making them.

Finney was one of my idols when I was a young lad. I preferred him at centre-forward where he was a natural who could do things others could not do. The only problem was that England had Nat Lofthouse – spoiled, you might say, by an embarrassment of riches. Too often, England failed to sort out their team selection, which was done by committee, and paid the penalty for it with poor results when it mattered most.

I played with both Matthews and Finney in charity matches and it was a stroll because I did not have to run – the ball came straight to my feet or my head.

I have often been asked to choose who was the best right-winger at the time and I always joked that it was Harold Williams because he made so many goals for me.

When you think about the balls they used to play with, you have to wonder what they might have done with a modern ball; I think they would have had it on a piece of string – they could have done anything with it. As it was, when we practised before testimonial games, I used to tell Stan to have that hard, cutting leather string facing the goal and not my forehead. Yes, he was that good.

No wonder we struggled against them with ten men. With Alf dazedly struggling along the wing for the rest of the match, we held the score to 4–1 but left the ground wondering what might have been.

After the game, there was the usual cry for substitutes to be introduced but I was not in that camp at the time. I was not a supporter of substitutes. Injuries were all part of the game I had grown up with – why change it? I still believe in the basics of my theory but nowadays people pay so much money to watch football it would be wrong to have matches with eleven against nine.

Also, everyone has a bad game now and again and it's good that the off-form player can be swapped. I have changed my opinions a lot since my playing days.

One of the biggest problems was when the manager forced an injured player to carry on on the right wing for nuisance value, often aggravating the injury. The player could be out of action for longer than he would have been had he come off to get treatment.

Substitutes have been incorporated well into the modern game; using them tactically is an art in itself. The fact that substitutes need to be used properly was brought home to me when I watched Sir Alf Ramsey getting it wrong once or twice when he was new to it and clearly hadn't adapted as well as he might have done.

I had my share of injuries but, thankfully, not many serious ones. A couple of damaged cartilages were the worst, and that was lucky because we knew very little about warming up properly or diet. We would kick about for ten minutes on a freezing cold day and then go straight out to play. That left us open for all kinds of muscle strains, aches and pulls. We didn't warm down, either; it was unheard of. We went straight into the dressing rooms for a bath or shower, if there was one, and then into the bar.

Everything was done on a shoestring. Wales did not have a lot of money and all they could afford was the basic strip of shorts, shirts and socks. We had to bring everything else, including soap and towel for the bath. Because of the shortage of money, we used to have a small squad, usually no more than fourteen, but there were often double that number of Welsh officials with the party.

On one classic occasion, one of the players was left off the plane to France because there were not enough seats. Not one of the non-playing officials volunteered to give up his place, and the player had to wait for the next plane to join us. They were good people, but they were totally unaware of their place in the game. They thought they were much more important than they really were. It went on like that for years but it has changed now. We could have taken more players had one or two officials stood down, and we would have been covered for injuries.

We had been afflicted by cruel luck against the English but, more often than not in football, luck tends to even itself out, as it did for us in our next match a few weeks later against Scotland at Hampden Park. The Scots climbed all over us and in no time were two up. I managed to pull one back from a Bill Foulkes cross but, soon afterwards, the gap was restored and we were looking down the gun barrel at 3–1 and given no chance.

That is the pure joy of football. No one could have predicted what happened next. Allchurch scored one of his greatest ever goals, dribbling his way through what seemed the entire Scottish team before scoring with a twenty-yard shot.

It seemed we had pulled the tiger's tail for the Scots swarmed all over us again. I was a spectator on the halfway line when I wasn't back helping our overstretched defence. Suddenly, the ball broke to me and I set off. Most of the Scots were in our half and I managed to evade the one and only challenge and lined up against George Farm in Scotland's goal. Somehow he managed to throw his body in front of my shot but, miraculously, it came straight back to me and from what was now a ridiculous angle, the ball went into the net. What seemed like seconds rather than minutes later, the final whistle blew. We were almost embarrassed to claim a draw having been so comprehensively outplayed – but we took it.

Which was our true form? The half an hour against England or the struggle against Scotland. The critics had no doubts as we went on to lose 2–1 to Northern Ireland at Wrexham and 2–0 to Austria in Vienna with the great Ernst 'Clockwork' Ocwirk tearing us to pieces from midfield.

My dislike of substitutes at the time was magnified when, in September 1954, we had our opportunity to avenge the earlier thrashing by Yugoslavia. We would have done so but for those damn substitutes. We were forced into what was by then the usual agreement, with a substitute goalkeeper allowed at any time and one player up to the forty-fourth minute to replace an injured player.

We were deservedly leading with a goal from Ivor Allchurch. Dangerous right-winger Petakovic had been marked out of the game by Alf Sherwood and we were looking good for a win until Petakovic suddenly sank to the ground with no one near him and wriggled about in agony until he was replaced by a Vaselinovic. We all thought it seemed a ridiculous con and laughed at the antics, but in the end, the laugh was on us as the substitute went on to hammer a hat-trick in the second half and sink us. No wonder I was against substitutes; that incident just turned me further against them.

Not only did I not believe in fouling the opposition, neither did I like cheating by players or their coaches – nor did I like to see opponents hurt my team-mates. The nearest I came to losing my temper as a player was in the infamous Battle of Wrexham against Austria on 23 November 1955.

The trouble began in Vienna in 1954 when we lost 2–0 and the Austrians were upset because we challenged their goalkeeper, something that was routinely accepted in Britain but not elsewhere on the Continent, particularly, it seems, in Austria. They retaliated and the game became something of a roughhouse. As usual, I concentrated on my football, but eventually I was the victim of an awful tackle from behind that turned my leg black and blue. I am glad that I kept my temper although the Austrian who fouled me looked rather disturbed when I told him exactly what I thought of him and what I might do to him. Words and threats usually worked for me – one of the advantages of being bigger than most. The referee did nothing about it but the offending player's own National Association promptly banned him for a month – an outstanding gesture that should have been a good omen for the return fixture in Wrexham. Sadly, it wasn't.

The game began as though it was going to be a classic, with quality football played by excellent players. The Austrians were soon one up, and deservedly so, and then one of their players was injured in a challenge and stretchered off to hospital. But it was not this incident, an unhappy fluke, that provoked the mayhem that followed. That was the result of Trevor Ford and Derek Tapscott continually challenging their goalkeeper. The Austrians felt it should be a foul every time one of them went near, but nothing was given.

Gradually their patience wore thin and football was forgotten as the game developed into a rough and tumble. The Austrians showed that they could play the game equally well this way as the legitimate way.

Once again, I tried to remain aloof and play football until I saw my brother Mel go down in a tackle, clearly in pain and seriously injured. I admit here and now that my initial instinct was to go and hit the Austrian involved. Clearly, brotherly love was influencing me, along with the general tenor of the game. But as Mel was carried off, I kept my temper in check and carried on, wondering all the time how my little brother was.

However, Mel's injury had absolutely nothing to do with the mayhem going on all over the pitch. Like the Austrian hurt in the first half, he was simply a victim of circumstances, injured in what was a perfectly fair and legitimate challenge. My reaction, while understandable when your brother is hurt, was totally wrong and had I hit the player involved, I would not have been able to live with myself. Would I have even wanted to play on? Fortunately, I never had to answer that question because my natural instincts stopped my temper from bubbling over. It taught me a lesson and underlined my personal principles for playing football.

We lost the game 2–1 and there was a nasty taste in the mouth afterwards, which had nothing to do with Mel's injury. The Welsh were bitter about the Austrians, complaining of their underhand tactics while the Austrians were describing us as 'Welsh Assassins'. It made me stop and think. Often in the past we had accused others but now we were hearing the same complaints about ourselves. The fault lay on both sides with the officials having to take their share of finger pointing for not keeping a tight grip on the game.

The main fault, however, lay at the feet of the international governing body FIFA for not laying down precise laws about challenging the goalkeeper. Every country had their own interpretation with the Continentals solidly against it while we were all for a good, honest, shoulder-to-shoulder charge.

In the end, a sensible compromise by the ruling bodies helped everyone. Goalkeepers, if anything, are too well protected these days, but who wants to see them hurt? I prefer the compromise.

We needed to stand strong in both of those games and Alf Sherwood was as resolute as ever. He would have played anywhere for Wales and was a great example as captain.

Another landmark in my international career came on 10 November 1954 when I played my first game at Wembley. I couldn't wait to play there. I had played at Hampden Park, which at the time was a bigger ground than Wembley, but I was disappointed because I found the surface too bumpy. By contrast, Wembley was smooth with really springy grass. There was also a terrific, non-threatening atmosphere and every game was like a cup-tie.

It was not the easiest surface to play on because you sank into the lush, thick turf, a bit like an expensive carpet, and it meant that you had to hit your ground passes slightly harder than usual, but for accuracy of passing there was nowhere like it. It was as reliable as a snooker table and I loved it.

It was a tiring ground because the studs bit so deep and I could see why England had built up such a good record at their fortress. It was a tester. If you were sensible, you paced yourself and did not try to do too much running. If you weren't fit, it found you out. It would grab your legs and make you suffer. Even when you were fit it was no use charging about chasing everything because your legs would go from under you long before the ninety minutes were up. Some people went so far as to say that Wembley was a dangerous ground because there were so many injuries in high-profile matches, but few of them were the fault of the ground, just with players trying to turn too quickly, running too hard, too early and trying to put in too much effort. Walley Barnes, Jimmy Meadows and Colin Grainger all suffered serious injuries within the space of a few years through turning quickly but I never heard one of them blame Wembley for the injury. Anyone who did was talking nonsense. It was as safe as any ground in the world. Injuries were caused by players turning when their studs had a good grip in the turf, and that usually means trouble.

I do not believe that there were any more injuries at Wembley than anywhere else and I say this despite the fact that Wales were dreadfully unlucky there. In fact, it was something of a hoodoo. In 1954 we were once again the better team early on. Ten minutes before half-time, Ivor Allchurch put me through and I scored my first ever goal at the world's most famous stadium – a moment of great pride. But five minutes before the interval, Ray Daniel was led off with a cut eye and before he reached the dressing room, Derek Sullivan was carried off unconscious after an accidental clash of heads.

Although both came back on after the break, we were weakened, and Stanley Matthews seized the opportunity to take us on. The surface was slippery and he was at his best. Before long, he had slipped through our defence and placed a perfect cross on to Roy Bentley's head for the equaliser. Bentley scored a second and although we came back well to equalise as I scored my second, Bentley went one better and completed his hat-trick just seven minutes from the end. There was little or no time for us to hit back.

It was annoying to lose to England again, especially as I felt that we were the better team, but we made up for it to some extent in our next match when I scored a hat-trick in a 3–2 win over Northern Ireland in Belfast.

Players being injured against the English was getting to be a habit. Two years later, we were again reduced to nine men for a while when

Mel went off with a stomach injury while Jack Kelsey, our goalkeeper, also went off to be replaced by Alf Sherwood. To add to the problems, England winger Colin Grainger went off half an hour before the end with a chipped anklebone. Mel and Jack both came back but all Jack could do was hobble on the wing and England went on to win 3–1. It was such a big pitch that being a man short left a team with an awful lot of running to do on that strength-sapping surface; but the injuries came about because of the usual football incidents and not dirty play nor the lush pitch.

On 22 October 1955, a date writ large in my memory, we at last beat England for the first time in seventeen years. Unfortunately, it was not at Wembley but in front of our own fans at Cardiff. We won 2–1, even though Roy Paul was reduced to a limping passenger. It was a special occasion with 60,000 Welsh fans in full voice as Derek Tapscott put us ahead and Cliff Jones added a second within a minute. I scored – but this time through my own goal. It was not enough for England and we won a great victory.

The team that day was: Kelsey (Arsenal); Williams (WBA), Sherwood (Cardiff City); Mel Charles (Swansea Town), John Charles (Leeds United), Paul (Manchester City); Tapscott (Arsenal), Kinsey (Birmingham City), Ford (Cardiff City), Ivor Allchurch (Swansea Town), Cliff Jones (Swansea Town).

We were walking on air after that victory but it must have gone to our heads as we went on to lose in Scotland, and could only draw with Northern Ireland in Cardiff, and all four countries finished the Home International Championships level on four points. Had we beaten the Irish, we would have won the title. We scored after only ten minutes through Roy Clarke. I gained possession in my own six-yard box and as I was about to hoof the ball clear to relieve the pressure, a gap opened up in front of me. I moved forward and no one seemed to bother, so I carried on my run and before I knew it I

PLAYING FOR WALES

was past the halfway line and into their half with the huge crowd cheering for all they were worth. I made it all the way to their penalty area and when goalkeeper Norman Uprichard came off his line to close me down, I slipped the ball towards Trevor Ford who cleverly let it pass under his foot for Clarke to score.

Happily, the BBC cameras were there at the time and the goal, described as one of the best for Wales, was recorded on film, every step I took. For many years it was used in the introduction for BBC's Saturday evening sports programme 'Sports Special'.

The strange thing was that when Wales weren't involved, I used to be happy to support England in all internationals, especially the World Cup. It happened the other way round in 1958 when England were knocked out and we stayed in. Everyone in England seemed to be supporting us in Sweden as we lined up against both Mexico and Brazil.

It's an amazing story. Our skipper Ray Daniel was at odds with some of the selectors. His bad luck was my good fortune because, in April 1957, I was named as the Welsh captain and led the team out to a rather uninspired goalless draw against Northern Ireland in Belfast.

For such a tepid game, it was probably one of the most important for me because sitting in the stand that day was Signor Umberto Agnelli, and I am still baffled about what he saw in me to encourage him to watch me ever again; that's how disappointing my first game as captain was.

Signor Agnelli was to give me problems when my dream came true and Wales eventually reached the 1958 World Cup finals in Sweden, but in 1957 it did not look as though it was going to be a problem as Wales were knocked out in the qualifying rounds by Czechoslovakia. But then Israel were left in limbo when all their qualifying opponents, Turkey, Indonesia, Egypt and Sudan, all withdrew. FIFA in their wisdom decreed that Israel could not qualify in such a way and decided the names of the second-placed teams from all the qualifying groups would go into a hat – or rather the gold Jules Rimet Cup – and whoever was drawn out would play off against Israel for a place in the finals.

With Uruguay proudly refusing to be involved in such a lottery, into the draw went the Republic of Ireland, Wales, Bulgaria, Holland, Romania, Poland and either Italy or Northern Ireland, whoever came second in Group Eight.

The draw was made in Zurich ten days before Christmas and what a present it turned out to be for Wales as ours was the name to come out of the Cup. We needed to beat the Israelis over two legs to claim a place among the sixteen best teams in the world.

We felt that we deserved it having been in such a tough group and going so close. We had beaten the Czechs 1–0 at Ninian Park with a goal from Roy Vernon. I played in the back line along with Mel to try to hold a team that included the brilliant Josef Masopust, Ladislav Novak and the international football and ice-hockey player Vlastimil Bubnik. I didn't mind playing at the back – I would have played anywhere – and it was some struggle against such a powerful team. Our Arsenal goalkeeper Jack Kelsey was in brilliant form and was largely instrumental in us keeping a clean sheet.

They were one of the better teams in Europe at the time and they were well aware of the fact. They arrived in Cardiff with a list of what they wanted – ten footballs for training; a trip to the seaside (honest!); English cigarettes; a look around the civic buildings of Cardiff; 300 postcards of views of Cardiff beauty spots, with stamps; and finally and cheekiest of all, to watch us in training.

After that, we played East Germany in Leipzig, and Czechoslovakia in Prague seven days later. Unbelievably, the Welsh Association took just twelve players to East Germany, including

Derek Tapscott who had an ankle injury, but picked a full team of eleven selectors for the trip. I was in Holland with Leeds at the time, and joined up with the party two days before the game, having travelled via Amsterdam and Frankfurt. Although one of the selectors pulled out, when you added manager Jimmy Murphy, trainer Jack Jones and doctor Bill Hughes, the players were comfortably outnumbered. It was crazy but that's how it was – selectors first and players second.

When the team arrived in Berlin, they were taken by coach to Leipzig through Check Point Charlie while the selectors were driven to their hotel in limousines. I found the entire scene very intimidating, not least the stadium, which was bulging with over 110,000 people packed inside and hardly a Red Dragon to be seen.

I had just signed for Juventus as a centre-forward but Jimmy Murphy kept me at the back and moved Mel forward. It paid off when Mel opened the scoring but our joy was short lived as Günter Wirth, an outstanding player, soon equalised.

We weren't playing well and I was certainly below my best against a one-armed centre-forward named Willi Troger. I was sorry for him and determined not to be physical, but he was very quick and scored East Germany's second goal. I immediately went up front but we failed to rescue a game we were expected to win.

We were left licking our wounds in a very ordinary hotel in Leipzig for four days before travelling to Czechoslovakia in a very old Dakota. It was hardly the right build-up for what had become a crucial game against the best opponents in the group.

The shortage of players came home to roost as well, with Tapscott still struggling and Reg Davies sick with a sore throat. It forced the selectors to call Ray Daniel up from Sunderland as a replacement, something of a shock as his ban for accepting an illegal payment from his club had only just been lifted.

It was a mess. Ray did not even have a decent pair of boots –
Sunderland had sent a new pair to Heathrow instead of his old
broken-in ones. He tried a pair of mine but they didn't fit. He was
forced to train in the new boots and at the end of the first session he
was in agony with his feet blistered and his body aching all over.
The great middle distance runner Emil Zatopek was staying at the
hotel and he fashioned some pads to fit inside Ray's boots to try to
relieve the pain.

Worse was to follow as Tapscott showed little or no improvement
and the selectors were forced to send home for another player. This
time they went for the young Swansea centre-forward Des Palmer,
who had never played at this level before.

The build-up was a total farce and the match itself was even
worse as we went behind to a Daniel own goal. It was a pity because
apart from this error, he had a very good game although we were
lucky to escape with a 2–0 defeat. Daniel was in so much pain that
he took off his new boots, threw them to the sidelines and played
the last fifteen minutes in his socks.

So, with the Czechs winning their last two matches, we were out
of it although we managed to beat East Germany 4–1 – a game I
missed because Juventus decided, and I agreed, it would be a stupid
risk for me to play what everyone thought was a meaningless match.

Then came our reprieve and suddenly we were in with a chance
again. We were to play Israel in Tel Aviv on 15 January 1958 with
the return at Ninian Park on 5 February. Fortunately, Juventus agreed
to release me for both games and we also had Ivor Allchurch back
after he had missed the last seven games for Wales.

There was a crowd of more than 36,000 for the first game, but
we were the better side and fully deserved our two-goal first-leg lead.
Ivor scored the first and Arsenal's Dave Bowen the second, making
the second leg something of a formality back in Cardiff. Their

goalkeeper Yaacov Chodoroff was a bit special and for a while he threatened to keep the score at 0–0 but in the second half we collided and while I was fine he was left dazed with a broken nose and a sprained shoulder. He played on but finished up in the local hospital, unsure of the score and talking only Hebrew.

We won 2–0 with goals from Allchurch and Cliff Jones, and celebrated into the early hours of the morning – justifiably so as we were off to Sweden for the World Cup as representatives, not of Great Britain and Europe, but of Asia and Africa.

The next day manager Jimmy Murphy made his way back to Manchester and reached the Old Trafford ground before he discovered from the manager's secretary, Alma George, that the Manchester United plane had crashed in Munich on the way back from their European Cup match in Belgrade.

Fate had dealt him a crushing blow, but had also possibly saved his life. But for the draw to find a team to play Israel, he would have been sitting on that aircraft next to Matt Busby. His place had been taken by coach Bert Whalley – one of twenty-three to die. Busby himself barely survived as eight of the Busby Babes, three club officials and eight journalists perished in the Bavarian snow.

Jimmy had gone from the heights of football ecstasy to the depths of despair. He was straight on a train to Munich where Matt Busby whispered to him, 'Keep the flag flying, Jimmy. Keep things going until I get back.'

It takes some sort of character to overcome an incident so grievous and heart-rending as that, but not only did Jimmy manage Wales in their preparation for the World Cup but also Manchester United's decimated and rebuilt team. Under Jimmy, United amazingly finished ninth in the First Division, reached the FA Cup final where they lost 2–1 to Bolton Wanderers and beat AC Milan at

Old Trafford before going out of the European Cup in the second leg of the semi-final.

I don't believe Jimmy was ever given the rightful recognition for what he did in United's direst hour of need, but then he was not that sort of man. He shied away from publicity, always happy to let others do the talking while he worked with the players. That was when he was at his happiest. Now he was attending the funerals of his friends Bert Whalley, the coach, and Tom Curry, the trainer, while trying to rebuild the shattered team. Despite his natural public shyness, the team became known as 'Murphy's Marvels'.

The son of a Welsh mother and an Irish father, Jimmy Murphy was a real character, a one-off. I was very close to him and when I was at Leeds we would often meet in Manchester to talk about the Welsh national team and whom we thought were the good and not so good players.

The players loved and respected him. If you wanted a drink a couple of days before the game, it was fine, but you were warned the booze had to be left alone the next day. Jimmy would have a drink with you when the time was right. He was one of the boys but remained respected and above the usual tomfoolery.

His team-talks were something special and became legendary, as he did. His style of motivation was unique. When we played the Germans, he told us, 'Gentlemen, these people bombed your houses, killed your mothers and fathers, killed your brothers and sisters. Go out and get your own back!' The players responded well – jaws dropped at first but then they clenched their fists, ready to wreak revenge for previous sins. It sounds harsh now but don't forget the war had not been over for that long, and it was still relevant, as it was for the Dutch for many years afterwards.

Jimmy was brought up in the Rhondda Valley and when he wasn't playing football he was playing the organ in the Treorchy

Parish Church. Football was his consuming passion and he played for the Welsh schoolboys before joining West Bromwich Albion until the outbreak of the war. Like me later, he was the youngest player to pull on the red shirt of Wales, aged twenty-one, and he went on to be capped fifteen times.

During the war, he was a Desert Rat serving with the Royal Artillery and he told us that after the North African campaign he arrived at the Bari transit camp in Italy where he relieved a certain Stan Cullis as the sergeant in charge of sport. It was there he met and became friends with Matt Busby.

He did so well for United and Wales that Juventus sent me over to ask him if he would become our manager. He said no not only to Juventus but also to Brazil and Arsenal to stay at Old Trafford. He told me he was sorely tempted by the Highbury offer but, in the end, he decided to stay loyal to Matt Busby, who gave him a job after the war, having heard him exhorting his troops before going into battle.

He worked until his death on 14 November 1989, aged seventy-nine, a day I cried. His is a name remembered with pride not only at Old Trafford but by every Welsh soccer lover for he was the man who took us on such a great adventure to Sweden, and almost upset the greatest odds in football history.

Wales had a very good team in those days with Kelsey, Paul, Sherwood, Tapscott, Mel and me. Then there were the Allchurch brothers, Ivor and Lenny, and Terry Medwin. Paul was great on long balls, the angled ball that found the winger. Despite those great leather balls, he could pick out his man time after time. I particularly liked playing with Ivor Allchurch and Reg Davies, who played it very simply, while Ivor was a bit more technical. He was world class. Sherwood was solid, and I also liked Ray Daniel, but the best was Roy Paul, a great player.

Despite having a good team, we didn't do what we should have done; maybe we didn't have enough games, and sometimes clubs wouldn't release players while at other times the players didn't want to play, and that includes me. I loved playing for Wales but I missed a dozen or more matches because I could not face the hours and hours of travelling. I wasn't injured and the club didn't stop me; it was just me saying no to friendly internationals. This is something I haven't admitted before. Sometimes I would say no because I was too tired and too sore after the game on Saturday, and the match was too far away. I was knackered and the travelling would make it worse. If I was carrying a knock, it would stiffen up over the journey and make me even more susceptible to injury when I did play. I would not have been able to give of my best and sometimes I decided I was better off resting my kicks and bruises to prepare for the next weekend.

It is different now when you can get anywhere in a short time. That was not the case then. There was a lot of changing of airplanes, trains and even boats, and an awful lot of hanging around. It would often take a full day or more to travel from Milan to Cardiff and then another full day or more to get back, according to the connections. I can understand the problems Dennis Bergkamp has because he does not like flying, but at least he has a fast train service and comfortable, quick cars to take him when he does play away from England. Wales were very understanding when I said I couldn't play. It was said it was never my choice and Juventus, always and without demur, shouldered the blame.

I suppose you could say I picked and chose my games, sometimes with the stern help of Juventus and sometimes completely through my own decision. Juventus, of course, did not want me to go anywhere. It was all give and take, a game of chess. I knew the games I wanted to play, when Wales might really need me, and I would play those off against the games I missed to keep Juventus happy. It meant that when I said yes to a game, they would let me go. However, they were all big games in those days and now I regret missing any. Thirty-eight caps is a small return and I wish that I had won my fifty.

Trevor Ford missed the World Cup finals in Sweden, because he had been banned by the Welsh FA for comments he made in his autobiography. Although he was nearing the end of his career, I am sure he would have been good enough to go to the tournament. His international career began in 1946 with a Victory Shield appearance against Northern Ireland and lasted eleven years. What difference would he have made to our World Cup bid? He was absolutely fearless, aggressive and full of energy, which frightened lesser men, and, in particular, lesser goalkeepers. But for all his teak-toughness, he was never sly. What you saw was what you got and he wasn't in trouble with referees as often as some.

He was a centre-forward first and last, so much so that he once declined to play inside-right at Cardiff, offering to play centre-forward for the reserves instead. All he thought about was scoring goals in any way inside the laws of the game. He would charge goalkeepers, block them and chase them wherever and whenever he could. Goalkeepers were genuinely frightened of him and he was booed at almost every ground on which he played except, of course, his own; and every one of those fans who booed him would have loved to have had him leading their attack.

To me he was a hero, a wholehearted trier who gave his all, prepared to tackle every lost cause and take on defences on his own. How he would have loved playing in Italy. He would have given as good as he got but, of course, the moment he touched a goalkeeper that would have been it.

His assets were his speed, his strength and his shooting power. He began as a gangling youth but when he emerged from the army he was two inches taller and a couple of stone heavier. It was the army that converted him from a wing-half to a centre-forward. In fact, he began with Tower United as a full-back and was chosen to play in that position for the Welsh schoolboy team, but he broke his leg and missed out.

Like me, he began with Swansea, turning down both Arsenal and Cardiff, but fell out with them over preparations for a cup-tie, and moved to Aston Villa for £10,000.

He never lost the Welsh feeling. The dragon must have been tattooed across his heart for he sent his wife Louise home to Swansea so that his first son David would be born a Welshman. So it was a surprise when he moved to Sunderland for £30,000. The club gave him a house by the sea and a job outside football.

He eventually moved to Cardiff for another big fee but it was a continually troubled time. In the end he rebelled against a sliding scale of wages – the maximum then was £15 a week – and was suspended for refusing to play inside-forward.

His turbulent life continued when he was banned sine die by the FA for revealing in his book, *I Lead The Attack*, that he and other players had received irregular payments of up to £100 from his former club Sunderland. That ban was eventually rescinded on appeal.

Because the ban prevented him from playing in the Football League, he signed for PSV in Holland and helped them to second place in the Dutch League, scoring 51 goals in 54 games in 1958. They loved him in Holland but doctors there told him that so bad were his injuries he would have to stop playing. So, aged thirty-six, he returned home and signed for little Newport County for £2,000. It was a mistake. They were struggling and so was he, scoring three goals in eight games before another row caused him to move to

Romford in the Southern League. Although they offered him a contract, he retired from football and went back to live in Cardiff.

His superb fitness saved his life in 1969 when he was involved in a serious car accident in Bridgend, trapped behind the wheel of his car.

I have often wondered what might have happened had Trevor not been banned by his own association for the 1958 World Cup. He would have loved it and the other teams would have been frightened to death of his robust style. One thing I know for sure is that had he played I would not have been subject to such a fearsome kicking from the Hungarians. He would have made sure he deflected a lot of the attention. And then . . . who knows?

In fact, he wasn't the only one not to go to Sweden: Ray Daniel and Derek Tapscott were also missing. Ray Daniel wasn't dropped because of the own goal he conceded in his last game, against Czechoslovakia in Prague, but because he'd sung some songs in West End shows that were considered risqué by some religious members of the international committee. While Derek Tapscott did not withdraw through a knee injury, as he said at the time, but he later confessed it was due to the pressure he had been put under to transfer from Arsenal to Cardiff, which made him feel blackmailed.

It saddened me hugely when I heard of Trevor's death as we completed this manuscript. He was a lifelong hero of mine.

CHAPTER TEN

Sweden and a boy named Pele

The World Cup was a dream for me but, for a while, it looked as though I was going to miss it completely. Italy had failed to qualify and the Serie A clubs were contemplating a summer knock-out tournament.

It was not just me plunged into depression – the host nation Sweden had half a dozen players in the Italian League while the Austrians would seriously miss Ernst Ocwirk, who was playing for Sampdoria at the time.

When I returned home to Swansea in March for Mel's wedding, I was convinced there were serious problems. I already knew I would be out of the Home International against Northern Ireland because the game was sandwiched between two important league fixtures and we were chasing the title.

At the same time, it was being rumoured that I was about to join Manchester United as Jimmy Murphy tried to rebuild the team shattered by the Munich disaster, but the closest the rumour was to the truth was that I had offered Jimmy my help in any other way. It was a well-meant gesture.

It was not until a week before the World Cup tournament began that I was finally told I could join the Welsh team, who were already preparing in Scandinavia, and then only for the first-round games. Presumably, they expected Wales to be out of the competition after that. It had taken a personal appeal to Signor Agnelli to release me for the qualifying games and Juventus were reluctant to lose me for the new cup competition. It was the traditional club versus country business, but I did feel on this occasion the World Cup should take precedence, and I made my point as forcibly as I could. I was backed by a campaign that spread from Wales through England and into Sweden.

I could understand Juventus's concern. They had no interest in this World Cup and I had finished the season as the top scorer in Serie A and we had won the championship for the first time in six years. They had invested a great deal of money in me and, according to the press, I was now valued at £150,000, which would have made me the most expensive player in the world had they sold me for that sort of money.

The cup, as far as I was concerned, was a run-out for the reserves and the crowds were not going to be affected in Biella, Verneli and Turin, which would all be sold out whether I played or not. What's more, Milan, Inter, Lazio and Atalanta had all released Swedish players to compete in the World Cup. In the end, they respected the fact that I wanted to play for my country and allowed me to go, albeit reluctantly. It took a lot of persuasion on my part and I had to remind Agnelli he had promised me I could play in Sweden if Wales got through the play-off.

I was ready to move heaven and earth to play for my country in this, their biggest ever tournament, but Juventus were paying my wages and I had to do what I was told. I would not have walked out on the club if they had refused but it would have affected my attitude and therefore my form. It was in their interests to keep me happy and let me play.

Eventually I left with their blessing and, because of delays, arrived in the early hours of the morning at a nearly empty Bromma airport. There was no one from the Welsh party to meet me and it took me a while to find out which hotel they were in. I was just preparing to sleep on a bench at the airport when Dewi Lewis, a reporter from the *Western Mail* in Cardiff, turned up and took me to Soltsjobaden where the team were staying.

The selectors, bless 'em, had never experienced anything like this before. They did not know what was going on. But you would have thought, after all the fuss they and others had made in a bid to secure my release, they would at least have had someone to meet me at the airport, if only a driver. Failing that, a message would have gone to let me know where in Sweden I was heading for.

The officials again outnumbered the players and Jimmy Murphy was wild about it. His anger was understandable because we did not have enough players to cover for injuries. But the officials were good people who meant well. They all claimed they picked you when you had been left out. When Wales played in France, Italy or Spain, it was their holiday as well as a football match and they loved it.

I expected a lie-in when I finally arrived but Jimmy Murphy soon had me up. When I walked into the breakfast room, the selectors and their wives started to sing 'For He's a Jolly Good Fellow'. Needless to say, the players did not join in the chorus and how they laughed at this spontaneous show of emotion – but I could tell they were pleased to see me.

Soon afterwards, I was shown a copy of the local paper, *Aftonbladet*, which had launched a stinging attack on Juventus. It took me by surprise because I was not aware feelings were running so high outside my own circle. The article read:

When John Charles arrives in Stockholm he will be greeted with ecstasy by thousands of his Swedish soccer fans who are all talking about his magnificent show for Juventus here last season. It is indeed an especially joyous message that the Swedish public will see the world's most expensive player again.

What treatment he got from the Italian club in return. They played him a dirty, underhand trick and it is good to know that he has stood up to them and got his way.

It was clear that Juventus first of all gave him permission to travel but then they went behind his back and got the Italian Federation to ban him from the World Cup competition.

This was because the Italian Cup came into being and the bosses of Juventus discovered that without Charles they would not be a very attractive team for the public. That is why they got the Italian Association to place an embargo on him.

Now, of course, Juventus have got wind of the storm of hate that would blow up in Britain if Charles were not allowed to play in the World Cup finals.

And with the player himself taking a firm stand – he might even have offered reprisals if he was refused permission – he is on his way.

We in Sweden were particularly interested in Charles' case for we have got four of our Italian professionals in our camp now training with the Swedish side for the World Cup.

There has been no discussion like that which arose around

John Charles and Juventus at any time and that is where we feel the FA of Wales are to blame.

It is not difficult to think out a reason why Wales had difficulty in getting John Charles. The FA of Wales were content to send a letter to Juventus to try to get an agreement by correspondence instead of by personal contact.

Sweden sent their most influential football man to Italy, despite the fact that he had a thousand important jobs to do at home, and he succeeded in getting the release of the Swedish players without undue difficulty.

How can the FA of Wales expect to get the release of Charles by letter only?

They certainly seemed to like me and I guess the reason why I got such a good press when it looked as though I wouldn't play in the finals was due in part to Juventus's tour of Scandinavia the previous year.

Apparently, the Italian Federation gave me permission to travel for the first-round games only after Juventus and the teams they were due to play raised no objections, but I felt it was a little unfair to blame the Welsh selectors who, to be honest, hadn't a clue what to do to obtain my release and left it to me to argue the point.

It was not a great way to prepare for the greatest competition in world football – but at least I was there and I was going to play. I was pleased not only for myself but for Jimmy Murphy who had put so much into Wales despite working every hour God sent to rebuild his beloved Manchester United.

Wales played a couple of friendly games against local opposition to warm up for the tournament, and after missing the first, I played against Soltsjobaden. I scored four goals out of something like nineteen but I injured my knee in the process. The joint ballooned up but I carried on playing and while it was a little sore I was ready to face Hungary two days later.

We were drawn in a group with the magnificent Magyars, now rebuilding after the revolution and short of a few of their top players, hosts Sweden with their clutch of Italian players, and those perennial underdogs Mexico.

We were booked on the first flight out after the final group game, which was how much of a chance we were given, even by our own huge team of selectors. All the home countries had qualified and there was not too much pressure on us because we were considered the unlikeliest of the four contenders. The Munich disaster had touched us all, as young Welshman Ken Morgans was lucky to survive. However, England had suffered the truly severe loss of Roger Byrne, Duncan Edwards and Tommy Taylor, while the exhausted Bobby Charlton did not play in a single game in Sweden. To make matters worse for England, they decided to leave out the veterans Stanley Matthews and Nat Lofthouse, and not to take a bright young centre-forward, Brian Clough.

Our record of playing away from home was not good – the first game we had won abroad was the play-off against Israel a few months earlier. Up until then, in our entire history we had lost all nine games we'd played outside the British Isles. But two were due to go through and the big question was how good were the Hungarians after losing so many of the players from the 1954 finals in the uprising two years later? Those players who remained were in the twilight of their careers – goalkeeper Gyula Grosics, Jozsef Bozsik and Nandor Hidegkuti were all in their thirties – but Hungary were still strongly fancied to beat us in the Jernvallen Stadium in Sandviken, close to the Arctic Circle.

The journey there seemed to take forever and it was hardly the best preparation for the game, particularly as, when we eventually stepped off the bus, the first thing we saw was the Hungarians training on the ground. We went straight into the dressing room to get changed and then out for the match. There was certainly no time for nerves.

Mel was picked at centre-half to look after the tall Lajos Tichy and I was up front as our battering ram. We were in all yellow as we had lost the toss for colours, and we lost the toss for kick-off as well. That was unfortunate because it meant that we were playing into the sun, and within four minutes we were a goal down through Bozsik who scored from a Hidegkuti pass. So much for the old men!

For a while they pummelled us and whenever the ball came forward, I seemed to have two Hungarians clinging to me and kicking lumps out of me. As usual, my attitude was that the best way to reply and to hurt them was to score, and my opportunity came midway through the first half from a Cliff Jones corner. Colin Webster took the centre-half away and I was left with a free header, which went in off the post.

The goal gave us confidence but the Hungarians were still more of a threat than us, and it needed goalline clearances from Mel Hopkins and Stuart Williams to keep the score level while, once again, Jack Kelsey was superb in goal, truly world class.

As for me, they kicked me from pillar to post right from the kick-off. They held my shirt, my arm or anything else they could get hold of. One of them even put both arms round my neck when I tried to jump for a cross. I thought it was bad in Italy but this was much worse, and Uruguayan referee Codesal did little about it other than awarding free kicks. He missed a penalty when Matrai tripped Cliff Jones, waving play on, and we had to settle for a draw.

The small ground suited us but I have to say I was disappointed with the Hungarians. I had gone to see them when they beat England at Wembley in 1953 and marvelled at their play as they won 6–3, but this was a different team who wanted to kick more than play.

The game was draining and we hardly managed a song on the long journey back to our hotel with the next game, against Mexico, just three days away. Mexico, despite their history in the World Cup, were expected to be the whipping boys of our group, having lost to two Portuguese club sides on the way out. They had been thrashed 3–0 by Sweden in their opening game, they had injuries and, according to the British journalists, they were an unhappy bunch. Suddenly, we were odds-on favourites to win our game in the Rasunda Stadium in Stockholm and claim a place in the quarter-finals.

The Mexicans made a number of changes and, before the game, Jimmy Murphy ranted and screamed that they couldn't play football and were only good for riding horses. Only Jimmy had seen them, and we knew nothing about them. There were no films to watch in those days.

The majority of the 15,000 crowd were for the underdogs, Mexico, but that was hardly an excuse for the way we played. We were very poor and did not settle even when Ivor Allchurch put us in front in the first half. The Mexicans were a much better side than we had been led to believe; they certainly passed the ball well.

Colin Webster upset the Mexican and the Swedish fans with his over-robust tackling and Jimmy Murphy not only gave him a good ticking off after the game but also left him out of the next one, against Sweden. If Hungary were the villains when we played our opening game, we were seen as the bad boys in this one.

We were as bad in the second half as we were in the first and I could not shake off my marker Jorge Romo but, all the same, we looked like taking the points with Ivor's goal until they snatched an equaliser in the eighty-ninth minute.

I hardly saw the ball throughout the game, got in a couple of tame headers and didn't contribute as much as I should have done. No one did. Jimmy Murphy was furious and went around muttering under his breath, saying we were bloody rubbish. It wasn't a good performance by any stretch of the imagination, but the point was good. We had to accept it was one of those days and we would have to put it right in our third match, the toughest of the three on paper. We felt we were still in with a chance when Sweden beat Hungary 2–1.

The press hammered us – the manager, the team and me. In the space of seventy-two hours we had gone from hero to zero. They had their teeth into us and we were accused of everything from being playboys to over-indulging in the luxuries offered by the Grand Hotel.

Of more interest to us was FIFA talking about goal difference settling the places rather than a play-off, which had been agreed before the tournament. It made a big difference to Murphy's strategy. He was looking for a draw against a Swedish team that had already qualified, which would guarantee us a play-off place. To this end, he picked me up front but instructed me to play virtually in midfield, and this against a Swedish team that rested Liedholm, Mellberg, Simonsson, Gren and Hamrin. That suited Jimmy's plans down to the ground and after fifteen minutes I was dropped into the back line to partner my brother after I had gone close with a header.

I had cut my eyebrow and was being very well marked by Gustavsson, a very good player with Atalanta in Italy who always gave me a tough game because he was not only good in the air but also tackled very strongly. I was quite happy to drop back and get out of his way. I liked Gustavsson a lot and got to know him even better when Colombo joined Atalanta. I used to go to watch them and we would all go out for dinner together after the game.

We survived with our third draw of the competition, but the game couldn't have been very good to watch. We had some luck when Skoglund hit the underside of the crossbar – it looked harder for him to miss than to score. That was it. It was not greeted with great applause, far from it. Dewi Lewis said it was like watching a Sunday afternoon tea party while the local papers called me a flop.

The press were entitled to have a go but Jimmy wanted me to play a bit behind the game like Di Stefano. It was all part of our tactical plan because we knew if we stopped Sweden scoring we could stay in the World Cup. We set out to play a defensive game and I honestly felt sorry for the people who had paid to see it. I could understand it when they jeered us from the pitch.

The most amazing sight was saved for the day after the game when the selectors had to fly back home and were not sure they would be able to book seats back out to rejoin us. They were crying their eyes out. It was unbelievable. They had to take the seats they had booked in advance. No one thought, 'What the hell, we'll stay and sort it out afterwards.' It was a shambles. They were back the next day. What a farce!

Later that night we heard that Hungary had crushed Mexico 4–0 in Jernvallen and they would be our opponents in the play-off for a place in the quarter-finals. Scotland were out but also through to play-offs were England and Northern Ireland.

We had just two days' rest after our slog against Sweden. I had four or five stitches in my head wound but a little thing like a cut wasn't going to keep me out of this game, and this time I was to play centre-forward. It was a game we had to win because if it was still a draw after extra time, goal difference would count and that would put the Hungarians through.

The odds were in our favour as we were able to wear our red shirts and Hungary had to make the long trip to Stockholm.

We also won the toss, which meant Grosics would be facing the setting sun and not Kelsey. Amazing how things can reverse themselves and, in fact, our only problem was the selection of a Russian referee, who Jimmy, with his own logic, was convinced would favour Hungary.

A big disappointment was the fact that the 50,000 Rasunda Stadium was virtually deserted when we kicked off with only a couple of thousand dotted about the terraces. It was dead with no atmosphere at all.

Jimmy's worst fears about the Russian referee, Nikolai Latychev, were soon realised. In the opening stages of the game I could have scored a hat-trick but Grosics made a staggering save and then I was pulled down in the area twice in the space of a few minutes. Both were penalties and neither was given. Russia had invaded Hungary and I wondered if this was some sort of apology!

It was to count because Tichy, who was proving to be one of their best players, scored his fourth goal of the tournament to leave us trailing 1–0 at half-time and needing to do something we had failed to do in our previous three matches – score twice.

But we were playing well and the Hungarians were becoming desperate. They were kicking me black and blue again and when I was presented with another chance I was held down by Sipos right in front of the referee – but again he waved play on.

At corners, one of the Hungarian defenders would hold my arms while another would crash into my back. It was blatant and obvious but the Russian referee ignored it and when asked about it afterwards said, somewhat strangely, he was playing the advantage rule. Whose advantage, I wondered.

I had to go off the pitch for treatment after being chopped down once more but when I came back on I was quickly in possession and spotted Ivor Allchurch all on his own. I lobbed him a pass and he struck a superb goal. Ivor was that sort of player; he could hit the ball with right or left foot. It was a goal I will never forget.

We were level but this was not enough. We were encouraged when the Hungarians started to have a go at each other, showing they were clearly unhappy. Their tackling became even worse and I seemed to be their main target. They were kicking me to pieces and I was receiving no protection from the referee. They were kicking everything and everybody. In all the games I played in Italy, England and Wales, this was the worst I ever suffered. I was continually knocked to the ground but I was determined I would not give them the pleasure of seeing me lose my temper or retaliating. I just tried to smile but, twenty minutes from the end, I chested a ball down and as I did so, Sipos kicked me on the back of my right leg. That was the one that finished me and I could scarcely raise a trot or kick the ball after it. I was a passenger.

The rest of the team could see I was unable to contribute but the other ten raised their game and with little more than ten minutes left, Terry Medwin scored a cheeky goal after a terrible mix-up in the Hungarian defence. I was in the clear but he chose to shoot, which was a good decision considering the state I was in.

There were unbelievable scenes in the dug-out and in the stands when the goal went in with manager and trainer hugging each other and the selectors leaping up and down in the otherwise empty stand.

After the goal, the tackling became even more ugly but still the referee took no action until our reserve keeper Ken Jones picked the ball up and booted it out of the ground. He was not only booked but also fined by FIFA, and by his club Cardiff City, for ungentlemanly conduct.

Eventually, even the Russian could take no more and sent Sipos off after he had kicked Hewitt so badly he had to be carried off and taken to hospital. We finished with ten men a side and in the dying minutes it took a wonderful save from Jack Kelsey to keep us in the competition.

Jimmy was running up and down the touchline shouting for the referee to blow time and taking an occasional swig out of the flask he kept filled with whisky. It was an incredible moment when the whistle blew. It was Wales' first-ever win in the World Cup and it had put us into the quarter-finals to face the favourites, Brazil. We did not know whether to cry or laugh as we made our way to the dressing room where the selectors burst through the door doing a jig and singing.

I was thrilled but I was not surprised because I knew we were capable of getting the result and there was a feeling among the entire team that we could do it, even if the media and everyone else had written us off.

I could not help but feel a little sympathy for the Hungarians for they had played against a backdrop of terror and fighting in their home country, but they had won few new friends with their underhand tactics.

We weren't the only British side to pull off a shock in the play-offs. Northern Ireland beat the much-fancied Czechs 2–1, but England, with only nine fit players, lost 1–0 to Russia. Ask them what they thought about the introduction of substitutes. Had they been allowed, England might well have gone on to win the tournament.

Although there were only two days before our next game, the selectors insisted on holding a celebration party in the Grand Hotel. It was terrible. The players drank too much and there was a fight between a local Swedish waiter and Colin Webster, with the waiter ending up in my lap in a shower of glass. All sorts of threats were being bandied about on the wounded waiter's behalf, and the manager of the hotel, so I organised a quick collection of £2 each from all the players and Colin apologised to the waiter. It was all very embarrassing but this is what footballers get up to at times. It was fortunate for all of us that the story did not get out because we would all have been branded hooligans. We would have gone home in disgrace instead of as heroes – imagine if it happened today. Jimmy was furious when he found out and wanted to send Colin home straightaway but I persuaded him we might need him because of injuries, not realising how prophetic those words were.

I took a few kicks in my time, but that was the game then, wasn't it? In the Hungary game, they did stop me because they kicked the hell out of me, knowing I would not retaliate. I could not have done so even if I had wanted to because my leg was hurting so badly I couldn't catch anybody. I was sore and my legs were black rather than blue from the pummelling they had taken and I began to have serious doubts about whether I would be able to play against the Brazilians. I kept telling people I would, but time was running out. Masseurs were working on me and I did everything I could to make that team.

Jimmy took us on a picnic to get us away from football. He told us to forget everything. It was all right for the others but it was hard for me. I would have been a lot better off having another day on the treatment table, but things were not so sophisticated in those days.

Jimmy gave me every opportunity and left it open right until the last minute. Just before the kick-off I gave it one last try but it quickly became obvious that I would be a liability. I couldn't move my right leg properly. I could hardly walk and I certainly could not run or jump. Had there been substitutes, it may have been different; I could have taken a gamble. But I knew if I started and it all went wrong, Wales would be reduced to ten men against the best team in the world. Sadly, I told Jimmy he would have to count me out. I couldn't let the side down by pretending I was fit.

Then came the problem for Jimmy of who to pick. There was no Trevor Ford, and Mel had played so well at centre-half it would have been foolhardy to move him. So, in the end, he had to pick Colin Webster, the player he had wanted to send home.

Missing the game against Brazil was undoubtedly the biggest disappointment of my footballing life. I wasn't just disappointed, I was devastated. But it was the right decision as subsequent events proved because I could not play again for another two months and I missed the start of the Serie A season.

I was told by one of the selectors that I could go home as I couldn't play. I ignored him. I was going to sit on the bench with Jimmy, but it was agony. It was murder watching the game and not being able to play. It was all I could do to stop the tears for both myself and for the team. Those had come earlier when I realised that I could not play. I admit I cried . . . and cried. It took me a long, long time to get over it.

What a forward line the Brazilians had that day with Garrincha on one wing, Zagalo on the other and two teenagers through the middle, Jose Altafini, who became a friend of mine in Italy, and a seventeen-year-old boy named Pele, who had already captured the imagination of the world. They were a good team from goalkeeper Gilmar forward. Didi in midfield was the star in their firmament.

Playing our third game in five days, no wonder we were second favourites against a team who were better prepared than any that had gone before them, but Jimmy, standing in the dressing rooms in the Ullevi Stadium in Gothenburg, rubbished every one of the Brazilian players as I stood next to him, and sent the team out feeling that glory was within their grasp. They were so pumped up we could have been ahead within minutes of the start when Jones whipped in the ball and Webster fired into the side netting. In fact, we controlled the first twenty minutes, much to the surprise of the 25,000 fans who half filled the stadium.

I watched Colin miss two early chances and honestly felt that, had I been there instead of him, I might have had one or even both of them. I turned to Jimmy and told him I would have scored. That's not putting the boys down because they were all heroes that day, stupendous, and I was feeling sorry for myself.

Brazil gradually worked themselves into the game and for a time it seemed only the magnificent Jack Kelsey stood in their way although Mel was also doing his bit, shackling Altafini so well that the Milan-bound striker hardly had a kick. So well did Mel play him, Altafini did not play for Brazil again despite being one of the most expensive, gifted players on the planet.

That performance, allied to a solid World Cup generally, resulted in Mel being named in the 1958 World Cup XI. Pele praised him as the best centre-half in the tournament.

I went into the dressing room at half-time and told the boys they could win it. Brazil were perplexed and clearly unsure of what they were supposed to do against this unrated team who should never have even been in the finals.

We started the second half just as we had the first, but again Brazil gradually settled and came back at us. Then there were all sorts of heroes – Mel Hopkins shackled Garrincha and Williams closed down Zagalo and behind them all was the brilliant Kelsey, playing even better than he did against Sweden.

We survived until seventeen minutes from the end when Pele received a ball from Didi, turned inside Mel in one sweet movement only to scuff the ball. That was enough to put Jack Kelsey off and he stood transfixed as the ball rolled slowly into the net followed by a tearful Pele who picked it up and kissed it to mark his very first World Cup goal. Pele admitted afterwards it was one of the luckiest goals he ever scored, and one of the most important.

Jimmy was devastated and called Pele everything before turning to me to say quietly, 'After all this, we're going to lose.'

There was no way back. After the goal, Brazil relaxed visibly and played some sweet football with Altafini, for once, escaping Mel's attentions to hit the crossbar.

That same day, Northern Ireland also went down, losing 4–0 to France. In the semi-finals, Brazil beat the French 5–2 in a stunning game in which Pele scored a hat-trick while Sweden came from behind, surprisingly, to put out the holders, West Germany. Pele scored another two in the final as Brazil again won 5–2 against the hosts. By then, I was on the Italian Riviera, licking my wounds and recovering from the battering I had taken.

The hurt has not improved with the passage of time and often when I watch games on television my mind drifts back to that tournament and I think to myself what would have happened had I played. Of course, there is no answer to the question, only more grief, and we will never know. But because of Jimmy Murphy and the team spirit, I felt we could have beaten them on the day – not two or three times, just on that day. We were a very together bunch of players, and although they were undoubtedly the best team in the world, there were times during the game when I thought we were going to win.

Mel, quite rightly, took the plaudits and goalkeeper Jack Kelsey deserved a great deal of praise for his outstanding performances. Jack, who played for Arsenal between 1949 and 1962 and earned forty-one Welsh caps, was one of the bravest goalkeepers I ever came across. Perhaps that bravery sometimes bordered on lunacy. They say all goalkeepers had to be mad in those days when challenges went unchecked, and Jack was in the true tradition of this great line of custodians, never displaying any fear whatsoever. Away from the pitch, he was mild mannered and softly spoken, but a legend, for all that.

The pinnacle of his illustrious career came in 1955 when he was selected to represent Great Britain against the Rest of Europe, playing alongside Danny Blanchflower, Stanley Matthews, Billy Liddell, Jimmy McIlroy and yours truly.

Goalkeeping was tough in those days with the heavy ball, heavier pitches and even heavier challenges from centre-forwards such as Trevor Ford, Peter McParland and Nat Lofthouse. Consequently, goalkeepers were injured as often, if not more often, that outfield players, and Jack missed his share of matches. He was eventually forced to retire because of a serious back injury sustained diving at the feet of the Brazilian centre-forward Vava in 1962.

He was a real one-club man and stayed on with Arsenal, running the club lottery, opening the shop, advising on goalkeepers and eventually becoming commercial manager before retiring after forty years at Highbury.

I suspect Jack had more than a little to do with Mel going to Arsenal in March 1959. They payed a club record fee of £42,750 for him plus youngsters Peter Davies and David Dodson. Mel's promise at the Gunners was cruelly cut down by two cartilage operations, and he often played carrying injuries. Nevertheless, he started the 1961–62 season as first choice centre-forward and scored two against Everton and a hat-trick against Blackburn Rovers. He went on to score 17 goals in just 23 league and cup games that season before moving on to Cardiff City for £28,500 in February 1962. George Swindin wanted to build his team around Mel at centre-half and he made his debut against Sheffield Wednesday in August. Mel suffered from the same problem as I did – managers were not sure whether to play him at the back or up front. The funny thing is that Mel, like me, preferred to play at centre-half.

For Cardiff, he scored 25 goals in 79 league games and then eventually lost his place to his big brother. We played together a little before he moved into non-league with Porthmadog in the Welsh League (North). He returned briefly to the League with Port Vale, playing seven games for them. His last club was Haverfordwest before he hung up his boots.

Mel played a big part in guiding his son Jeremy who played for Swansea, Queens Park Rangers and Oxford United; and, to maintain the Welsh tradition, Jeremy also won nineteen caps for Wales.

How good was Mel? Ted Drake was prepared to pay £40,000 to take him to Chelsea and said that at one time he thought he was going to be a better player than me; and Mel's was one of the first names on Manchester United's list after the plane crash in 1958. Jimmy Murphy, of course, knew him well from the Welsh team.

Although Mel scored just six goals in all for his country, he holds the individual scoring record for Wales with four in a match against Ireland in 1962. The day he won his first cap was a red-letter day for the Charles family. That was against Northern Ireland in Belfast in April 1955 and Mel had an outstanding game at right-half while I scored a hat-trick.

Before I left for Sweden, Agnelli had warned me that the World Cup matches would be the last games I would play for Wales for a while, and when the president heard about my injuries, he was even more adamant. A combination of Juventus's reluctance to allow me to play and my anxiety about travelling long distances between games meant that between the end of the World Cup and October 1961, I missed twelve games for Wales, although I did play against Scotland in November 1959, before returning in a 1–1 draw with England at Ninian Park.

I did, however, go on the summer tour in 1962, as I was about to leave Juventus and return to Leeds. We played against Brazil twice and Mexico. I played centre-half in both Brazil games, the first in fabulous Rio and the second in Sao Paulo. We lost both games 3–1, with Pele scoring once in the first game and twice in the second. One of my greatest treasures was a picture of Pele and me together in Brazil. He was, without question, the best player I ever saw on any continent, a great goalscorer and a very humble man. We finished the tour with a 2–1 defeat against Mexico in Mexico City where I played centre-forward and I managed to score a goal.

With all my moving around England, Italy and Wales in the following years, I played only four more games for Wales. In October 1962, while I was back at Leeds, we lost 3–2 to Scotland, despite scoring my last goal for the country, then while I was with Cardiff City, we lost 2–1 in Scotland in 1963 and we beat them 3–2 in Cardiff the following year.

My thirty-eighth and last game for my country was a World Cup qualifier against the Soviet Union in Moscow in front of 105,000 Russians on 30 May 1965. I didn't go out on a high – we lost 2–1.

CHAPTER ELEVEN

Three titles and a restaurant

Being coach of Juventus was not the most secure of positions, regardless of results. While I was there, I played for the Yugoslav Ljubisa Brocic, the Italian Carlo Parola and the Swede Gunnar Gren. This was over five years during which time we won three league titles and two Italian Cups.

Brocic was in charge when I arrived at the start of the 1957–58 season. He came to Juventus after spells with Red Star Belgrade and with the Yugoslavian, Albanian and Egyptian national sides. Although it was Umberto Agnelli who brought Sivori and me to the club, it was Brocic who made it work, and restored 'La Vecchia Signora', the Old Lady, as the club was known, to what they considered their rightful place at the top of the table, winning the Scudetto in 1958.

We took everyone by surprise that season, and so for the next one, they were prepared. It was tough as every team targeted Sivori and me and we slipped to fourth in the table, mainly through drawing 10 of our 34 games; we lost only two more than when we won the championship. Reluctantly, we handed over our hard-earned crown to AC Milan. I managed just 19 goals in 29 league games and just one hat-trick in a 4–3 win against Genoa.

There was great expectation in the European Cup, especially as Italy had provided one of the finalists in each of the previous two seasons, losing in both cases to the great Real Madrid side of the late 1950s. We were drawn with Wiener SC in the preliminary round and were considered odds-on favourites to progress. There were no problems in Turin where we won 3–1 and everyone, ourselves included, considered the second leg to be a formality. Some formality! We collapsed and were beaten 7–0. But this game was the most frightening episode of my career. I was kicked so much by the Austrian defenders that I heard the doctors in the Molinette Hospital in Turin discussing whether or not they might need to amputate my legs. For a while it was genuinely touch and go whether I would lose my left one. When we returned to Italy, I was in a lot of pain and still had a big swelling on my leg. Eventually, I became feverish and had to spend a month in hospital, receiving injections every few hours because of the pain I was suffering. Even though I knew my leg would be saved, it was still some time before I was reassured that I would be able to continue my career.

We had a great side but, in fact, never got very far in the European Cup during my time there. It is hard to understand. We were drawn against a lot of communist countries and they seemed to be fitter, stronger and more ready to adapt than we were. I can hardly point the finger because I failed to score a single goal in the competition. I often wondered how much better we might have done if there had been greater competition for places in the team, as there was in England.

The squad would be picked at the start of the season and, more often than not, the coach would stay with the same group of players. It was an odd situation. Often players who were out of form would retain their places to help them regain their edge, rather than being dropped. There were no substitutes in those days and coaches would build a team and keep it together. It meant if there was an injury to a senior player there would be near panic, even though there were plenty of good reserves just waiting for their chance. If someone was out through injury, as soon as they were fit again they would be hurried back into the team, and quite often we would play a season using only the fifteen or sixteen players nominated at the start. They loved to keep the same side playing week after week, and it wasn't so difficult as we had only thirty-four league matches, plus a handful of European Cup games. For the Italian Cup and the friendlies, they would usually give the reserves a run-out.

The Italian Cup has never been a big deal but with the League having slipped away we desperately wanted to win something, so in 1958–59 we took it much more seriously. We saw off Alessandria 6–2, Fiorentina 3–1 and Genoa by the same score to reach our first Copa Italia final since 1938.

The Cup may not have been important in the early stages but by the time it reached its climax there was a crowd of almost 68,000 to watch us play Inter Milan. We were hungry to make up for our league form and were off to a terrific start as I opened the scoring. Cervato added a second before Milan pulled a goal back. After the break, Cervato scored his second and Sivori clinched a 4–1 victory. It wasn't the League, but it was better than nothing.

Brocic was replaced for the 1959–60 season by Carlo Parola, already a firm favourite at Juventus, being a local boy made good. He had gained a reputation as a tough man marker with the Bianconeri (or 'black and whites' as the club was nicknamed) at the

Stadio Comunale in the 1930s. Parola played over 330 league games for Juventus and for a while was skipper, but his main claim to fame, according to local legend, was as the inventor of the scissor kick. He worked with technical director Renato Cesarini at first and later with Gunnar Gren.

My first contract expired after two years, at the end of the 1959 season. I had a long chat with Agnelli and asked for more money. He was quick to respond, saying, with a big smile on his face, that they would have to sell a few more Fiats to pay me. The fact that he agreed so quickly probably meant I could have pushed for more but, as far as I could see, there was no reason to ask for any more. I was not a greedy person and I was happy with what he gave me, and I was loving it in Italy. I may have missed the bacon sandwiches at first, but I had very soon become accustomed to the pasta, the osso buco, the Chianti and the wonderful lifestyle.

I was valued at £140,000 by Juventus, a bit more than my mate Jimmy Greaves whose transfer fee at the same time was £95,000. Either they rated me quite highly or they were hoping to discourage other clubs from trying to sign me.

Winning the Copa Italia gave us a lift for the 1959–60 season, which proved to be my best ever as we regained the title and retained the Cup, losing just four games all season. Sivori and I scored 50 goals between us, Sivori leading the way with 27. We again finished eight points clear, this time ahead of Fiorentina.

In the Cup, we beat Sampdoria 5–4 after extra time and had another narrow squeak when Atalanta held us to a 2–2 draw; we got through on the drawing of lots. We then beat Lazio 3–0 to set up a final against Fiorentina, our nearest title challengers. The game was played at the start of the following season in Milan and what a thriller it was. I opened the scoring but Fiorentina came back and went ahead. We seemed to be heading for defeat until I grabbed the second and we snatched the winner in extra time when Micheli put through his own goal.

In 1960–61, we won back-to-back championships, this time chased home by neighbours AC Milan and Inter, finishing four and five points clear respectively. Again Sivori and I shared the goals, Sivori scoring 25 in another fine season for the talented Argentinian while I weighed in with 15. But there was no double this time as we were put out of the Cup by the eventual winners, Fiorentina, in the semi-finals.

The two Milan clubs dominated the 1961–62 season, with Milan winning the title and Inter coming second. Rather than challenging for a third successive title, we finished a distant eleventh, at some stages battling to steer clear of the relegation zone. I managed just twenty-one league appearances, scoring eight goals in a season that was much interrupted by injury.

We lost our Swedish manager Gunnar Gren after only two matches and the club brought in their old defender Parola to replace him. That was good for me because he was a former international centre-half and knew I liked playing at the back even more than at centre-forward. He was the first manager to pick me solely as a defender. Under the others I had played as a centre-back, but only through circumstances and usually when we were defending a narrow lead in a major match. They would switch me about, but it was not very often I started a match wearing the number five shirt until Parola came in. This change in my role also meant he could switch the talented young striker Bruno Nicole from the wing to centre-forward.

I enjoyed playing at the back more regularly and was particularly pleased with my performance that season against Roma when we won 1–0. I damaged my eye during that game and had to play with a patch throughout the second half like some lost pirate. Not that Parola played me at centre-half all of the time. Sometimes he would pick me at inside-right and other times at centre-forward. There was often a place up front that needed filling because Sivori was suspended so often!

It would have been interesting to see how that season would have panned out for me if I'd been able to play the whole campaign at the back, but it was wrecked when I picked up a knee injury against Spal and then aggravated it playing for the Italian League in Glasgow. It was so bad I was sent to a clinic in France in a bid to be ready for the game against Real Madrid on Valentine's Day 1962. I made it with ten days to spare, as I played in the local derby against Torino and scored one and made one to prove I was ready for the game against the world's top club side. We flopped in the Italian Cup, too, but had our best-ever run in the European Cup.

In 1960–61 we had played CDNA Sofia of Bulgaria and coasted through our home leg 2–0 only to lose 4–1 away from home. We were devastated again and couldn't believe how badly we had played. Clearly, we didn't travel well, but in 1961–62, we broke the mould when, for the first time in Europe, we avoided an away defeat. Having been drawn against the very good Greek side Panathinaikos, we drew 1–1 in Athens and then beat them 2–1 in Italy. At last we were out of the preliminary round and in with the big boys of Europe – but there was still a big question about our ability to do the business away from home, and when we drew Partizan Belgrade there was much shaking of heads about our chances against this very tough, rugged side. I was out injured for the first leg and, in just ten minutes, Sivori was helped off after being targeted by their defenders. Nevertheless, we came away with a 2–1 victory, and gained our revenge over their physical assaults by scoring five in the second leg.

Then came the big one. We were drawn against Real Madrid and faced them at home in the first leg; 66,000 people paid a massive £60,000 to watch Di Stefano and Puskas and the rest of their world-class stars take us on.

Much thought went into the tactics and after great deliberation I was asked to play centre-half to mark Alfredo Di Stefano. Was it necessary? They came with an eight-man defence, designed to submerge our attack, which they did to great effect. What made it even more humiliating was that they broke away to score an undeserved winner through Di Stefano when I had moved up to my normal centre-forward position, looking for a winner. Di Stefano had hardly moved forward all match and Del Sol stayed back giving our strikers, Sivori and Nicole, no space in which to work. We had to be careful; especially with their two speedy wingmen, Gento and Canario, who were always lurking, ready to take you on. It wasn't a pretty game and our supporters were deeply upset when the fabulous Di Stefano skipped through to score.

We were written off, which was hardly a surprise. Having lost at home, we were given absolutely no chance of upsetting the great Real in front of their own packed crowd at the Chamartin, now the Bernabeu, Stadium. No team had ever beaten them in a European tie there before.

This time I was picked at right-half and we were amazed to see Real Madrid protecting their one-goal lead with another massed defence. We couldn't believe our luck and, after thirty-eight minutes, Sivori scored and we held out to win 1–0. So the scores were level over the two legs, and we were rewarded with a play-off.

Clearly, the Madrid public thought the game was won in their own stadium because the crowd were 30,000 down on capacity. It was a bad-tempered game and Real seemed unable to adjust their tactics once we had gone in front. The Real players obviously knew about my damaged knee because they seemed to target me and I spent some time off the pitch after I'd got caught in a late tackle. I was not one to criticise referees, but I felt that the well-known French official Maurice Guigou did not really do himself justice and I found I had little protection. He seemed to agree for, after the game, he publicly apologised and considered quitting the game until being persuaded otherwise. Real attacked but they were disjointed, and as we no longer had to take risks we shored up our defence. It was all hands to the pump and we held out.

Up until that game, Real had played 19 home games in Europe, won 18, drawn just one, against bitter rivals Barcelona, and had scored 82 goals and conceded just 11. It felt like we had won the European Cup.

On our return home the next day, there were so many people at the airport and at the ground to welcome us back that you could not move. Wherever you looked there were masses of people. We fought our way out of the airport to the coach, and all the way back to Turin the roads were lined with supporters. There was a big square in front of the Juventus offices and whenever we won a title, beat Torino or, in this case, Real Madrid, the crowds massed there to pay homage to the club and its players. We were heroes but the job was only half done. We still had to win the play-off to take our place in the semi-finals.

There was no sleep that night. There were bands playing every-where, including outside my house. This was special not only to us players but to every one of our supporters. It was great but I felt like reminding them of how they had berated us when we lost the first leg. I also felt like telling them how much I would appreciate a couple of nights' sleep before playing Real again.

The match was played at the Parc des Princes in Paris, and how we were to regret that home defeat. We kept the same team but Real made changes with Luis Del Sol going back into the attack, Rafael

Felo, an attacking midfield player, taking over at right-half and Pachin playing on the left. Now they were being written off as too old and past it. What nonsense! The criticism and their defeat in their own stadium spurred them to the heights. It took them just thirty-five seconds to score as Di Stefano and Puskas, with his fabulous left foot, combined to feed in Felo and he drove the ball home. It was a fantastic pass, angled through the defence, and Felo's pace was blistering.

What a shaker that was and immediately I was moved from my attacking right-half role to centre-forward where I found myself marked by the glowering Uruguayan-born Spanish international centre-half Jose Santamaria. This was my third position in three games.

Santamaria was solid, you couldn't get past him. He was like the Leaning Tower of Pisa and he leant all over me. Referee Pierre Schwinte gave us absolutely nothing that match. It is wrong to blame referees for a result and certainly Real were the better side on the night, but I have often wondered what would have happened had I been awarded a penalty when Santamaria brought me down in the area, instead of awarding a free kick outside the area; or if Felo had been sent off after the same incident when he caught me so badly in the side that I had a severely bruised thigh and could hardly walk, never mind run, for the remainder of the match.

I finished the game limping heavily from the treatment meted out to me. I was kicked and punched, not the sort of thing you expected from the best side around. They were a great side but they could certainly look after themselves. The consequences were serious, as I again missed games and we did not win another game for the rest of the season as we struggled to recover from our defeat. My legs were bruised from top to bottom by the end of ninety minutes and I had to be carried from the bath to the bus; I could not walk once they had stiffened up.

But, credit to a great team, Real were still fantastic. They had won the European Cup from 1956 to 1960 inclusive. Di Stefano was the best centre-forward I ever saw while Gento and Puskas were superb. Di Stefano retained his form in his thirties and was a wonderful player with one of the cleverest footballing brains I have ever come across. He seemed to be able to read the game two moves ahead. He had pace and dribbling skills, and the ability to keep his body between his marker and the ball. Puskas was every bit as deadly. An out-and-out striker, he had the best left foot in the business. Add to these Del Sol, Gento, Kopa, Didi and the rest and no wonder they were rated as the best club side ever – and now they are at it again, dominating Europe as only they have ever done.

It is a shame the British took so long to recognise the qualities of continental and South American football. It wasn't until the advent of the great Hungarians of 1953, and then the 1960 European Cup final between Real Madrid and Eintracht Frankfurt at Hampden Park – a ten-goal thriller won 7–3 by the Spaniards – that the British public woke up to the fact that there were wonderful teams and players away from our shores.

My Juventus team-mates were pretty good. Newspaper-talk may have focused on the 'Three Kings' – Sivori, Boniperti and me – but the team was packed with outstanding talent. Goalkeeper Carlo Mattrel, a local youngster of 6ft 3in, was very agile. We had two great full-backs in Corradi and Bruno Grazena. Centre-half Chivato, who came from Florence, was not very big but he was good and very strong, as he had to be in that league. The two wing-halves were my close friend Umberto Colombo and Flavio Emoli. They never stopped running; they would run all day. In today's terminology, they both had a good engine. You need those people in a team; they could also play a bit and were both full internationals.

We had Stacchini on the right wing, or Bruno Nicole who played through the middle when I couldn't play, and on the other wing we had a flyer – Stivanello could run 100 yards in even time. He not only had terrific pace but also had a great left foot.

They were good mates as well as good team-mates. Everyone supported everyone else. Whether that was because we were a winning team or whether it made us into a winning team I am not sure – but I'll settle for it. My special mates were Boniperti, Colombo and Sivori. Colombo and I have always remained in touch and he regularly invites me over to visit. My other great friend was Benito Boldi, a full-back, and we have remained close.

Boniperti was adored by Juve fans and hated by the rest. They called him 'Mariza', meaning woman, because he was pretty; and when we went to Turin or Milan their fans would chant 'Mariza, Mariza'. He was a hard man and he didn't like it one bit, and someone would suffer for it.

There was a bit of style about the other players' nick-names. Centre-half Rino Ferrario was called 'The Lion' and Carlo Mattrel was called 'Premio Combi' after the great Italian goalkeeper Giampiero Combi.

I had nicknames, too – far too many of them. I would have preferred to stick with John, Jack or Giovanni but I had so many names I was supposed to answer to. Apart from the Gentle Giant and King John, I was also known at different times as the Prince of Wales, Il Re and the King of Soccer. I couldn't keep count of the names and often didn't even know when someone was talking about, or to, me. I suppose, looking back, it was all very flattering to be called a king in a foreign country, and I will be eternally grateful for the friendship the Italian people offered me.

Colombo, my great mate, had left by the time we hit the buffers, transferred to Atalanta.

It was with Colombo that I opened King's restaurant. The idea came to us when we were trying to decide where to go to eat one day; one of us wanted one thing and the other wanted something else until, in the end, one of us said the only way round it was to open our own restaurant. We both claimed to have had the idea first when the restaurant was a success, but gave the credit to the other when it collapsed!

It is the sort of thing that is often said in jest but this time we liked the idea and three or four months later we had our restaurant. It was right in the middle of town, above a cinema. We both used to drop in every day. Colombo told me, 'John, you cannot miss a day, they want to see you there.' It was hugely popular, packed every night, and quickly became the place to be seen. We would invite the other players to come and join us for dinner and the punters loved to be able to boast about whom they had seen eating there.

The restaurant continued to prosper even after Colombo was suddenly sold on to Atalanta. The downturn came when I left Italy and went back to Leeds. We kept it going because we thought it would remain as popular as ever, but later I was told that Colombo and I were the attraction and, in fact, the diners didn't like having to climb stairs to reach the place. When neither of us was able to keep an eye on things, it quickly went downhill. Being the good friend he is, Colombo persuaded me to quit and took over the responsibility. What was originally a very good idea had suddenly become a financial millstone around my neck, swallowing up not only the money it had made but also most of my savings. Colombo saved me further losses but suffered heavy losses himself. I don't even know whether the restaurant still exists. I have never been back to have a look, even though I have been back to Italy many times since then.

In Italy, they believe that success deserves money. Defeat meant you lived on your weekly wage, which had gone up to £120 per month by the time I left, plus an increase in bonuses. When you won the big one, the sky was the limit. On one memorable occasion, the chairman upped our bonus to £100. Then three rich supporters got together and threw in even more money. It came to £300 – ten weeks' wages!

It was not unusual for rich supporters to show their gratitude by rewarding the team when we won well, often with expensive items such as wine instead of money. People would drop off gifts on the doorstep, and when we went out, the meal would be on the restaurant and there would be as much wine as we could drink from supporters in the establishment. I didn't complain. I was living an incredible lifestyle with a wardrobe of more than twenty suits, a similar number of pairs of shoes, some seventy ties and a wide selection of hand-made shirts. More than one fan even offered me his wife! I was no millionaire but I was certainly living like one and enjoying every minute of it. They called me the King and they treated me like a king, even the Torino supporters. As long as you were winning, anything was possible; they would give you the earth. Lose and friends were hard to find. If we lost, we paid for everything; if we lost to Torino, we didn't dare go out.

There was an incident when I ran through Torino's defence and accidentally elbowed their last player. He collapsed in a heap and instead of carrying on unimpeded, I put the ball into touch. It was an instinctive reaction and had I thought about it, I would probably have carried on and tried to put the ball in the net. But I stopped and went to the injured player to see whether he was all right. Suddenly, the crowd were clapping and applauding me. I was a hero to our biggest rivals. That's when I became known as the Gentle Giant.

That night, I could hear the cars outside my house tooting their horns and a crowd gathered. I was frightened to death but I invited some of them into the house. They wanted nothing more than to shake my hand and ask me if I would play for Torino when I left Juventus. It was all a bit overwhelming. There were no complaints from the manager, either, unlike when Paolo Di Canio did a similar thing for West Ham, putting the ball out of play instead of shooting. Harry Redknapp nearly shot him!

On other occasions it was the Juventus supporters who drove up to the house. They didn't want anything other than to drive past and hoot their horns, hoping to see me after I had scored a goal or two or when the team had enjoyed a good win. Football was everything. The jubilation and rewards when we became the first club to beat Real Madrid in a European Cup-tie in their own Bernabeu Stadium were staggering.

The supporters were even better in those days than they are now. They were fantastic, if a little frantic, until the gangs started to take over the terraces. It was the same in England, and it was extremely bad for a while, driving supporters away. When clubs and police took action, the situation improved in both countries, but there are some signs of trouble returning. So clubs beware — if it does, the golden goose will not be laying any more golden eggs because no one wants to be connected with a club surrounded by hooliganism. Family fans will stay away. That's not me being clever because we have all seen it happen before.

Because of the lack of international communications in the late fifties, the Juve fans did not know what to expect when the club signed me. They didn't know what club or country I played for, and I was fortunate to be accepted so readily. Luigi Scarambone, the secretary of the Italian League, said in 1961, 'Wales should give John Charles a medal. He put it on the map. No one in Italy knew where it was before.' That was another exaggeration because there were Italians in Wales and England long before we started to play football.

When Joe Baker and Denis Law arrived at Torino, they were amazed to be offered double bonuses for the two games against us, and for the games against the two Milan sides. Our bonuses were scaled in a similar fashion and bore little relationship to reality.

It was the same when the chairman gave me a new car shortly after Peter was born. I went out of the house to find that my car, which was pretty new and quite expensive, had disappeared. I ran back inside to tell Peggy it had been stolen. Then a 2200 Fiat was driven up to my front door and Signor Agnelli telephoned to tell me there was a new car outside the house, saying I needed it because I had a bigger family.

All the players had different cars. Obviously, they preferred you to have a Fiat and, as far as I was concerned, it would have been foolish to refuse, but some of the others liked to be different and would choose other makes.

Agnelli used to take us to the Fiat factory now and again to introduce us to the workers, who were also our fans, at least the majority were. It would give them a lift and production would increase for a few days, just as it would if we won a big game on Sunday. They would all be at work bright and early on Monday to taunt the Torino fans and get stuck into their work. It was no problem to us as; in many ways, we were working for each other.

The luckiest bonus I ever had was against Inter Milan. It was in my second season with Juventus and we had hit a bad patch as we approached Christmas. Our form at the San Siro Stadium didn't promise much of an improvement. We were losing 2–0 with three minutes to play when the infamous Milan fog suddenly dropped like a curtain. The game was called off; despite there being such a short time to go, there was really no other choice. It was a fog like no one had ever seen before, billowing in great blankets, submerging the terraces and the pitch. There was one unforgettable moment when one of our players was running the ball down the wing with the fog following him, gradually catching him up and swallowing him. We could hardly see a foot in front of us. It was even difficult to find our way back to the dressing room, and getting back from Milan to Torino took forever.

The following Wednesday the game was replayed and we won it 3–1. Signor Agnelli was so thrilled he gave us a huge extra bonus and then took us all out for dinner instead of going back to the hotel straight from the game. We celebrated but not the way English teams would have done under the same circumstances. We drank a little wine, but not a lot.

There was a great incentive to stay fit because when you were injured all you received was your basic money, no bonuses. A long injury could hurt severely. I had a couple of cartilage operations and for those six or seven weeks there was no bonus, just the salary and the slice of the signing-on fee. If I'd been injured for longer, that would have stopped after a while. The rules were if the injuries were caused by 'irregular conduct', which could be translated as anything, the player would lose half his monthly salary while he was out. If the injury lingered on for three months, wages would stop completely and, worst of all, if the injury lasted into the next season, the player would remain bound to the club but suspended without pay until he was active again.

Just in case that did not sway everything in the clubs' favour, Italian regulations stated: 'If at any time, because of grave action, either sporting or social, or inadequacy of performance, the player does damage, direct or indirect, to the club, the agreement between the club and the player will be broken completely by his own fault, and the club has every reason to exercise its right to claim for damages.'

Italian clubs paid massive transfer fees and wages to top players from all over the world, and to some extent they still do, but in return they expected, no, demanded, a return on their investment, and if you failed, they would cut their losses, sell you off and start all over again with someone else. They could transfer you to another club without even asking your opinion. Their contracts bound you every inch, body and soul, to the club, so making you the best-paid slaves in the sports industry. Whenever English players asked me about the prospect of playing in Italy, I would tell them to forget it unless they were prepared to obey the rules, both on and off the pitch. You had to accept that you belonged to the club.

Any step out of line and the players were hit with big fines. I was punished after losing to Arsenal in London. After the game, a few of us went to the Talk of the Town in Leicester Square for a night out. We were fined £12 each; had we won the game, we would not have been touched. It was something you had to expect, like it or not, and playing for the Bianconeri the fines were big because the bigger the club, the bigger the fine.

Some clubs would pay half bonuses to players not selected in the team. There was one Roma player who played in every game for his previous club but earned more from bonuses with Roma as a permanent reserve. That is how abstruse the system was. There was no similar problem at Juventus because they simply did not pay bonuses to those not in the team.

Strict? Of course it was strict. Each club had its own rules and regulations but they hardly needed them as the Italian Federation set down the expected behaviour in Article Seven: the duties of the player. It read:

> The player must obey all the rules as to the style and technique prescribed by the club and its officers; fix his place of residence where told by the club; always conduct himself in a correct

manner everywhere and live a decent moral and physical life; conduct himself in an irreproachable manner sportingly and socially; undertake to play, except in the case of a force majeure, which would be agreed by the club, or on the advice of the medical officer, every game which he should, whether they are in the championship or friendly match, either in Italy or abroad; undertake to play in whatever team of the club in any position; take part in all training in the method, at the places and times fixed by the club; respect the statutes and rules of the Football Federation and of the club; not to take part in any game, even for benevolent causes, for other clubs, committees or organisations without the consent of the club.

That was pretty well catch-all and strictly enforced when results went against us. There were also other club rules such as no drinking or dancing after Monday. I couldn't go for a drive in the countryside or down to the seaside without express permission from the club.

If the club said all players would have dinner together, there were no exceptions, regardless of what was happing with your family, including birthdays and other celebrations. But I found that as long as I told them what I was doing or asked permission, they were very reasonable. Juventus was a hugely friendly and happy club. It was not so good for those who lived a carefree or ill-regimented life. It could be hell for them, as was proved by some of the other British players who followed me to Italy.

There were other big differences on a more basic level compared with life at an English club. You were expected to generate good publicity for the club and while I was there no Italian player was ever paid for an article in an Italian newspaper or magazine; the same applied to the Italian Television Service. If we were asked to do an interview, we were expected to do it, no fee involved.

Despite seeming to have missed our chance in the World Cup in 1958, Wales were given a reprieve and took on Israel. Our 2–0 win at Ninian Park ensured that we would be going to Sweden.

As ever, the Wales team is shown its place by the committee. On one remarkable occasion, when we flew to Paris for a game, one of the players was turfed off the plane as there weren't enough seats and none of the officials was going to give way!

A rare venture forward for me in the 0–0 draw against hosts Sweden in the 1958 World Cup. Jimmy Murphy had asked me to play deep, and I had a quiet game.

Getting a tackle back against the Hungarians in our violent play-off for a quarter-final place. We won the match to take on Brazil, but I had been kicked so badly that I was unable to play.

Denis Law battles to hold me off during the 1959 Home Championship tussle against Scotland at Hampden Park.

Shaking hands with Bobby Robson after the Italian League had beaten the English League 4–2 in Milan in 1960. These inter-league matches were hugely popular.

My brief return to Leeds in 1962 was not a happy one, as I struggled to settle back into the English way of life.

EMPICS
TOPHAM PICTUREPOINT

POPPERFOTO

Within ten minutes of my return to Italian football, I scored this goal for Roma against league leaders Bologna, but it created a level of expectation I could not live up to.

TOPHAM PICTUREPOINT

NI SYNDICATION

Celebrating with the Cardiff City team after winning the Welsh Cup final against Bangor in May 1964, guaranteeing us a place in the European Cup-Winners' Cup next season.

Various business ventures

Outside my sports shop in Cardiff – I worked there in the mornings before commuting to Hereford where I was player-manager. Serving behind the bar at the New Inn near Elland Road. Norman Hunter is first in line, with Gordon McQueen, Bobby Collins, Len Browning and Eric Kerfoot all waiting for a pint. The Gomersal Park Hotel, which Glenda and I ran from 1983–86.

TOPHAM PICTUREPOINT

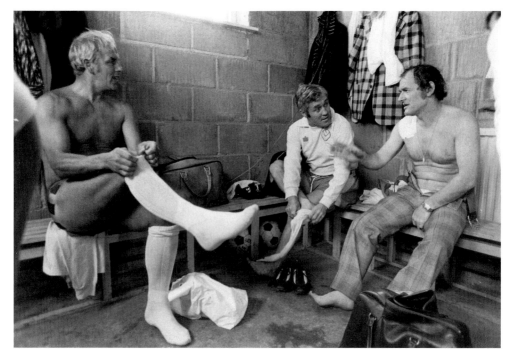

I carried on playing friendly football for many years after I'd retired from the game. Here I line up alongside Bobby Collins and George Meek for a game between ex-Leeds and ex-Italian sides.

Jack Charlton, Kenneth Wolstenholme, who helped me so much in my transfer to Juventus, Cliff Morgan and Michael Parkinson line up with me at a function.

Umberto Agnelli welcomes me to watch Juventus training. The club has been so good to me all these years after I left, and I feel honoured that the fans still remember me.

The 1958 Welsh World Cup team reunited. From left: Ken Jones, Stuart Williams, Terry Medwin, Colin Baker, Mel Hopkins, me and brother Mel.

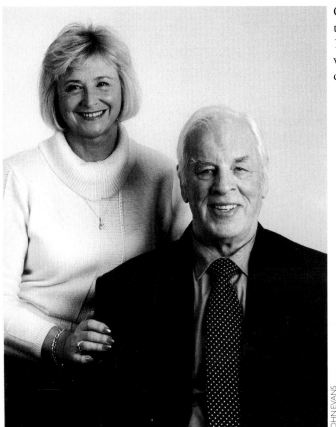

Glenda and I first met twenty-five years ago, in 1978, and she has been a wonderful support to me during my recent troubles.

JOHN EVANS

Receiving the CBE from Prince Charles in the 2001 Birthday Honours list – I feel it is not just an honour for me, but for Wales.

HY MONEY

Still enjoying life...

We were not allowed to promote commercial products although there were exceptions. Sivori was given special permission to endorse a make of football boots and footballs, which earned him a massive £2,500, and my boots were made by Pontofola d'oro in Ascoli. They were fantastic, lightweight, more like slippers than football boots. Sivori and I were allowed to appear in a film called 'Idoli Controluce', translated into English as 'Idols in Contrast', while Colombo and I were permitted to open our restaurant.

I was also allowed to make records and promote them with on-stage performances. Perhaps they knew something. The records did not sell particularly well, although well enough to make a few bob, and I went on a summer tour of two weeks with one-night stands on the Adriatic and Mediterranean coasts and in the South of Italy. I enjoyed every minute, travelling with my impresario-cum-pianist-cum-driver-cum-songwriter. It was great fun singing to the tourists, relaxing on their summer holidays. But I hardly made my fortune; in fact, I probably lost out on it all told.

I was slightly embarrassed about my new 'career' to start with and did not even tell my family back home in Wales about it, but the Italian public seemed to like my records even if my wife Peggy didn't. One of the best things to come out of the entire business was appearing alongside the fabulous Nat 'King' Cole on a Saturday night television show.

Twice I didn't get paid at all when I sang in a particular restaurant. When I got up to perform, the restaurant was empty, but there were hundreds outside just listening to the music. The owner was distraught and said he could not pay me because he had no customers and I would have to do an extra night for him. I agreed and the same thing happened again with about twenty diners and literally hundreds of others outside. I finished up working two nights for nothing. I should have sent my jack-of-all-trades out with a hat to collect from the tourists; I would have made more money busking outside on the seafront.

My feet earned me more money than my singing voice, but whenever I am in Italy I invariably get asked to sing and I still do the old Frankie Laine number 'Sixteen Tons' and my own 'Love in Portofino'.

It all began at a party with some Italian friends when someone suggested it was my turn to do a number. For some reason, they liked my deep, Welsh baritone and told me I should take lessons. I took no notice of it but the next morning the same friends called and took me to the Rai-TV Italian state-controlled radio studios where I was introduced to the resident bandleader William Galassini. Much against my better judgement, I was persuaded to sing for him. I played along thinking it was a hoax, especially when they produced a tape recorder and asked me to warble a few hit songs into the microphone.

But it was no joke and even I did not recognise my voice when they played the recording back to me. Eventually, I agreed to learn how to sing in front of an orchestra. Then came the records. I made two. The first had 'Sixteen Tons' on one side and 'Love in Portofino' on the other. That song was specially written for me by a good friend of mine, singer and composer Fred Buscaglione, who, sadly, died in a road crash in 1960. The second record had me singing 'Non Dimenticare (Don't Forget)' and a song called 'The End'.

As far as I was concerned, it was the end. Although I appeared in front of the television cameras and went on my little summer tour, I wasn't too keen when Galassini told me he planned a new series of songs to match my voice. To me, it was just good fun and good relaxation, something that was sorely needed after the intensity of the football.

In Britain, footballers were admired but they were part of the working community, earning not much more than the bloke next door who worked down the local factory and paid his money to watch you on a Saturday afternoon. In Italy, for me, it was different. I was big and easily recognised. I played for a top, successful team and I was looked upon as a star. I was careful not to let the adulation go to my head because I had seen the effect of that on players in both England and Italy.

David Beckham certainly wasn't the first footballer to go to film premieres. I was usually invited to the Rimini Film Festival, along with other top players, and rubbed shoulders with Claudia Cardinale, Carlo Ponti, Marcello Mastroianni, the gorgeous Sophia Loren and Bernardo Bertolucci. Outside the theatre, the fans were always there welcoming the film stars but when I arrived they would start chanting 'Giovanni . . . Giovanni . . . Giovanni'. I don't know how much the film stars appreciated me stealing their thunder but if they did take offence they never showed it. They accepted that footballers were popular and the new stars. We got on well with the film people and they liked to be seen in company with footballers. A regular stream of them came to King's restaurant, and they always asked if Colombo and I were going to be present. It wasn't really my scene. Colombo used to drag me along; he enjoyed the involvement.

Italy was undoubtedly my home, and my best years in football were spent playing for Juventus, rather than my beloved Leeds or even my country. It was special, it was about winning. When we lost, no one talked. I was lucky we won so much while I was there. But you knew that if your standards slipped, you would be out. It was like buying a new car – if your engine was knocking the club would dump you and go out and buy a new one.

I had very little feedback about what was happening in Britain. Newspapers were hard to come by and there was little or nothing on radio or television about what was happening in Leeds, Liverpool or Manchester. Anyway, my mind was directed towards becoming part of the team, the city and the country, integrating and making things work. That's probably the reason why they were the happiest days of my footballing life. Juventus were a big, big club and, like Manchester United now, they had more supporters outside the city than within, even down south in Naples and Palermo, and beyond in the world wherever Italians travelled. I remember one time in Palermo, the night before the match, we had an hour's sleep because our fans were outside the hotel, dancing and singing. They never meant any harm; they were just overjoyed to see Juventus in their city. In other places, opposing fans sang to keep us awake!

It is amazing that, even now, everyone seems to know me. That's how it was when I was there; they remembered everyone because it was part of their history. Italians love football and they are nice people. They have some mad ones among them but name me a country that does not.

I followed the rules and loved every minute of it; as far as I was concerned, it was like being in the army – accept the situation and get on and enjoy yourself. It must have been appreciated because they always welcome me back with open arms whenever I return to Turin, and I am delighted to see that a painting of me in action remains on the wall of the players' lounge in the Stadio delle Alpi. I was invited back for the final game of the 2000–2001 season as a VIP and I was stunned when the entire crowd stood and chanted my name again. I have to admit it brought a tear to the eye and a lump to the throat as the years rolled back. Juventus is a club that recognises and rewards its favourite sons over the years, just look at Boniperti. It doesn't happen often in sport, and especially not in football.

CHAPTER TWELVE

The biggest mistake of my life

Like most things in life, I did not realise at the time how wonderful life was for me in Turin. I had everything a man could ask for, doing what I wanted to do in the lap of luxury surrounded by friends. The greatest mistake of my career was to leave Italy and come back home. Had I stayed, I would have maintained my fitness and carried on. But, if you carry that to extremes, maybe I shouldn't have left Leeds in the first place.

The decision to leave had nothing to do with money. Peggy no longer wanted us to live in Turin and I had already made the decision to play out my remaining years in the game in familiar surroundings when the maximum wage was scrapped. Peggy had not settled in Italy as well as I had. She complained of feeling lonely because she was left on her own so often when I was in ritiro (the rest period they organised after a game when the team would go back to the hotel to unwind and discuss the match), and pre-season, and she was insistent that the boys should be educated in England. I always said the reason I was leaving was that I did not want to overstay my welcome, but the truth was I was looking after my wife and children. Peggy was a Leeds girl with all her family at home. Sometimes you have to put the family before yourself, and with such an ordinary season behind me, the summer of 1962 seemed as good a time as any to quit. I did not foresee the struggles that lay ahead.

Once I had decided to leave and heard that Leeds United were interested, there was never any other club in it, even though they were in the Second Division and I had offers from First Division clubs. Swansea was the land of my fathers but Leeds was my football home and, once I had accepted that a return was inevitable, it was the obvious choice. I'd been happy there before, and it was Peggy's home town and the birthplace of two of the three children. I had scores of friends there and long ago had lost the feeling of being an exiled Welshman among the open-hearted Yorkshire folk.

I retained no bad vibes about Italy, far from it. It had been a great experience and I was never treated in any other way than exceptionally well. There were no complaints about the country, the people who watched the game, those who played it or those who ran it. They were the best five years of my professional life. It was not until I returned to Leeds that I realised just how much I had enjoyed Italy and the way of life it had given me. I had met a lot of good people, made many friends and lived in a style way above my means, thanks to the generosity of the Agnelli family and the club.

Juventus were desperate for me to stay although they always knew there was a possibility I would return home. Originally, I signed a two-year contract, then another for two years and then a one-year contract that would free me, if I wanted to go, in May 1962. From Christmas 1961 I tried to talk to Agnelli about it, but his reply was always 'Domani' – tomorrow.

He was so keen for me to sign for another year that when I was due to go to South America with Wales, he said they would let me go as soon as I signed a new contract. He had earlier refused to allow me to play for Wales against Spain in Cardiff and Madrid, which had annoyed me. Now, in desperation, I said I would sign but only if they offered me a ridiculous amount of money. I felt sure he would turn his back on me but to my surprise he agreed. He called my bluff and I had to admit to him that my wife wanted to go home no matter how much I wanted to stay or how much he was prepared to pay.

Agnelli allowed me to travel with Wales and, despite the shortage of time, I left with everything ready to return to Britain. I had been away for one day when the newspapers in Italy announced a statement from Agnelli saying that I had re-signed for the club.

They did not tell me, either, that Don Revie and three of his directors were in Turin to see me. I would not have known if I had not seen them leaving their city centre hotel as I drove past.

Juventus did not give up and Agnelli sent vice-president Remo Giordanetti to see me to explain that they had been unable to sign a replacement and offer me a £14,000 signing-on fee which, with salary and official bonuses, would have taken me past £18,000. Add on the unofficial bonuses and the money would have easily approached £20,000 – a staggering sum at the time. I was tempted, but I didn't tell Agnelli. I was doing it for my family.

Sadly, there was a bitter wrangle over money when I finally left. Albert Morris, the Leeds United director, smiled when he walked out of the Juventus boardroom and told me that the deal had been completed. What he did not realise, and what no one had told him, was that Juventus owed me a lot of money, a total of £7,860, which was a massive amount in those days. When I signed for Juventus, there was a clause in my contract that read:

As an alternative to the above mentioned option, Juventus shall have the option at the expiration of this agreement or at the expiration of the further said agreement entered into (such option to be exercised within thirty days) of arranging for the transfer of Mr Charles to a British or Continental or South American football club to be approved by Mr Charles, and provided he does not then wish to retire from playing soccer. If Mr Charles is so transferred to a British football club, Juventus will pay to him upon such transfer 12 per cent of the amount received in consideration of such transfer and in the event of Mr Charles being so transferred to a Continental or South American club, Mr Charles shall receive the whole of the amount received.

Teddy Sommerfield had insisted on including that clause because he predicted that Juventus might sell me on at a big profit and he believed I should share in it. Although Teddy was no longer my agent, I did not have to be much of a mathematician to work out that as Leeds had paid a club record of £53,000 for me, I was due a share of £6,360. Juventus had also promised me £1,500 if the club did well in my final season, but insisted that they would only pay me the money over the course of the following season, if I stayed with them.

For a player to have an agent or a lawyer was banned in England at the time, but so complex were the contracts in Italy that they were absolutely essential. I could not have come out of the Italian deal successfully without the help and work of Teddy Sommerfield. Experts understand the small print; laymen like me do not. Had Jimmy Greaves and Denis Law understood their contracts, or had some help with the explanations, things might have turned out differently for them. Teddy had the entire Italian Federation rulebook translated into English for me to read. Some of the rules were stupid but when in Rome . . .

I had a letter signed by Agnelli himself when I joined, stating that he made himself personally responsible for all the payments owed to me. I still have the letter. As I was sure that he was a man of great honour, I always believed that I would receive my dues eventually. Agnelli was very upset but we never fell out. Every day he tried to talk me out of going in the nicest way; and he would send someone important on a regular basis to try to persuade me not to go. He wanted to keep me and he was prepared to do anything within his power to persuade me to stay.

I don't blame Juventus for trying to keep me and I don't blame myself for fighting for what I was due. The Italians began to get a bad name over the sagas with Denis Law, Joe Baker and Jimmy Greaves, but they wanted to leave before their contracts had finished. Mine had finished.

The Italians were also accused of making illegal approaches for players through the newspapers – so what else was new! It was going on then with English players as it is now.

When I was finally allowed to go, the club were generous in their praise for me, describing me as one of their greatest ever players for technical skill, professional seriousness and dedication to the club. It left a lump in my throat.

I could have stayed and carried on for years more at centre-half. I always felt it was an easy position in Italy. I would have loved to play at the back as I had done at the start of my career, facing the football and using my height and strength in defence; and I'm sure things would have carried on after I had finished playing. The grateful, wealthy Agnelli family always looked after players who saw out their careers with the club. Boniperti is a prime example, as he remained involved with the club, eventually becoming a director.

I was thirty-one and had enjoyed five great seasons. I was not fed up with the football and certainly not with the way of life. I was still very fit. I had won three titles, two Cups and been Italian footballer of the year, a rarity for foreign players; I may even have been the first. It was, if I remember, voted for by the players and I have never been so flattered, considering all the star players in the country from all over the world. Juventus appreciated the honour and rewarded me in their usual generous manner.

When you think about it, we had everything – two cars, two homes, a 25 per cent share of the restaurant and a great life. We were idolised. Our flat was six minutes from the ground and I had bought another flat on the coast. It was mine, but it was bought with the wages and bonuses Juventus had given me. It was lovely for the kids and only a two-hour drive away. We would go down in the week if there were a couple of days clear, and Peggy would take the boys there during the holidays. We would have a couple of weeks back home in the summer as well.

The boys were the main reason Peggy wanted to come back to England, but even that proved to be a mistake. They loved Italy. They all spoke Italian as well as English, and they really missed the life there, as well as the sun.

All in all, it was a traumatic return. For a start, Agnelli had made it hard for me to leave. Apart from the £18,000 contract I'd been offered, I could have had what I wanted, and if I had been on my own I would certainly have stayed. As it was, I had to fight hard for the money they owed me. But we had a little money in the bank and Peggy had made up her mind. We were well off compared with footballers in England, and Leeds were generous. They found me a beautiful £8,000 home in Wetherby with three garages, central heating and terraced lawns, but I missed the Italian sunshine and the trips to the beach, and I made sure I had access to the Italian daily sports papers so I could keep in touch.

At the club, things had changed dramatically. Don Revie had swept through like the proverbial new broom, and I was flattered that he saw me as part of the future. He paid a club record fee for my services and the people of Leeds seemed as excited as I was by my return. We were all to be disappointed. For some reason, I never recaptured the form I showed for Juventus.

I wasn't as fit as I should have been and I did not fit in with the other players. They weren't jealous, even though they knew I had once again been given a big signing-on fee. It wasn't their fault, it was mine. I found it difficult to adapt. I thought it would be easy with everything I had done and learned in Italy, but things had changed – I had changed.

With all the moving and the negotiations, I had done little or no training before the start of the season and when the fixtures began I was overweight and felt a bit ponderous. Losing weight has always been difficult for me, being such a big man. Had I been training through the summer as usual, it would have been so different. At my age and my size, I needed that pre-season training. At the club, training was still from ten until noon, but I wanted to do more to try to regain my fitness and get my weight down so I trained every afternoon on my own and on Sundays, too. I didn't want anyone to accuse me of not trying or of returning home just for the money. I felt that once I regained my fitness I would have no problems, and I set my heart on becoming a favourite of the Leeds crowd again, but try as I might, it would not go for me. I just never caught up.

Every move I made was watched not only by our own fans but also by radio, television and newspaper reporters. They were expecting a lot from me and I couldn't give it; the glare of publicity showed that up. They wanted me to add punch to the attack but I found everything so different from Italy and the things I had become used to.

For the opening game of the season in the Potteries against Stoke City, 27,118 turned up to see what this John Charles thing was all about. I didn't play badly but neither was I inspirational. I was competent and the club were more than happy with the 1–0 victory, which gave us a good start in the quest for promotion to the top flight – an old story as far as Leeds United and I were concerned.

The first hint of trouble came with my first game at Elland Road. The club had more than doubled the price of tickets from three shillings to seven shillings and sixpence. The result was a fans' boycott of the game with only 14,119 turning up to welcome me home. That was sad. It was a disappointment to everyone and it showed in our play as we lost 4–3 to Rotherham, a game we were expected to win. After the game, Don Revie blamed Jack Charlton for one of the goals and Jack lost his temper and threw a cup at his manager, who promptly walked out of the dressing room while Jack struggled to calm down. It was a symptom that things weren't yet quite right in the changing room. For me, it was scant consolation that I scored my first goal for the club since my return. I suppose I was very fortunate in that even when I was not playing well the goals still came; indeed, I scored in the next two away matches, against Rotherham in the return and in the local derby against Huddersfield. But I was disappointed with my overall form and continuing lack of fitness, despite the extra work I had been doing. I felt I was letting down not only Don Revie and the faith he had shown in me, and the directors for the money they had spent, but also the fans who were being charged twice the fee to watch the game. It was a lot of pressure.

The people at Leeds did give me a hard time at first, but soon realised I was trying as hard as I could and warmed to me. I was grateful for that. One of the reasons for the antipathy of the Leeds United fans towards me was because the board wanted the supporters to pay for my transfer. Of course, it was a lot of money, and it wasn't as if they had given the supporters a vote on whether they wanted me and, if they did, were prepared to pay for me. But the players were all friendly, and there was usually one who would act as a minder in case anyone decided they wanted to try to knock me out of the game.

I had loved Turin and my flat with a view of the Alps was just six minutes' drive from the city centre. There were loads of really good restaurants within walking distance. Our apartment at the seaside was only a hundred miles away and the only real problem I could do nothing about was the fog, which could drop like a blanket. While Peggy had missed her friends and relations when we were in Turin, those same friends and relations had also advised us to stay put and told us we would find it hard to settle back in Leeds. They were right, and the move fell woefully short of our ideals, for both of us. It didn't take us long to realise we had made the biggest mistakes of our lives. In five years we had become Italian by association, totally in tune with the Italian way of life, the food, the good weather and the general ambience. The climate back in Leeds nearly killed us, and although I knew it was unfair, I couldn't help comparing everything with Italy.

It was the same with my football. Some critics lashed out at me when I began to suggest maybe I should go back to Italy. They pointed out I had no problems for Wales against Scotland at Cardiff, but then I was at centre-half linking up with Ivor Allchurch and Roy Vernon. At Leeds, I was at centre-forward and the style of play was nothing like the style of play to which I had become accustomed. Italian football is slower with a more deliberate build-up in midfield, but that did not mean it was not as good. I found it hard to adjust to the long-ball style with players scuttling around at 100 miles per hour. It might have been attractive to watch for the British fans, but I found it hard to play a game in which I was asked to run, run, run.

There was a classic example in favour of my argument when the Brazilian World Club champions Santos played at Sheffield Wednesday and showed that the game does not have to be played at breakneck pace but with players moving into space and letting the ball do the work.

I simply could not get used to the style Leeds played, and the harder I tried the worse it became. Gradually, I realised what a dreadful mistake I had made. In the five years away, I had become an Italian footballer and I did not fit in with football at home.

The great irony was that Peggy was missing Italy as much as I was, and the boys' education in Italy was as good, if not better, than they were getting in Leeds. All my good intentions had gone out of the window and I decided I had to go back to Italy. I can understand how disappointed Don Revie and the club were when I told him my decision. It was not long into my first season back but, in truth, it was not working for either the club or me. The best solution was for us to cut our losses.

If I had stuck with Leeds and not gone to Juventus originally, I would have been happy; equally, when I rejoined Leeds, had I stayed with Juventus I would have been happy. I would not have lost the pre-season training and I have no reason to believe I would not have carried on as I had in my previous five seasons before eventually moving to centre-half. Each time, circumstances forced the decision, and every year you inevitably lose a little something, either in terms of fitness or pace. I was no different from the Leeds supporters. I wanted to be the same as I was in my twenties, and it is hard to accept you are getting older.

Revie was very good to me even during the bad times. He could see straightaway that I was lacking in general fitness and match sharpness, and he put me on a special training programme, designed to be tough and to extend me to the limit. As was his way, he also put me on a special course of massage, something he believed in deeply, to keep the muscles and the body generally flexible and supple, helping avoid strains and pulls. My fitness improved a bit with playing and training, but I wasn't quite there. It would have taken me a long time to get back to what I had been. The edge had gone, mentally more than physically. Don was very understanding and I liked him a lot. We talked a great deal. I was sad because I felt I had not only let down Leeds but also myself. Revie had put a lot of faith in me and stayed strong until the end but I was unable to return the favour. Maybe it would have been different in the First Division where the style of football was different. I missed Italy, that was the truth, and I could not settle with the style of play, the heavy pitches and my own lack of fitness, which was not helped by the fact I was also struggling to sleep.

He was very intense as a player, a manager and a person, and he could be a hard man, very much a sergeant major type, maybe even a bit of a bully, but to me he was down-to-earth. He was the sort who preferred egg and chips for dinner to prawn cocktail and steak Diane. If he didn't like you there could be a problem, and I could understand why some people did not like him. But he was a good coach and a deep thinker, and he had the right people around him, especially Les Cocker. He and Revie both died long before their time. Les was a ferocious little man who even scared me. Say the wrong thing and he was down your throat.

If Don had a fault it was that he saw things in black and white with no shades of grey. Clearly, he was an outstanding club manager and it was an interesting insight to see him at what was the start of his highly successful career at Elland Road. He built Leeds from nothing into the best team in Europe. You could see they had the makings of a great team. There were quality youngsters there including Billy Bremner, Johnny Giles, Norman Hunter and Paul Reaney. It was all down to him, getting the right players and getting them to want to play for him. Looking back, it was very sad that I did not settle and play a part in what became a great side.

Don tried to do the same thing with his country as he did with his club and it didn't work because they weren't all his players. After a game, he would lose them and couldn't talk to them. Footballers are strange people. They think as a group and if they are not with the manager all the way, it won't work. As it transpired, Revie was the right man in the wrong job. He eventually fell out with the Football Association after an unhappy and bumpy period with England.

It was a sorry time for me. Apart from my problems at Leeds, it was the time when King's was really struggling. It had gone from very good to very bad very quickly and, despite Colombo's intervention, I was in the process of losing a great deal of money, everything I had saved in Italy. What with marital problems as well, it was no wonder my form took a dive. If you are not happy in your home life, it is very difficult to make it work in your job, whatever business you are in. I tried to kid myself that football was a release but my form did not concur with the statement and, on reflection, it was clear these two massive setbacks affected me hugely.

I never asked for a transfer but it was mutually agreed. Fortunately, Roma wanted me and they offered £70,000, a fee that not only gave Leeds their money back but also a nice little profit on the side. When they came in, there was no problem. I think Leeds were glad to see the back of me because it had not worked out. It was nothing to do with them but all to do with my emotional problems caused by the business going bust in Italy, marital problems and injuries.

I'm not looking for excuses, simply giving legitimate reasons.

The Italians did it properly, making their approach through Alan Hardaker at the Football League who informed Revie of the interest. Revie announced publicly that he and the club did not want me to go, adding that I should be given time to settle down and saying how hard I was training. But I knew, as Revie did, that the time had come, and with the club being offered such good money for my services, it meant they had gained from my arrival. Had I stayed, there was a good chance their money would have been wasted and lost.

Millionaire chairman Harry Reynolds eventually emerged from a two-hour board meeting to announce that in view of the fact that neither Peggy nor I could settle, they were prepared to enter negotiations with an Italian club. Roma's president, Count Francesco Marini Dettina, was on the doorstep with a sack full of money ready to take me back to Italy.

I had been back at Leeds for just ninety-one days. I had learned my lesson the hard way and I couldn't wait to get back to Italy. I had no one to blame but myself and that was what persuaded me to go back. That was the second mistake I made, and the third one was to go to Roma.

The burden was still on my shoulders there. I had more knee problems and had to undergo surgery. It was a long hard road going from Footballer of the Year to injuries, loss of form and ongoing damage to my marriage, but I survived it. Those are the bad things in life. They come to test you as a human being and I managed to overcome them.

Perhaps it might have been different had Leeds accepted an offer from Torino but the bid from Roma was too good to refuse and on 2 November 1962 at a minute to 7 p.m., I shook hands and was on my way from Yorkshire to Italy for the second time in my life.

CHAPTER THIRTEEN

Rome –
the eternal city?

I was excited at the prospect of going to the Italian capital to play my football. Whenever I had played at the Olympic Stadium against either Roma or Lazio I had been impressed.

I was desperately sorry it had not turned out as everyone had hoped back at Leeds but it was my mistake and I was delighted to be going back to Italy. Contrary to some sniping from fans and newspapers, it had nothing to do with money. I was going back because I felt my future as a footballer lay in Italy.

I left some considerable turbulence in my wake. To placate the fans, Leeds offered refunds on season tickets or the chance to pay for two games less the next season. The third and somewhat controversial choice was for the money to go into the Leeds transfer fund.

I was quickly forgotten. Revie signed Don Weston from Rotherham for £15,000 as my replacement and he obliged by scoring a hat-trick in his first thirty minutes for the club in his debut against

Stoke City. Leeds eventually went on to gain promotion in the following season and never looked back, winning the League twice, the FA Cup and a host of honours in Europe.

That was now my past. The future, I hoped, was Rome. The city was splendid, a sightseeing paradise, and I knew from experience that the restaurants were wide and varied; those I had visited were very good. However, like many places, it was good to visit but not so good to live there. I found it to be a cold place to live in comparison with Turin where I seemed to know everybody. I would have loved to have gone back to Turin, of course, but Torino did not offer enough. I had hoped that Juventus would come back in for me but in my heart I knew they would not. They did not bring back players who had left them because they considered you had let the club down by going. No matter how hard Juventus had tried to keep me, once I walked away, they ripped up the contracts and I was no longer one of them; at least, not until I stopped playing altogether and then they welcomed me back with open arms.

It was very flattering that a club of Roma's size came in for me at the age of thirty-two, near enough. They wanted me to play centre-forward but I would have much preferred to play centre- half. In the previous few months, I had lost my edge as a striker.

The manager was Luis Carniglia, known as 'Yiyo'. He was some character who had played and coached all over the world. He played in Argentina, Mexico and France and then managed in France, Spain, Italy and Argentina. He was in charge of the fabulous Real Madrid when they won two of their first five European Cups, with such players as Di Stefano, Kopa, Gento and Santamaria under his control. He had also managed Fiorentina and Bari before joining Roma and leading them to the 1961 Fairs Cup, beating Birmingham City in the final.

I was looking forward to working under Carniglia but I was

virtually his last act; he was replaced by Udine-born Alfredo Foni after being in charge for just seven games. Foni came into management with a fabulous playing record. He formed a formidable defensive partnership with Rava, which helped Italy to win the 1938 World Cup, and two years earlier he had won an Olympic Gold medal in the Berlin Olympics. But as a coach he disappointed; so much so, the Roma players called him Buffoni.

I was welcomed back to Italy in grand style, and for a few brief weeks I began to think that I had been smiled on once again. I was not to know what lay in front, and neither did the fans as I made my debut in place of the Argentinian Pedro Manfredini on 4 November 1962 and scored in the 3–1 win over the league leaders Bologna. There were 90,000 in the Olympic Stadium with record gate receipts of £27,500. Everyone was delirious and coach Foni said, 'With goals like these we will soon pay off the transfer fee and the very presence of John Charles should increase our home gates by at least 5,000.'

I felt I was back and began to look forward to the remainder of the season, especially as our good form continued. I scored the equaliser in a 2–2 draw at Fiorentina and then in the next game. Ironically, the first game in which I failed to score was against Torino in Turin, another 2–2 draw, on 25 November.

To underline my return, I was twice picked to play for the Italian League in that first month. I was one of five 'stranieri', strangers or foreigners, in the side that beat the Scottish League 4–3 in Rome. I managed to set up a couple of goals and although I did not score myself, I was fairly satisfied as Del Sol, Haller, Petris and Hamrin outscored Divers, Cooke and Millar.

Two weeks later, I was back in England playing for the Italian League against my old mates from the Football League at Highbury. A stunning crowd of over 35,000 paid £8,743 to watch. I celebrated by scoring a couple of goals but we lost 3–2 to goals from O'Grady of Huddersfield and the Spurs pair of Greaves and Allen.

I was back on the scoresheet a few days later when I scored a second-half equaliser against Genoa. I felt my fitness was returning and I had not lost my goal touch, even though I would have been happier playing at the back with the ball in front of me. There is nothing like a goal or two to cheer up a footballer, and the club and the supporters seemed happy enough with my contribution. It was a false dawn.

The dressing room was full of South Americans, with Carniglia having brought in Ghiggia, Schiaffino, Da Costa, Manfredini, Angelillo and Lojacono, and I assumed it would be like playing with my old friend Sivori, but they were nothing like him and I have to admit I was nothing like the player I had been.

The signs at the start were excellent, and when I scored against Bologna, everyone in Rome believed my arrival signalled a change in fortunes for the club. That in itself became a burden because suddenly it seemed that all their dreams would be fulfilled; they believed they had signed the man who was going to lead them to the promised land. Roma were, in truth, a midtable side, no better than that, and I wasn't going to make the necessary difference on my own.

That became apparent when I began to struggle with injuries; those and my personal problems soon began to take their toll. Apart from being sidelined with niggling injuries, my marriage to the mother of my four sons was falling apart.

I felt I was under almost unbearable pressure, and was devastated when I was dropped by the club, something that had never happened to me in all my time at Juventus. A leg injury kept me out of the game for a long time and even threatened my career for a while. It was a hard struggle back and in May 1963 I played outside-left against Leeds in Rome, a game that I assume was part of the transfer deal.

As at Leeds, I take full responsibility. What was sad for me was that I was on the top of my form when I left Juventus and everything went downhill after I left. Looking back now, I believe that just the very act of leaving Juventus had a massive effect on me. They were, and probably still are, one of the best clubs in the world and you cannot help but compare everything and everyone else with them. Nothing matched up to them.

Add to that the fantastic lifestyle and the fact that life was just so sweet. The money was good, they were very fair and if I wanted to go back to Leeds or Swansea to see family or friends they usually said 'yes'. It was only when I wanted to play for Wales that I had the occasional problem. I understood that they didn't like me going away, risking injury, and not being sure how well we were being looked after. In any case, I didn't always want to do the travelling.

For Wales, I was playing centre-half and although I was not playing brilliantly, I was doing a job and it was much easier than playing centre-forward. I am sure, had I been able to work myself back into football in the defence at Roma, things would have turned out a lot better – except I was not happy anyway. Rome was too big for me, and our accommodation was a long way from the ground. It took an eternity to get there through the mad Rome traffic. While Turin was my home, this was a foreign country to me. They were different people in the capital and Roma was a different club from Juventus. Lots of little things added up to make me very unhappy but I guess, had I been really fit and on top of my form, I would have got used to the situation and the environment.

For the first time in my life, I was feeling sorry for myself. I was still trying to tell myself that things off the field did not affect what

I did on it, but they did, especially when allied to my general lack of fitness. I probably tried too hard to get myself back into shape too quickly at Leeds and Roma.

It is difficult to know why they signed me. I knew that Roma had a dream that they could replace the Milan and Turin sides at the top of the Scudetto, and the president believed I could deliver this for him. They remembered me from when I played against them, but they already had a top centre-forward in the Argentinian Pedro Manfredini, who was the top scorer that season. So, because of Manfredini, I was played as an inside-forward even though I would have much preferred to have gone back to my old centre-half position.

Initially I had been happy to be back in Italy and I honestly thought I would live out the remainder of my life over there. But Rome was so different to Turin, and people complained that I spent too much time in restaurants enjoying myself. I had to eat but I never went over the top. Maybe my diet wasn't the same as other players but I knew what was good for my weight and me.

The real problem while I was there came with the injuries I suffered, and I was in and out of the team. This led some people to claim I was too old and had come to Rome to finish my career. It did not help that Peggy also disliked Rome, and she spent a lot of her time away at our seaside villa. She had new friends and said she did not like the expensive apartment the club had put us in.

When it was decided I would leave Roma to return home to Cardiff I could not immediately get hold of her to tell her the news. Once in Cardiff I felt that the best thing for all the family would be for us to get divorced and I had actually visited a solicitor to start the proceedings before Peggy turned up unexpectedly at my parents' house. We sat down and talked into the early hours while the kids slept and eventually we decided to give it another go.

It was not long before I came to the conclusion that I could not stick it out. Everyone told me everything would turn out all right but it didn't matter what anyone else felt, I hated it and wanted to leave. I was another year older, unhappy and unsettled. I was never going to give of my best in those circumstances. I was depressed and in serious need of a little tender loving care, and what better place to find it than back home? When Cardiff came in for me, I was overwhelmed. It was the perfect move, back home to Wales and to a club where I knew the chairman and where my brother Mel was playing.

CHAPTER FOURTEEN

Back to Wales

It was an amicable parting when I left Roma. The supporters were fine but I suppose they were glad to see the back of me because I wasn't the John Charles they had expected or, indeed, believed they had signed after the opening game against Bologna. I was not at my best and they weren't a good side. They were comfortable but not challenging for honours, so they were hardly going to be able to carry me until I regained my fitness and my form.

I had been very friendly with the previous Cardiff chairman, Fred Dewey, and with both George Swindin and his replacement as manager, Jimmy Scoular. Dewey was a Welsh selector and I got on very well with him. He knew I was unhappy in Rome and, as soon as he found out that Roma might be prepared to sell me on and cut their losses, he told Cardiff to try for me.

However, I was still wanted as a centre-forward for the glory and for the goals. I tried to persuade them I would serve them better at centre-half but Dewey and Swindin were insistent they wanted a goalscoring star and I was the man.

I signed for Cardiff in the summer of 1963 for £20,000, so my ten-month stay cost Roma some £50,000. I played just ten Serie A games for them, scoring four goals – not a bad return of goals per games in the Italian League, but it just goes to show how statistics can lie.

Cardiff chairman Ron Beecher wanted me but, quite rightly, was not prepared to pay silly money they could not recover through the gates. He did offer me decent wages of £40 per week, the same as my old Welsh team-mate Ivor Allchurch, which was a lot more than the rest of the squad were earning, but some way short of the money that top stars like Johnny Haynes were receiving. My old friend Gigi Peronace was again involved in the deal but the Roma president wanted £30,000 and would not shift; neither would Beecher.

Huddersfield announced their interest but I had set my heart on returning to Wales with Cardiff City. By announcing publicly they were the club I wanted to join, it put off Peterborough, my home-town club Swansea Town and Manchester City.

It took another fortnight of careful manoeuvring by Peronace and Beecher to see the deal through at the price they wanted. Then Gigi sent me a cable saying 'Catch the first flight to Cardiff' and I finally signed on the dotted line on 9 August 1963.

With the new season just two weeks away, manager George Swindin was keen to see what sort of shape I was in after my injury-ravaged season in Italy, and he plunged me straight into the team to play a friendly against Bath City. Twerton Park was filled to overflowing and everyone, it seemed, had come to see John Charles score a goal for his new club. I did but they were disappointed because it was an own goal as I tired towards the end of the game and it gave the non-leaguers a 1–1 draw.

Nevertheless, I felt fitter than I had done for a long time; I had shed the excess pounds and was 6lbs under my fighting weight. I was ready for the new season but the authorities were not and, for a while, it looked as though my league debut would have to be put on hold.

The problem lay in a contract wrangle between Leeds and Roma over money still outstanding from my move the previous November. Leeds claimed they were owed £10,000 by Roma for the original transfer and the Football League were refusing to accept the registration. The £10,000 was the sum guaranteed by Roma for Leeds' close-season tour of Italy during which they played Roma in front of a 15,000 crowd. The money should have been paid within a week but Leeds received only their expenses and complained to the League who put a block on the transfer until Cardiff paid part of my fee direct to Leeds.

The problem was not resolved until twenty-four hours before our opening game against Norwich City at Ninian Park. I was cleared to play just in time and in front of a crowd of over 21,000 I lined up at club level for the first time alongside my brother Mel.

This time I put the ball in the right net – but what a freak goal it was. Just before half-time we were awarded a free kick around the halfway line and my effort bounced over the head of goalkeeper Kevin Keelan and into the net. We went on to win 3–1.

It was exactly the sort of start the chairman had hoped for and the next game, against Manchester City, attracted even more fans to our ground with over 25,000 paying to watch. I struggled after pulling a muscle but still managed to score an equaliser in a 2–2 draw. Although I say it myself, it was one of my better goals and that in itself was very satisfying, but the injury was a curse and forced me to miss too many games as the old body took a while to heal. I still managed to play thirty-three league games in the first season at Ninian Park and score eleven goals, even though I played a number of those games at centre-half.

At times, we looked more than capable of gaining promotion – we beat Newcastle United 4–0 at St James' Park with both myself and my old mate Ivor Allchurch scoring in a 4–0 win in front of almost 40,000 Geordie fans – but that was a long way off. We finished in the bottom half of the table without ever looking like joining the chasing group.

We did not do a lot better in the cup competitions. Leeds knocked us out of the FA Cup in one of the clubs' regular meetings in the competition at the time, while Wrexham, of all teams, put us out of the League Cup. I played in the 2–2 draw in the first game at Ninian Park but missed the two replays.

How many memories the game against Leeds brought back! When I was at Leeds, Cardiff seemed to knock us out in the third round every season. Perhaps they were looking for revenge. Anyway, it was a tough, bruising game at Ninian Park against a side favourite to win the Second Division and return to the top flight under Revie.

They were an extremely hard side then, and won few friends with their style. I have bad memories of the game for when I clashed with centre-half Freddie Goodwin he broke his right leg. It was an awful sight and it was to be the end of his career. Jack Charlton did not play because he was already out injured and Leeds sent on Paul Madeley, a talented young central defender. He went on to play many times for England and form part of the bedrock for Leeds' success in the years to come.

The only sniff of success we had that first season was in the Welsh Cup. It was a competition I had not been involved with before, but it was important because the winners were guaranteed a place in the European Cup-Winners' Cup and the chance of a top draw and a big gate. We beat Ebbw Vale 6–1, Chester 3–1 and then, after a replay, Newport 1–0 with a goal from Mel. That took us to the final, played over two legs; an aggregate win would seal a place in Europe.

But nothing is ever straightforward, and before the game, George Swindin lost his job because of our indifferent season in the League. That had an effect on the team and we crashed to a 2–0 defeat at Bangor's Farrar Road ground. Fortunately, we managed to pull ourselves together and I enjoyed one of my better games as we won 3–1 at Ninian Park to force a replay at Wrexham. Given the lifeline, we won comfortably with Peter King scoring twice, and we went off for our summer break eagerly awaiting the first-round draw for Europe, and looking forward to starting the new season under the irascible Jimmy Scoular.

Before then, however, we made a trip to play in Italy, with our trainer Ernie Curtis now in charge. My team-mates were astonished to see the welcome I got when we arrived at Milan airport, with so many people calling out my name and trying to touch me. It was such a heart-warming response. Then, on the day of our game against Juventus, I was presented with a diamond brooch, a gold medal and an inscribed parchment. It may have been a friendly, but everyone was keen to play their very best – and how the Cardiff side responded. We went 3–0 up by half time, with Mel scoring the first, me the second and Ivor Allchurch adding a third. My goal may have been against the home side, but you wouldn't have thought it to judge by the way the 40,000 crowd chanted my name. It was a wonderful sound. At half time, someone parachuted down to present me with another gift – a beautiful watch. Sadly, after all the emotion we couldn't keep it up in the second half, and as we ran out of steam, Juventus came back to draw level at 3–3.

At the end of the game, I was carried off the pitch and after I was changed I was again carried to the coach by the fans. Talk about your feet not touching the ground! Many of the crowd then jumped into their cars and followed us back to our hotel.

When Cardiff played Roma, the supporters were again incredible to us, although the response wasn't quite as spectacular as in Turin. Nor was our performance on the pitch, when we lost 4–1, despite taking the lead. Our third game, against Latina, also ended in defeat. But for Cardiff the trip was very useful experience ahead of our forthcoming continental campaign. On a personal note, I was so pleased to have been welcomed back in such style.

So for Cardiff's first ever appearance in Europe, we drew Danish Cup winners Esbjerg in the first round, held them to a goalless draw away and won the return, which I missed through injury, with another Peter King goal. Then we drew the plum – Sporting Lisbon. No one gave us a chance, least of all the Lisbon club, but we liked the role of underdogs and produced our finest performance in the years I was at the club, winning 2–1 in the away leg. I played sweeper, the first time I had ever played the position between the goalkeeper and our defence. I was happy to get my own back for I had faced many such formations in Italy when there always appeared to be one more defender ahead of me than there should have been. Despite a deep cut to my head, I had one of my better games as we defended against wave after wave of Portuguese attacks. I had a plaster protecting the four stitches in my head wound but that was not going to stop me. I went into every challenge as though my very life depended upon it. Farrell and Tapscott scored our two breakaway goals and we returned home to Wales as heroes; but the job was only half done.

When we won that first game in Lisbon, we were at the wrong end of the Second Division and playing against a team who had thrashed Manchester United 5–0 the previous season.

Unsurprisingly, Sporting were still firm favourites, but in front of 25,000 fans at Ninian Park, we drew 0–0 and moved into a quarter-final tie against Zaragoza from Spain. I again played sweeper.

Once again, we played way above ourselves in the away leg and came away with a superb 2–2 draw. There were visions of a place in the last four, especially as we held out until the last fifteen minutes when former Real Madrid player Canario sent me the wrong way and went through to score a superb goal.

I went up front to try to retrieve my error but it wasn't to be. I was surrounded with Spaniards and hardly had a sight of goal. But it was a great adventure and the win in Lisbon is a cherished moment from my three-year stay with the club.

The results in Europe were not mirrored domestically. Injuries were a major problem for me and I missed around a third of the 1964–65 season as we again finished below halfway in thirteenth position. I played mainly at the back in my twenty-eight league games and, consequently, did not contribute hugely towards the 'goals for' column with only three to my name.

We went out of the FA Cup to Charlton and the League Cup to Southampton but, once again, the Welsh Cup came to our rescue. We won it again, beating Wrexham in another play-off. We had won 5–1 at home, lost 1–0 away and clinched our place in Europe with a comfortable 3–0 win at Shrewsbury's ground.

Cardiff told me at the end of the season that I would have to take a cut in wages, but I turned down the terms and left. Mel and I had started up a scrap-metal business and I planned to concentrate on that. Several clubs were queuing up for me, but I decided I did not want to uproot the family again to move to Bournemouth, the best of the offers. However, not long after I left the club, Cardiff came knocking on my door; they had raised the money, so I carried on playing.

I was selected at centre-forward and to show I had not lost the instinct, I scored on the opening day of the 1965–66 season against Bury – the only goal of the game – and then I got a couple at Derby County in a 5–1 win. I had my mind on an Indian summer but I was injured in a 6–4 defeat at Rotherham and was out of action once more. In my eagerness to get fit, I even opted to play for the reserves for the first time in my career. I did not mind – it was football.

In Europe, we drew Standard Liège of Belgium, a game that failed to capture the interest of the Welsh fans; fewer than 13,000 saw the Belgians take a 2–1 lead back home for the second leg in a game where, playing at centre-forward, I hardly got a kick, which we lost 1–0 in front of over 30,000 delirious Belgians. Towards the end of that game, I limped out of the action with a very badly damaged knee after a clash with defender Vliers, and once again I was back on the treatment bench, watching the football from the sidelines.

The injury was so bad, I was out of the game for three months before being told that to have any chance of playing again I would need an operation. When the surgeon at the Prince of Wales Hospital cut into my knee, he extracted so many little slices of bone it was like filleting a fish.

While I was trying to recover from the injury I spent a lot of time with a willing learner and good worker, who was hoping to make the grade as a forward. A tall skinny, local lad, he was always hanging around, and often joined me for workouts. I gave him what tips I could on how to make the best use of his height when heading the ball. We also played together a few times in the reserves. He said I helped him a lot, but I reckon John Toshack would have made it anyway. He went on to play almost 200 games for Cardiff, scoring going on for a hundred goals before moving on to fame and fortune with Liverpool. He certainly didn't pick up any tips from me so far as management was concerned, as his terrific record in that role proves! It was a case of in with the new and out with the old, as he was soon to establish himself as the club's centre-forward.

That challenge proved to be the end for me in the Football League. I never really recovered from it and finished the season with eight league appearances against my name, and four goals. While I was recuperating, several clubs inquired about signing me – sadly not Swansea, as I would have loved to play for my home-town side – and it was disappointing that the season came to a close just as I was beginning to feel ready to play again. I was given a free transfer by the club, and received a few offers before Bob Dennison of Hereford United came to talk to me.

I discovered later that Cardiff had tried to sign me from Juventus before I joined Leeds United. Bill Jones, manager at the time, told me that their original offer had been turned down by Juventus because it was not high enough; they had immediately increased it by cable but received no reply. It was mystifying. I knew nothing about it at the time but because Peggy was from Leeds and I had spent so many happy years at Elland Road, they were always favourites.

It was interesting playing regularly with my brother Mel. The only times I had played with him previously were with Wales and on the local playing fields back home in Swansea. Playing for your country and for a club is vastly different and I thought it might be significant but, truth be told, there was no real difference between playing alongside him and anyone else. He was a friend, another footballer, but it still felt strange that after all those years we should finish up playing for the same team back in Wales.

I was at Cardiff from 9 August 1963 until 1 June 1966, making just 69 appearances and scoring 18 goals. Once again, my goals per game ratio was better than my performances.

I enjoyed my time at Cardiff but, to be honest, I did not really click there. It wasn't anything to do with the players; I knew and liked them. It was me. I couldn't do the business. Beecher was a good chairman and I got on well with the managers, but we never had quite the success we had all hoped for. It was very depressing that I had nothing but a string of failures after leaving Juventus.

Although I was not performing to the standards I would have liked, I was still enjoying playing. This was my game and I was not going to give it up easily. My days in the Football League may have been over, but not of playing football. While I was able to run around, I wanted to carry on and I didn't mind at what level. If necessary, I would have played back in the parks where I started. I had no ego about it. I felt privileged to be able to play at all, and I was a very lucky man to have been paid to do what I loved to do best.

But I didn't have to go to the parks because the biggest non-league club around, Hereford United, came for me and I signed on 4 July 1966, having turned down several Football League clubs, including Notts County and Brighton.

Hereford was a pleasant little market town with a population of a little over 50,000, built by the River Wye. It is steeped in history with a Norman cathedral, which shows off a medieval map of the world, and King Stephen's chair. But mostly it is a farming community with market gardening, apples for local cider and lush grazing grounds for the world famous Herefordshire breed of cattle. Hereford's mascot is a live bull.

Hereford played in the Southern League, and it was my old Welsh international captain and team-mate Ray Daniel who counselled me. He said that they were the best club he had ever played for. That was certainly good enough for me and, in any case, their sole ambition was to gain entry into the exclusive club of the Football League. It wasn't the most convenient location because I was still living in Cardiff and commuted to Hereford on a daily basis.

Once again, I managed to pop one in on my debut, scoring early in the second half in a 5–1 victory over Bedford. Soon after I arrived, the club brought in former England winger Eddie Holliday to provide me with some service. Things went so well that both Bury, of the Second Division, and an Italian club came in for me – not bad for an old man who was past it! But I was happy where I was, and I even received some recognition when I was selected to play for a World XI against Italy in Milan in 1966. Sadly, it poured with rain so heavily that the game had to be called off two hours before the kick-off and I finished up going to the movies instead. I knew the dolce vita was over when I was asked to sign four books and a Woodbine packet, but at least there were no photographers hiding under restaurant tables as there had once been.

For away fixtures, every club would ring up to make sure I was playing because of the interest I had created and the extra crowds who would attend. I remember being thanked at Nuneaton Borough because the takings were the highest for eleven years, some £700.

I managed to score twenty-five goals in my first twenty-four games, and still got a hell of a kick at seeing the ball go in the net. I was thirty-five by then, and conserving my wind and strength.

There were some emotional moments in the Cup, especially when we reached the first round proper of the FA Cup only to be knocked out 4–1 by Peterborough, the team who achieved what we were aiming for, election to join the big boys.

In the Welsh Cup, over 11,000 people turned up at Ninian Park for what proved to be a tremendous game of football against Cardiff. I managed to lay on a couple late on, but it was too late by then as we went out 6–3.

In April 1967, I helped the club to claim some silverware when we won the Herefordshire Senior Cup by beating Port Vale. It was a significant victory for me for two reasons. One was that Mel was on the other side for his brief stay at the Potteries club; the other was that a certain Stanley Matthews was playing, an old friend and adversary.

The disappointment came in the league where we failed to push on and could finish tenth only, with just eighteen wins out of the forty-two matches played. I scored thirty-seven of the seventy-nine goals but would have willingly sacrificed every one of them to have had a crack at the Southern League championship.

I also had my first run-in with the authorities during my time at the club. We had lost 3–2 to Nuneaton and in the build-up to their winner, our goalkeeper Peter Isaac had clearly been fouled yet the referee allowed play to continue, a decision that cost us the game. After the game I waited in the tunnel and told the referee what I thought of his decision. I didn't threaten him, or even swear at him, but I was still censured and warned as to my future conduct.

In my second season, our manager Bob Dennison left to take up a scouting position with Coventry City, and in December 1967, I was asked by chairman Bill Humphries to become player-manager. I had passed the FA coaching courses and was really thrilled with the appointment. With the passing of time, I had begun to think I might have a career in the game as a manager or a coach. I had been a footballer, I reasoned, therefore I could be a manager.

Of course, it does not always work that way and there are plenty of examples to prove it from the brilliant Bobby Moore and Stanley Matthews down. Often the better the player, the harder it is for them to adapt to coaching players of a lesser standard. At Juventus, Parola, who had been the best centre-half in the world, couldn't countenance others' fallibilities, even with top-quality players, and he eventually failed as a manager.

Like any role in any sport, it was great when you were winning, awful when you were losing. The worst part was having to talk to the chairman. The crowds were fantastic at Hereford, and if you had a run in the Cup, they were unbelievable. It was a real Cup club. The support came to Edgar Street from miles away.

In my first game as player-manager, we reached the first round of the FA Cup with a win over Barnet. We were drawn against league club Watford and showed our nerves by going three down after little more than half an hour. To our credit, we pulled ourselves together and did not concede another goal although I had my nose broken in our efforts to achieve a respectable score.

I began to learn about the complexities of management when I had the opportunity to sign Mel from Porthmadog – I didn't in the end – and I took some stick from the fans and the local newspaper when I dropped goalkeeper Peter Isaac against our neighbours Worcester and played Bob Appleby who was not himself convinced of his fitness. I suffered for that one in an unusual manner for when Appleby went off injured I had to go in goal. The crowd were shouting for the referee to award Worcester a penalty to see how I shaped up to it but what they had not realised was that I was quite comfortable in goal. I had played there on several occasions for Leeds United when our goalkeeper was injured and also on a tour of Zambia one summer.

The good old Welsh Cup, which served us so well when I was at Cardiff, came to my rescue in my first season of management when Albert Derrick scored the only goal to help us beat Newport County in the semi-final in front of 5,186 fans at Somerton Park. Better still, our opponents were to be none other than Cardiff, looking for their place in the European Cup-Winners' Cup the following season.

Wales was agog with the fun of it all and I found myself in demand by the media. I was telling everyone that Hereford was better known for its famous white-faced cattle and its cider apples than for its football club, but when the Sunday tabloid newspaper ran the story they carried the headline 'The Cows Are Better Known Than The People'. Boy, did that make me unpopular in Hereford until I was able to explain exactly what I had said and what I meant.

The odds were heavily against us and, sure enough, Cardiff beat us 2–0 at Edgar Street in front of more than 5,000 fans, and then thrashed us at Ninian Park 4–1. I had the consolation of scoring our only goal, much to the appreciation of the 6,000 paying attendance.

We could have no complaints about either defeat but we were upset at losing the Herefordshire Senior Cup to Charlton, 3–2 after extra time. It was not so much the result as the fact we had three goals disallowed and hit the crossbar twice. It summed up the disappointment of the season generally as we finished in a lowly sixteenth place.

We warmed up for the 1968–69 season with a long tour to Zimbabwe, then known as Rhodesia, where we played a staggering fourteen games. It could have been a disaster but it wasn't – we won twelve and drew two. I turned out in seven of the games in the packed programme and scored twenty goals, including five in a game, which gave the total a bit of an imbalance.

All went well until the New Year. We just failed to persuade my old mate Ivor Allchurch to sign for us. During my time there, I was able to sign some good players, such as Ricky George, Ronnie Radford, Dudley Tyler and Ken Brown, who all went on to do marvellous things for the club in its various well-publicised cup runs. I also bought Brian Purcell and Roy Evans from Swansea, and we switched on our new floodlights with a 1–1 draw against Swansea.

We also reached the first round proper of the FA Cup where we gave a creditable performance while losing 4–2 to another league side, Torquay United.

Then disaster struck – disaster in the true sense and not the exaggeration of football reporters. Purcell and Evans were tragically killed in a car crash as they travelled from their homes in South Wales to Hereford. I found it particularly hard to take, telling myself they would not have died if I had not signed them; irrational I know, but it was how I felt at the time. We held a memorial game for their dependants and 5,000 turned up to watch Sheffield Wednesday beat us 4–2.

Unsurprisingly, after this awful event our season spluttered to an unsatisfactory conclusion as we finished in fourteenth place, just two places higher than the previous season, when we had hoped for so much.

It was the local cups that breathed life into our season again, as we won the Herefordshire Senior Cup by beating Newport County 4–1 and 4–3. I scored all four goals in our first-leg victory at Edgar Street. The touch, thank goodness, was still there in front of goal, although it was missing when we lost by a single goal to Swansea Town in the semi-final of the Welsh Cup with John Bird missing a penalty in the first half.

Our slow climb up the Southern League continued the following season when we came tenth, but we went out of the new FA Challenge Trophy to Barnet and the FA Cup to Newport County, losing three minutes from the end. We gained revenge by beating Newport in the Welsh Cup but went out in the semi-final for the third year running, losing to Chester.

I was the club's top scorer for the fourth season running with twenty-two goals in fifty-one games. I suppose it was the constant flow of goals that kept me going when others might have retired, but I was not only enjoying playing football but also the competition.

On the managerial front, I felt that I was slowly putting together a decent side that could challenge for more than just the local cups, and I was proved partially right when we challenged for the title in 1970–71. We looked good in pre-season against league opposition, drawing with Exeter and beating Wrexham. We eventually finished fourth and I am sure to this day that our Cup-fighting ability cost us the top spot.

The FA Cup was once again the competition that captured the imagination, and after knocking out Kidderminster, we drew Northampton Town at Edgar Street. We did not let down the massive 10,401 crowd, for after conceding two sloppy goals right at the start, we battled back with goals from Alan Jones and Brian Owen in true Cup tradition to force a replay.

That replay was supposed to be our Cup final but we fooled everyone, including Northampton who had previously gone fourteen games without defeat in League and Cup. We beat them 2–1 and set up a second-round tie against Third Division Brighton, the club who had tried to sign me a few seasons earlier.

Almost 13,000 people crammed into our ground and for a while our fans thought we were going on to the third round proper when I headed us into the lead after fifteen minutes of the second half, but Brighton equalised four minutes later and then scored the winner.

As if this was not enough of a distraction from our league efforts, we also had a long run in the FA Trophy, beating Bury Town, Banbury and then the holders Macclesfield to reach the semi-final. We were drawn to meet Hillingdon Borough at Leicester City's Filbert Street ground and knew we were in with a superb chance of winning; 4,000 fans travelled from Hereford. The prize was a place back at one of my favourite grounds in the world, Wembley.

We blew it. Ricky George, who went on to earn fame in future Hereford Cup triumphs, missed a sitter early on, and Hillingdon cantered to a comfortable 2–0 win. It hurt me as much as any club defeat in England, Wales or Italy, and was almost as bad as the World Cup defeat by Brazil. It was my greatest ambition to finish my playing career at Wembley, but worse than that, we let down our marvellous fans.

I finally quit in September 1971 when the club were lying fourth and challenging once again. I was finding it increasingly difficult to combine playing, managing and running my business in Cardiff, not to mention all the travelling involved in trying to gain Hereford the upgrade to the Football League. My job did not begin and end in the Edgar Street dressing room. Hereford had a far bigger aim for me, and my main off-the-field duty was to go round all the Football League clubs to persuade them to vote for Hereford when re-election of the bottom club came up.

Hereford had given me a wonderful time in the autumn of my career. They were hugely ambitious and that was great for me. I was often asked how I could play in the Southern League after being on top of the world in Italy and playing in the World Cup finals. I couldn't understand the question. I loved playing football and that was what I was doing. Just as my level of performance dictated my standard of club when I was a young man, moving me up the ladder, so it did as I became older and moved on.

Joe Wade took over on a caretaker basis and it was flattering to hear there were thirty applicants for the job. Colin Addison was appointed as player-manager and I left him a decent bunch of boys. I had tried to find a blend of seasoned professionals and good, raw talent, young players who could learn from those around them. I felt I left Hereford in a much stronger and healthier position than they were in when I joined. Much of that was due to the backing of the board and the fabulous support of the fans.

I left Hereford because I thought they deserved a manager who was able to live in the town and give the club his full attention as they sought league status. They were the most go-ahead club in the Southern League at the time and I had no doubts that they would soon be playing their football in the Fourth Division.

In those days the Football League was almost a closed shop. At the end of the season, the bottom four clubs in the Fourth Division had to apply for re-election; almost inevitably they were accepted. Hereford wanted me to use my contacts and my influence to break the mould. I loved that job because it enabled me to catch up with former players who had become managers, and meet people I did not know other than by reputation because of my six years in Italy. It was great fun and a very happy period of my life. I got on particularly well with the great Stan Cullis of Wolves and then Birmingham, and Raich Carter. Most people were happy to talk to me and I was able to tell them how Hereford had developed, what a good club they were and how they deserved to be in with the big boys.

The town also had a remarkable FA Cup record, which, over the years, grew to almost mythical proportions. Victories over top-flight clubs Newcastle and West Ham in the 1971–72 season added to the legend. For years, no non-league club had even been close to breaking through; now they were making their big bid on the back of their record and my reputation. It did not surprise me that Addison took the club up with what was very much my squad of players but it was still one of the most nervous days of my life as I waited for the voting to be completed.

When the result was announced, Northampton Town had polled 49 votes, Crewe Alexandra and Stockport County 46 – and Barrow and Hereford had tied with 26 votes apiece. It meant going to a second vote and, to my relief, Hereford won it 29–20, so Barrow, who had actually finished above both Stockport and Crewe, were demoted. I felt as though I had won the Cup. It was a fantastic achievement for a great little club and I felt as though I had done my bit.

There were a number of other top non-league clubs in the hunt but Bradford Park Avenue, Cambridge City and Wimbledon managed just a single vote each, while Bangor City, Bedford Town, Boston United, Hillingdon Borough, Romford, Telford United, Wigan Athletic and Yeovil Town all failed to register a vote at all.

It was a great achievement by Hereford, but how much better it was when the Conference became virtually the fifth division with automatic promotion for the top club. Now there are play-offs for a second club to progress. Some clubs that have gone up have done themselves and their League proud but, sad to say, Hereford are back in the non-league zone, fighting to regain their rightful place.

I never had the opportunity of testing myself at the higher level as a manager. I was not surprised because my talent did not match my enthusiasm. I wanted to be mates with everyone and while I had no problem picking a team, I found it difficult to be the hard man and end players' careers. I enjoyed every minute at Hereford and was able to bring good players to the club from the League. They signed because of my involvement and I felt that I played a very large part in their promotion. That was good enough for me.

I left Hereford having played 173 times in the league and scored 80 goals. According to the records, I also played 78 cup-ties of various sorts and scored another 46 goals. I do not feel as though I let anyone down and they certainly gave me a great deal of pleasure.

I applied for a few jobs in football after leaving Hereford and I was mystified why no one wanted to use my experience.

The next stop on my football journey was another non-league club in Wales, this time Merthyr Tydfil at Penydarren Park in Mid-Glamorgan. I joined them in January 1972. I was very friendly with the chairman, Maldwyn Davies, another contact from my days playing international football with Wales. By then, I was forty-one years of age but I still felt capable of playing and Maldwyn took me on as a part-time player-manager in the lower reaches of the Southern League.

Some twenty-five years after making my debut, here I was still playing and still enjoying it. I was once asked why I did not retire at my peak. It was a question I found hard to understand. I said that perhaps those who did quit at the top had no wish to play and did not love the game. I did. I loved every minute of it. Why should I pack it in when I could still be useful? As for playing on public parks with few people watching – why not? Is someone suggesting that was beneath me? It can never be beneath the dignity of a footballer to play football.

Davies was a lovely man and he wanted a bit of glamour at the club, which was going through a bad time. He wanted a bit of success and he saw me as the man who could deliver it. Methyr was a good club with a long history. They had even had a spell in the Football League before the war.

I loved it there. We were in the Southern League playing a decent sort of football and it became a lot better when the former West Ham centre-half Ken Brown joined us. It was wonderful to think that we were doing something for the town. It also helped the club finances because the crowds went up, just as they had done at Hereford, rising from around 500 to 2,000. We must have been doing something right.

I watched them before I took on the job and almost changed my mind, but I was in charge of the team for my first match on 29

January 1972 against Barnet at home. We lost 2–1 but I was more satisfied than I had been the previous week; they played better than I had seen them play before.

My enthusiasm lasted precisely until the next game when we crashed 5–1 to Chelmsford in the FA Trophy and suddenly there was nothing left for the club but the battle to avoid relegation. It was very depressing and there were strong rumours I wouldn't be staying, especially as Dutch club Den Haag and Swansea City wanted me. But how could I turn my back on the club after just two games? It was not on. I was staying, relegation or not. I waited until 26 February for my first victory as we beat Worcester City 2–0, the club's first win since 6 November.

There was no money, a small squad, and electricity restrictions stopped us using the floodlights for our evening training sessions. With everyone, including myself, on part-time wages, we could only train in the evening. I worked for a while at Briton Ferry Steel Works as a public relations man to supplement my wages, and even helped to head off a strike. The workers were going to lay down tools and I was asked to chat to them and managed to persuade them not to.

On the long trip to Yeovil, our team bus broke down and we arrived twenty minutes late for a game we lost 1–0, a good result under the circumstance. We had been forced to change on the coach, and jump straight out and play when we arrived.

Most of the problems were down to the shortage of cash so I organised a fundraiser – an International XI of some of my footballing mates versus the club. They gave good value for money. The Internationals won 6–3 with both Ivor and Len Allchurch on the scoresheet along with Roy Saunders and me.

By the end of the season, we were just beginning to pull things together on the pitch, drawing at Romford and beating Bedford, but it was too little too late, and for the first time in my career I knew what it was like to be relegated from the Premier Division as we finished twenty-first. In some ways, it was better to be a step down because it gave me breathing space to rebuild the side as best as I could. The standard was obviously not as high and the travelling was considerably less. I scouted around and brought in Alan Smith, Bryan Rees and the former Welsh international Mel Nurse.

There was certainly a new atmosphere about the place, especially when we beat Fourth Division Newport County 3–1 in a pre-season friendly – only to be brought crashing back down to earth by losing our first game, away to Rugby. But gradually our league form began to pick up, and we had a couple of wins against Ton Pentre and Minehead in the FA Cup before being put out by Barry; we also drew 3–3 with Bournemouth in a friendly to open our new Jubilee Club, Merthyr's £25,000 clubhouse.

The improvements were there for everyone to see as we beat Hastings in the FA Trophy and reached the quarter-finals of the Welsh Cup where, almost inevitably it seemed, we drew my old club Hereford. We managed to hold out for a goalless draw at Edgar Street in front of more than 8,000 fans but lost the replay at home. We earned £3,500 from those two games, a fortune for a club such as ours. I was even able to resign from my job – I was by this time liaison officer at Baglan Bay – to go full-time at the club, combining the manager's job with the equally important post of fundraiser.

We might well have won promotion back to the top flight that year but for Mel Nurse breaking his leg against Kidderminster in March. Two months later he was named Player of the Year. Our only league defeat at Penydarren Park all season was in our final home game against Rugby. We had moved on.

It was quickly realised that a budget of £175 a week was not going to finance a big enough squad to challenge for promotion, and they let me bring in another former Welsh international, Barrie Jones, plus Nick Deacy. We really fancied our chances as we beat Bristol City 2–1 and played well against Derby (1–3) and Wolves (1–2) in pre-season friendlies. We began the 1973–74 season with a four-goal win against Dunstable, Deacy scoring two, but we never lived up to our early promise.

The FA Cup provided some fun. Wins over Barry, Glastonbury and Macclesfield sent us into the first round proper where we beat Weymouth. We were one match off a possible plum third-round Cup-tie against one of the big guns, and with a draw against Hendon we fancied our chances. I organised special training at a local school and the players had their best-ever preparation for a game – we lost 3–0 in front of a full house at Penydarren Park and Hendon went on to draw Newcastle at St James' Park. Once again, it was a case of what might have been.

Despite Nick Deacy scoring forty-nine goals we could finish eleventh only, and by September 1974, my new striker had been sold to Hereford for £1,500. It is a pity they did not have add-on clauses in those days because he went on to play a dozen times for Wales.

I felt I had taken Merthyr as far as I could and I let them know before the start of the season. Given their financial problems, I felt I had done a good job for them. I continued to follow their results, of course, and their greatest moment came in 1987 when they qualified for the European Cup-Winners' Cup and they went desperately close to putting out the Italian Serie A side Atalanta, losing 3–2 on aggregate having won the home leg 2–1.

As the manager, I was able to take on those who left clubs such as Cardiff, Swansea and Newport. Any player I fancied, I used to go and chat them up to see if they wanted to join me. I loved doing that, and I loved playing. I could stand up front while everyone did the running for me. I would wait by the penalty spot and if anything came in, I would try to knock it in.

The nice thing was that I was treated with respect. No one ever came out to try to make a name by deliberately kicking me. Of course, there were battles and fouls in a one against one situation but I was quite happy playing football at that level. I enjoyed it with the people, and the atmosphere was terrific. The knees, having carried so much weight for so many years, were a problem and gave me a little trouble, but I tried not to make a fuss about it.

There was nothing flash about playing for Merthyr but there was a very good spirit in the side. We used to stop off at a fish and chip shop on the way back from away matches and I would go for fish suppers for all the players to eat on the coach on the way home. We didn't run to meals in restaurants. I remember once, in 1973, stopping in Rhydyfelin after a game at Barry Town. We pulled up at a chippy and I popped out to buy the necessary nineteen or twenty cod and chips. Unbeknown to me, the fish-shop owner was from Naples, a man named Paolo, and when I walked in he stopped in his tracks and shouted for his wife Maria to come quickly.

'It's Giovanni,' he called. 'He has come to our shop.'

Needless to say, I went back to the coach with free fish and chips for everyone while Paolo and Maria went back to work to talk about the day the Gentle Giant came for fish and chips at their shop. I wasn't about to refuse the offer – Merthyr didn't have the sort of money to be too proud.

Long after I stopped playing, big teams such as Liverpool were still having fish suppers on the way back from matches but I doubt whether their dieticians would allow them to do so now. The fish suppers have probably gone the same way as many of the players' bars – into oblivion.

I eventually stopped playing in April 1974, aged forty-two. Just before I bade farewell to the game, I enjoyed one last little moment of glory, against Bromsgrove Rovers, when I chipped their goalkeeper Chris Hooper from the halfway line. He should have known better than to come off his line because he was very experienced and boasted a record number of appearances for the club.

At the end of that season, I was on my way to our holiday apartment when Harry Gregg, the former Manchester United and Northern Ireland goalkeeper, then managing Swansea, offered me the job of youth team coach at Vetch Field. I discussed the opportunity with Mel Nurse, who said I should jump at it. If I couldn't play for the club, at least I would finally have some role there.

We were living in Swansea and I thought maybe I could develop my own coaching skills while helping the kids, but I have to admit I didn't get the same buzz as when I was playing. I stuck it out and gave it my best shot – I needed the money. I had to look after Peggy and the boys, and there was little to spare. Footballers had little financial security in those days and the longer I could play, coach or manage, the better I felt. Apart from anything else, it meant I was keeping in touch with a game I loved and, in the end, it owed me nothing. In the two years I was there, we brought in some good youngsters, such as my nephew Jeremy Charles, Nigel Stevenson, Alan Curtis and Robbie James. They all played a part in the club's rise from the Fourth Division to the First. I hoped this would be the start of a greater role in the club, and when Harry left in 1975 he recommended me as his replacement. Sadly, it was not to be, and eventually in 1976 I decided the time had come to leave.

I had almost returned to Juventus in 1969 when they were trying to persuade Malcolm Allison to become coach and he said he would accept only if I was given a job at the club, too. My name was also linked with managerial jobs at Plymouth, Birmingham, Wrexham, Barnsley and Doncaster, but nothing came of them. I took charge of the Welsh Under-23 side in 1972, hoping it would develop into something with the senior national side, but it did not.

I gave it one more shot some years later when I was invited to become technical director of the Canadian Soccer League side, Hamilton Steelers. I wasn't there for long, just six months, and my time there finally convinced me that I was not cut out for this sort of management, even though the people were very nice to me.

CHAPTER FIFTEEN

The best

During all my years in the professional game, I came across a great many coaches and managers, former international footballers, men steeped in football tradition. Rarely were there two alike in outlook, temperament or ability. All of them had good qualities, some more than others, but picking the three best, in the end, proved no problem.

My first choice, Jimmy Murphy, may surprise some people because he spent much of his professional career as the number two to Matt Busby at Manchester United. However, he not only took Wales to their one and only World Cup finals in Sweden in 1958, but in the same year he had the emotional task of taking over from Matt Busby at Old Trafford following the devastating Munich air disaster, which decimated the team.

I have no doubt at all that Jimmy Murphy has to be up there with the best of them because he commanded the total respect of the players who played under him. He would never ask you to do something he couldn't do himself, and he knew what he was talking about. If he wanted you to kick with your instep, he would do it first.

He was not just professional in his attitude to coaching; as manager of Wales he always looked after all the players, putting them first, above and beyond the International Committee, who were often a law unto themselves.

He was a great man and everyone connected with him loved him whether at club or international level. When we pulled on the red shirt and played for Wales, we also played for him. He was one of the game's great motivators in the dressing room before a game and during the interval. He had a fantastic World Cup, taking us to within a goal of beating the eventual winners, Brazil, with a squad scarcely big enough to do the job.

He also did a marvellous job at Old Trafford. I think it suited him to be second in command, leaving the big man to look after the press and the board of directors while he looked after the players.

Second on my list is Major Buckley, a good man with a big heart, and the third comes from among my managers and coaches at Juventus.

Carlo Parola, the former Juventus player who became their manager, wasn't there for long but during that short time we became very friendly. It was good to be friendly with the coach because you knew you would be in the team, but seriously, while he was there we became very close and would talk about football all the time. A centre-half good enough to be picked for the Rest of Europe and for Italy, Parola was different, a good talker who knew everything there was to know about football. Although he had played centre-half, he was very attack minded. He thought we were the best team in Italy and therefore we should attack. It suited me, as a forward. There could be nothing worse in Italy than being a centre-forward with a defensive team, with the catenaccio defences. We could play that way if we wanted to, especially away to AC Milan or Torino, but they rarely pulled me back to defend. The standard at Juventus was higher than in England, the weather was better, but football is the same the world over.

Of the other coaches at Juventus, Ljubisa Brocic impressed me hugely. He preceded Parola and was there when I joined. I used to look up to him in every sense. He was tall with grey hair and we were in awe of the man. He was a great coach. Then there was Renato Cesarini, the Argentinian, Sivori's mate. He was technical director with Parola; he couldn't coach but told good stories. He was half the size of Brocic and we looked down on him in every sense.

It wasn't hard to coach Juventus because we had all the best players, but the Swede Gunnar Gren, who arrived when Cesarini left and took over from Parola, was an unusual appointment because football in Sweden was amateur. For him to come through Italian football and make an impact as a coach was remarkable. Like most Swedes, he was a gentle person but hard when he had to be. He was very good to me. He would take you to one side and have a chat if it was going wrong, but he was equally quick to tell you when things were going right.

Gren was experienced in the ways and wiles of Italian football, having served his time with Milan. When he played with compatriots Gunnar Nordahl and Nils Liedholm, they were known throughout the world of football as the 'Gre-No-Li Trio'. They won the Olympic Gold medal for football at Wembley in 1948 and were third in the World Cup in 1950. Prematurely bald, Gren was nicknamed 'The Professor'. He commanded total respect. He was an excellent coach and tactician, and good with the players, knowing how to talk to them and how to treat them.

He was also in favour of attacking football with two men down the flanks – my sort of man. I am sure it would have been a very different story if I had gone to a team that played catenaccio, and I'd had to forage on my own up front. It would not have suited me at all and I don't know if I could have seen it out under those circumstances.

We had a solid team that could compete with any one; we were awesome sometimes, yet how strange that it rarely worked in Europe. I am afraid we were 'homers'; away from home, we just gave it up. That wasn't Gren's fault; it was the same under all our managers, and he takes my vote behind Jimmy Murphy and the Major.

Of the British players I played against while I was at Leeds United, one of my favourites, and a good friend, was Tommy Taylor of Manchester United and England. The first time I met Tommy was in the juniors when he played for Barnsley and I played for Leeds; I was just settling in at centre-half and I played against him. Two big blokes, we had a terrific tussle and became firm friends. At eighteen, we went into the army together and played in the same side with another bustling centre-forward, Bobby Smith of Spurs and England fame. I was delighted we had two such talented centre-forwards because it meant I could play at centre-half, a much easier proposition, but you can imagine we had quite a good side, which I think frightened a few teams before the referee even started a game.

Tommy was a real handful to mark, and a natural finisher. He was also a hard bloke and gave me a good kicking in that first meeting when we were kids. I took it with a smile and that's probably why we became very good friends. There was a great deal of respect between us.

Another centre-forward who would give you a tough time was the great Nat Lofthouse, the Lion of Vienna. I don't think I got to sleep the night before I played against him the first time. I tossed and turned trying to work out how I could counteract him. I was so tired by the time of the kick-off, I was almost hanging on to his shirt tails.

He was an outstanding international striker and I was quaking at the prospect of playing against someone so good. He always played at the same intense level, never holding anything back whatever the game, whether it was for his club or his country. He was another hard player and he wasn't averse to giving the goalkeeper a whack or two, never mind the centre-half.

In those days, a lot of football fans went to games specifically to watch these bustling, hard, centre-forwards, players such as Trevor Ford, Bobby Smith and Nat Lofthouse, and they liked to see them put pressure on the goalkeeper now and again to keep them honest. As long as the keeper had his feet on the floor there was no problem, and if he flew into the back of the net still holding the ball, so much the better. That was allowed. The game was a lot more physical then, and as long as it was shoulder to shoulder that was all right. The game was different in those days. The problems came when the bad boys took advantage, leaving the foot in or leading with the elbow.

A centre-forward of a different type was Brian Clough. I liked him because he was a natural goalscorer. I also liked him as a person; he was charming and pleasant but I saw the other side of him with people he did not like. His career was cut short by injury but his loss as a player was football's gain as he developed into a great manager, who was, sadly, largely ignored by England. We remained friends and it was nice of him to invite me along to Derby's European Cup-tie against Juventus in Turin in 1973 – I had to keep a straight face as my old club won.

I knew Billy Wright pretty well. One of Major Buckley's discoveries at Wolves, he was a very difficult centre-half to play against despite being around six inches shorter than me. For me, he was the backbone of the England side at the time. He started off at wing-half and then moved to his best position at centre-half. He wasn't very tall but he was very strong. He was called 'push-push' because he would put both hands in the middle of your back at corners or free kicks, and he wasn't shy about giving your shirt a tug when necessary – but he was another who could play.

He was in a very good Wolves side at the time, a quality player in a quality team that included Dennis Wilshaw, Ron Flowers, Jesse Pye and Jimmy Mullen. They were a fine side and, with a lot of foresight, they pioneered bringing continental football to Britain by inviting European sides to Molineux.

The Spurs and Northern Ireland captain Danny Blanchflower was another quality player, and a lovely lad – even though he was Irish, as I used to tell him! He had the ability to run games in the way he wanted them to go. He was the guiding influence behind the great push and run Spurs side. He was so consistent and his distribution was superb. All of us had our good games and our bad games, but Danny seemed to play at a certain level all the time. I admired him for that.

Another centre-half I admired and respected was the huge Scot, George Young. He was a fine player, and one of the few I had to look up to. He was solidly built as well, and if you ran into him you knew about it as he was very tough.

When you think of it, every professional is earning a living from football; they all have their responsibilities, wives and families, mortgages, and it is not right that someone should deliberately try to injure a fellow professional. In what other profession can that happen, apart from boxing and the other contact sports, where the combatants start on an even footing, knowing the rules of the game. Where in the laws of football does it permit one player to kick another, use an elbow, go over the top or throw a punch? Nowhere.

Some players would take liberties because of the licence allowed them by referees. Everyone knew who the bad ones were, but you had to accept it because it was all part of the game. I knew who was going to kick me and, while I would not kick them back, I would use my body strength against them; and if I hit someone, he remembered it for the next time. Shoulder to shoulder, yes – but no kicking and no elbows. If I did not do it, they would just carry on kicking me and take advantage, not allowing me to play.

The worst place, of course, was Italy. That was one of the great drawbacks. I experienced things there that I had never come across in England – spitting, treading on insteps, treading on your toes while you were waiting to jump for a corner or a free kick. A little fellow would stand on your feet and you wouldn't get off the ground.

Every team in those days had their hard man who would threaten and intimidate. For example, at Leeds we had a right-back, Jimmy Dunn, a Scots lad who wouldn't let anyone past him – maybe once, but never again. He would quietly tell them that the ball might go past him but they wouldn't. Sometimes these threats were enough – after all, the game can be won and lost in the mind as well as on the pitch. We had another full-back, Jimmy Milburn, who we used to say would have kicked his own mother to stop her scoring, he was that tough. There was the Irishman Jim McCabe, a right-half who used to just stand on people. They couldn't move. He was a good player but he didn't like people getting the better of him. And that was just Leeds United!

Every team had one or two who would carry it too far, especially the guy who would leave his foot over the ball. In those days, the boots were like weapons; the studs were leather with nails. Major Buckley used to tell us on a frosty day to put a piece of cardboard on the bottom of the stud for the referee to see and clear for play. Then when we went on to the pitch, we clattered down the concrete tunnel so that the cardboard would fall off and the leather would wear down, exposing the ends of the nails. It wasn't so much a threat to the opposition, more a way of ensuring a good grip on an icy pitch – the Major didn't promote dirty play – but you can imagine what sort of weapon those studs were in the wrong hands – or should I say on the wrong feet.

For Wales, Jimmy Murphy was totally different. He would say to his team, 'If they kick you – kick them back!' But he accepted that I would not be kicking them back, then or ever. He would talk to us individually and as a team, but he never asked me to be dirty or throw my weight around.

It was the same in Italy. The Juventus coaches and the chairman knew what I thought of dirty play and knew I would rather not bother to play than get up to the underhand tricks that were so popular there. One nickname I never did mind was Gentleman John.

CHAPTER SIXTEEN

Life after football – and prison

I tried my hand at all sorts of things after I finished in football, and I wasn't very successful in any of them. I had opened a sportswear shop in Cardiff in 1972 but it didn't work out, despite the fact I added a sauna and a chiropodist, knowing how important these facilities are to sports people. Within a year or so, I had to close it down, having lost almost £10,000.

I was still with Peggy and the children. Twice divorce had threatened but we had managed to patch it up when we returned home to Britain to stay. While I was at Merthyr, we were living in Swansea but we eventually moved back to Cardiff and then back to Leeds. I invested £10,000 in buying the tenancy of a nice little pub called the New Inn in Churwell near my beloved Elland Road, probably no more than a mile away, halfway up to Morley. People passed us on the way to the ground and when they found out I was there, lots of them would pop in. For a while, the pub did very good business, attracting Leeds fans on matchdays, both before and after the kick-off. Even on other days, it was incredibly hectic there.

My old friend Harold Williams helped me to secure the place. He had a pub of his own, and he and his wife Ada used to get me behind the bar to teach me the business. It was a hard job – but not for me. I was the old type of landlord who spent a lot of time talking to the customers. If you don't enjoy that, there is no point in doing it. Most of the time I had my stool on the customers' side of the bar; someone else served the drinks while I talked football.

I always said I would continue to play football for as long as my legs could carry me because I loved the game so much, and I was quite happy to turn out at the Throstle Nest at Pudsey, not far from Leeds. It was a bit windswept and spartan, but I loved playing which I did well into the second half of my forties, along with little Bobby Collins, who loved the game as much as I did.

So as not to look too daft, a group of us old players used to gather regularly to raise money for the local hospital, sometimes it was as little as £100 but at other times it could be several hundred and each artificial kidney machine cost £4,000 – so we had to keep playing, didn't we?

They were great little matches and each of the old Leeds players would take it in turns to invite a side to play us. Bobby Collins brought a team from Scotland, George Meek, by then a toolmaker, brought a team with him from Walsall in the West Midlands, and I persuaded some of the old lads from Italy to turn out for me – or rather against me. Colombo, of course, answered the call and helped me put a team together, mixed with a few younger players to give the game a bit of an edge. I loved it.

We played almost every Sunday and I took a team to Italy and even to Russia to play. Apart from Bobby Collins, George Meek and me, we had Jack Charlton, Peter Lorimer, Alan Williams, Eric

Kershaw and Keith Ripley. It was a good bunch of guys and we enjoyed a game and a drink. Some of the boys trained a couple of days a week so that they could still look good, but what with the cigarettes and the whisky and lemonade, a sprint of ten yards for me was followed by a rest of twenty minutes.

Leeds United looked after me very well. They gave me a seat in the stand and everyone would talk to me. It didn't always work that way. When I was in Cardiff, they threw a benefit dinner for me but had to cancel it because of lack of support. That was depressing but I was philosophical about it. There was no reason for many of the supporters to remember who I was. Strangely, in later years, more and more people seemed to know who I was.

In seven years in Cardiff, I was invited to just one sports dinner. I suppose when you are just at the end of your career, you are brushed to one side, a has-been, but after a few years you start to become something of a legend and people want to know you again. You have to take it as it comes. You drift out and then you drift back in again. Nostalgia is suddenly big business.

After a couple of years in the pub, Peggy decided to leave. There had been difficulties in our marriage before now, but she felt that I was spending all my time at the pub, and that she hardly saw me at all now. So, after twenty-five years of marriage, she left me – it was one of the saddest moments of my life, but in truth we just did not get on with each other any more. It cost me a great deal of money, too. When I had my first £5,000 in the bank I naively thought I was made for life, but I did not account for inflation or the problems of my own making, and I did not know that Peggy was going to take a lot with her when she left.

It was always hard on her. I immediately took to everything in Italy, including the language. She didn't, and I can see it must have been difficult, stuck in another country with no close family or friends and only three very young children to keep her company.

My son Melvyn and his girlfriend Janet both helped me in the pub. Two of my other sons, Terry and Peter, had stayed in Cardiff. Terry, the eldest, was a schoolteacher and a rugby player. He had played at the top level for Cardiff and then went into coaching. He was doing all right and it would have been silly for him to contemplate moving. Peter eventually opened a take-away pizza place in Cardiff with his friend Adrian. Happily, it was very successful and they made a useful profit when it was sold a few years back. David, the youngest, stayed with Peggy, but I still managed to see quite a lot of him.

In Swansea, I had left my eldest sister Maureen, the first of us to pass away, my sister Avril, who now lives in Marbella, Mel and the youngest, Malcolm, who still lives there. Mel still refers to me as 'The King'. He has never shown any animosity or jealousy towards me, even though I once turned down the chance to sign him and took his place at Cardiff! He has no need to be jealous. He enjoyed a splendid career, especially with Arsenal and Wales, and a wonderful World Cup in Sweden.

One of the best things to happen to me was meeting Glenda in 1978. I had been running the pub for three years and it was not long after the divorce proceedings had been completed. Glenda came in for lunch with a friend who knew one or two of the former Leeds United players who regularly used the place. Although Glenda knew I was a former Leeds player, she didn't have that much interest; it was only because her brother Barry was such a big fan, and apparently admired me, that she knew anything about my past at all. That day I happened to be behind the bar rather than in my usual place on the stool in the corner, and when it was quiet we chatted as I drank my half of Guinness. We liked each other from the off.

She was, and still is, a very attractive lady and I was delighted when she came into the pub a week later. Gradually our friendship grew to such an extent that she came with me to the charity matches on Sundays. Wherever we went to play, they would arrange a meal or a buffet and it became very sociable for all of us, a chance to chat about the old days and for the fans to rub shoulders with players they had watched from the terraces in the past. Each of us had a party piece and I used to do my rendition of 'Sixteen Tons'.

That was a good period and the pub made decent money. Of course, it was a long way removed from the smart King's restaurant in Turin and the burden that had saddled me with; it was also a good deal friendlier and down to earth – more my style. I certainly enjoyed the pub, especially the social side and it being such a short walk to Elland Road. I went to all the home games and still do, thanks to the generosity of the club and my free seat. Saturday was always a great day when there was a home match. The place buzzed and there was great excitement in the air as everyone looked forward to the game and then came back afterwards to talk about what they had seen. Isn't that half the fun of being a supporter, knowing more than the manager, referee and all the players put together and then swapping opinions after the game armed with all that hindsight?

About eighteen months after we met, Glenda moved in with me along with her two sons, seven-year-old Dean and five-year-old Gary. It was nice to have a family again, but it did not work out at the pub. Melvyn and Janet moved into a pub of their own and Glenda did not particularly like working at the New Inn because she felt she was following Peggy, whom most of the customers remembered. I could understand her attitude. Apart from the ghosts of my previous marriage, she also thought there were too many hangers-on and she desperately wanted to get me away because I was getting a bit too involved with the drinking schools and the after-hours gambling.

Like all businesses, trade came and went as other places captured the imagination or offered a better deal to the fans and we left when the business started to go down. The chance came when the lease for the Gomersal Park Hotel came on the market. The hotel had stood empty for eighteen months when we took it over and, consequently, it needed some work doing to it; but it was a beautiful old house set in seven acres with ten bedrooms, and the owner had refurbished it completely.

We took the lease in 1983 and stayed there until December 1986. Neither of us will ever forget the first night we opened. I asked Glenda if she thought anyone would ever come because we were tucked out of sight of the road and it had no reputation as a hotel or a bar. Many years before, it had been a nursing home, then an unsuccessful hotel, which was why it had stood empty for so long.

However, it was a superb place and some lovely people stayed with us. We had a number of regulars including a man named Michael from Nottingham who worked in Cleckheaton. He stayed for a year. Alex, from Scotland, stayed with us for a long time, too. It became like an extended family.

We staged a lot of functions, especially weddings. We had a wedding virtually every Saturday of the year and did them very well. I used to get all the praise for how splendid they were but the truth was I would go to the football while Glenda did all the work. I would do the bar before the game and help afterwards, chatting and serving drinks, but of course, it was all down to Glenda while I took the credit.

However, problems began to grow with spiralling costs, and we had decided to move on when another opportunity cropped up. In 1986, we were invited to the centenary celebrations of Pontofola d'oro in Ascoli, the company that made my football boots in Italy. They were fantastic, lightweight boots, more like slippers than football boots. They presented me with a magnificent silver football.

Inside the ball was the company's emblem set on a silver square – six little ships in gold with a ruby set in each.

It was while I was there that I met Frank, an agent for a company in Canada. He asked if I would be interested in becoming Director of Football for a team called Hamilton Steelers in Stoney Creek, a small town just outside Toronto. I knew by then that our days at the hotel were numbered, so I told him I would be interested, and it was immediately arranged for me to travel to Canada for a week to meet the team owner, Mario, to talk about the appointment. He was very keen for me to join the club.

Both Glenda and I liked the idea, and the prospect of a change, and in March 1987, we travelled to Canada on a six-month contract. We had a wonderful time. Mario provided everything he had promised and we made many friends. The team were mainly of Italian origin and, of course, I got on well with them, speaking the language and knowing the Italian mentality. They did well and we travelled all over Canada. My old captain Boniperti had some friends in Toronto, hairdressers, and, in typical fashion, he got in touch with them and asked them to look after us. They were very kind and we spent a lot of time with them in Toronto. Stanley Matthews was in Canada at the same time, in the nearby town of Hamilton, and we saw a lot of him and his wife.

The only drawback was that Mario, like a good many chairmen around the world, wanted total control and told me what he wanted doing with the team rather than letting me have my head. The season finished in September and because of the interference and because Glenda's boys were unsettled, we decided to call it a day while everyone was still friends, and returned home.

We tried several other business ventures but nothing seemed to go right. I might have been a decent footballer, but I'm afraid that my judgement in business left something to be desired. Money had, and still has, little meaning for me. The problem is that it does for other people, and in March 1988 it all came home to roost when I was thrown into prison in Huddersfield for bad debts. It was the darkest moment of my life.

It wasn't the first time I had been in trouble. To my shame, I had been fined £25 in 1976 for handling leather jackets that, without my knowledge, turned out to have been stolen. I was naive and learned my lesson. The most depressing moment in my life came not because I had sold anything or stolen anything; it was simply that I had run out of money and could not pay my taxes. I owed the local council £943 in back rates on the hotel, and I found myself paying the penalty as the door clanged shut on me. It was the ultimate shame, absolute humiliation.

Three lady magistrates in Huddersfield sent me down. I told them I had been promised a testimonial by my friends at Leeds and this would help me pay off my debts. I am not sure they understood what I was talking about; football and testimonials were as foreign to them as I was and I was sent away for an incredible sixty days. Glenda and I were planning to get married in the April, just a few weeks later. What a wedding present I had presented my wife to be!

I had raised a lot for charity but I was not going to beg it for myself and I was prepared to do my time. I had never felt so low or so embarrassed. It was a long fall from grace from my days in Italy where I hardly had to carry a hundred lire note in my pocket because no one would let me pay for anything. I was on the scrapheap in a big way but I was determined to fight my way back, if not for myself, for Glenda, who had backed me and supported me all along.

But it was Glenda who had to go out looking for the money that would release me from my prison cell. It took her five hours to raise that amount, which she did by going to Leeds chairman Leslie Silver.

She took the money straight round to the magistrates' court, paid the bill and I was released.

We were married on 23 April and I was broke. We were living on £72 a week social security and supporting Dean, then sixteen, and Gary, fourteen, in a semi-detached house in Birkenshaw near Bradford, where we still live to this day.

That wasn't all that was done by Leeds to help me. I was given a joint testimonial, with Bobby Collins, that same month. Among those we approached to play were Michel Platini, Gaetono Scirea, Kenny Dalglish, Ian Rush, David Batty and John Sheridan. Benito Boldi, my old Juventus colleague, helped contact the players in Italy, and when they came for the game, Scirea, the Juve defender who had won the World Cup in 1982, landed at Leeds Bradford airport in his private plane, bringing with him Platini and Benito. Bernard Manning, a friend of mine, provided a Rolls Royce to collect them from the airport and take them to the game. I was delighted with the crowd of 10,000 that attended, which was good for that time, but imagine what sort of attendance that line-up would attract today.

I was so lucky to have Glenda at my side, and how I wished she could have enjoyed my great days in Turin when money was no problem. Poverty? Prison? Bad debts? Nothing could have been further from my mind when I was living in that beautiful apartment overlooking Turin, spending summer days on the Mediterranean coast in a holiday home, and earning an absolute fortune. Perhaps I should have left the money in the bank instead of investing it in the restaurant. On my return to England, I had just £6,000 in the bank and when I packed in the game, instead of being able to retire, there was nothing left.

If I had been born thirty years later, I would have been worth a million at least. But what is the point of worrying about what might have been? I was not complaining then and I am not complaining now. That's just how life goes.

I was never a businessman – always a footballer. It was all I had known from the time I left school in Swansea at the age of fourteen. I was used to having a drink or three with my friends, watching every game at Elland Road and expecting everything to work out, just as it had done in the past.

I have to hold up my hands and take the responsibility. Glenda tried to tell me but the lure of a football match and some good company afterwards always held sway. I discovered that, just as it was when I was a well-paid footballer, I had plenty of friends when I invited people back to the bar and let them help themselves.

I am not bitter and I am not blaming them. It was, as it had always been, down to me. It was my own fault and while it eventually brought me to my knees, I have to admit that I enjoyed my life, a drink and a packet of cigarettes and, indeed, I still do! And one of the best things to come out of that black, bleak time was when the Agnelli family sent someone over to Leeds to offer me a job. That was special.

CHAPTER SEVENTEEN

Later days

Glenda and I had gone down to Swansea to visit my family in April 1989 and were staying at my brother Malcolm's for the weekend when we received the call that everyone dreads. The phone rang in the early hours, and Malcolm heard from the policeman that there'd been a fire in our house that had started in the bedroom. He came up to tell us the news; the police were waiting to talk to us. Glenda raced downstairs for we'd left her sons, eighteen-year-old Dean and Gary, sixteen, to look after the place, and she was terrified that they might have been hurt. Our first concern was with them, and it was such a relief to hear they were fine, but the damage was enormous. The fire had taken the top off our roof, and the roof of our next door neighbours.

What had happened was this. Dean had been ill for most of the week with tonsillitis and had decided to use our bed while we were away because it had an electric blanket and he had been told to keep himself warm while he recovered. Dean switched on the blanket and went downstairs to make a hot drink while it warmed up, but when he came back up he found the blankets were smouldering. He quickly realised what it was and scooped up all the bedding and threw it out of the window, leaving the window open to help clear the smoke. Unfortunately, he did not realise the mattress had caught fire as well as the bedding. The rush of air from the open windows rekindled the flames, and it was fully alight before the boys realised what had happened. They immediately rang the fire brigade and ran next door to tell the neighbours.

We set off immediately for home, the four-hour drive seeming to take an eternity. Neither of us could believe the state of the house when we arrived there. It was devastated, and so were the boys, especially Dean who felt responsible. We were sorry for him, and for our neighbours, Mr and Mrs Marshall, who still live next door to us, for all the inconvenience. They harboured no ill will against us for all the trouble we had caused them. The most important thing to us was that the boys had not been hurt in the accident.

It took us four months for the builders to put the house back together so it was habitable, as only the lounge and dining room had been left largely unscathed. Fortunately, we were well insured, so we did not suffer financially. However, I kept all my mementoes and memorabilia in the loft, and they were all lost, including the fabulous silver football commemorating the centenary of Pontofola d'oro. Everything just melted.

The company ceased trading after their centenary in 1986, but started up again in 2001. We were invited to the launch of the new company and I was presented with a magnificent golden boot, and that one, I'm happy to say, is still around.

Fortunately, over the years I had given away all my international caps and shirts for charity, mainly through the former Leeds players who did so much for the community. At least all the rest of my history exists somewhere. In various houses, attics, some maybe in glass cases, there are my international caps, the blood red shirts of Wales and the zebra stripes of Juventus, as well as those I swapped.

But I don't need trinkets to know what I have done. I don't need the photographs, scrapbooks and the rest of the stuff that was consumed in the fire to remind me – I still have my memories. I don't keep them in my head; I keep them in my heart. That is where they belong.

Like most families, we have had a few ups and downs, not just confined to my battered old body. Glenda had a health scare with bowel cancer ten years ago, the same thing her father had and his brother, too. Fortunately, because of a good doctor, it was caught early and successfully treated.

I am amazed at the huge strides that have been made in coping with and curing cancer. You only have to look at Sir Bobby Robson, who has come through two serious bouts of the illness and is still managing at the highest level even though he is in his seventies.

Like Bobby, who was persuaded to go for a check-up by his wife, it was Glenda who pushed me to the doctors. If she had not, I would not be here now to tell the story. It was a matter of being aware and being on the ball and then doing something about it. The next thing is for the doctor to be on the ball and Dr Miller certainly was.

My body was rebelling after all the years of hard work I had subjected it to, not to mention the drinks and the cigarettes. The first sign came in 1993 when, at a dinner in York, I suddenly felt very ill. I was fortunate that there was a doctor present as a guest at the dinner and he immediately called for an ambulance. I was whisked off to York General Hospital where it was discovered that I had suffered a heart attack. I was kept in intensive care for some time, and remained in hospital for about a week until they let me go home. Touch wood, I have had no problems with my heart since then, but I guess I owe a lot to the doctor who acted so quickly that night.

Alzheimer's began a few years ago but before that I was diagnosed with blood cancer. In 1997 I had a tumour removed from my bladder but it was malignant and the cancer continued to spread. I underwent twenty radiotherapy treatments during the following year, but that didn't put a stop to it. So a year later, the doctors were forced into even more drastic action, giving me half a dozen chemotherapy treatments direct into my bladder. It gave me eighteen months' remission but the cancer returned a while back. I went back in for some more chemotherapy in September 2001, just before my seventieth birthday. I was due to have another six treatments, but I suffered really bad reactions to the first two, so they stopped it and I went back into hospital. Fortunately, it seemed to have been enough and it has now been twenty months since the last attack. I feel all right at the moment but who knows what the future may hold, as the doctor tells me it could return at any time. I go into hospital every three to six months for a check-up and a biopsy.

In contrast, I think I have coped well with the Alzheimer's which, of course, becomes progressively worse. It is a bit of a pest but I don't worry about it. If I sing the same song again at the bar, what does it matter? People just have to put up with it. I take no notice and don't expect other people to. I am not concerned about it; in fact, I am not concerned about anything. I just live my life, smiling at everyone. Glenda keeps an eye on things and makes sure that I don't make too much of a fool of myself.

Happily, it has not affected my long-term memory yet and, thankfully, I have not lost my grip of the Italian language, which means I can converse whenever I return to my second home, where

I am always made so welcome. I still retain the great memories of my football life and, as it is the short-term memory that suffers, I can forget about the cancer and the other bad things that have happened. It can be very convenient.

I have been smoking since I was twenty, when it was a fashion accessory, and I suppose I get through about twenty a day. I have tried to quit but I haven't the willpower. Anyway, it's too late to start worrying about it now.

Glenda says I am so laid back and it is probably a good job because if I weren't, there would be many more problems. I owe a lot to Glenda. I suppose I am lucky because wherever I have been and whatever I have done, I have always been looked after. My friends and family have been a great comfort.

For every unpleasant thing that has happened to me, there seems to be two or three happy experiences to balance the books. Nostalgia seems to be a growing industry these days and there is little doubt I have benefited from it. When I walked away from the game, I thought my memories were all that was left of the years I enjoyed so much, kicking a football around the fields of the world, but it seems the older I get, the more popular I become and, indeed, I seem to be a better player with each passing year.

There are great things happening year by year and it is nice so many people remember me. It was a great joy when, recently, I was voted the Greatest Ever Foreign Player in Serie A. To be voted above Diego Maradona, Michel Platini, Zinedine Zidane and Marco van Basten, to name just a few, was remarkable, considering so few would have seen me perform live. Perhaps it is an advantage not to be seen too much on television.

To be picked on top when so many great players have played in Italy before and since is a humbling experience, and flattering, because every football fan in Italy knows the history of the game back to front. It is so typical of those who follow football in Italy. It was just the same when I was there and they were all talking about the great players of the twenties as though they had seen them play the week before. The tifosi have a marvellous feel for the game and that made the award even more special. I have even been inducted into the Azzurri Hall of Fame in Florence – at the time, I was the only non-Italian represented.

One of the reasons the Italian people remembered me so well was that one of my goals, a flying header against Milan in the San Siro Stadium, was used in the opening sequence of the 'Sunday Football Show' on television for twenty years. It was a good job they didn't show one of my misses in front of an open goal or I would have come bottom of the list.

Goals are central to the debate over whether I was a better centre-forward than centre-half. All I can say is that I always felt like a centre-half. Whether I liked centre-forward better depended upon whether I was scoring goals. If you are on the target, there is no position to touch it; if you are not, I would sooner be a centre-half where the spotlight doesn't dazzle nearly so much. It is all rather mercurial. If I went for three or four games without scoring, I would feel as though the world was falling in on top of me. Then I'd score the only goal in a crucial 1–0 win and be back on top of the world again. One thing I do know is that playing centre-forward is the most glamorous position in the game – always has been and always will be.

My best goal? It was probably the header I scored against Fiorentina in the Copa Italia. We were losing 2–1 at the time and I went for a cross, cushioned the ball on my forehead and when goalkeeper Sarti came off his line I nodded it over his head like a circus seal with a beach ball. We went on to win 3–2.

I would have loved to stay at centre-half but I was a professional footballer. I played because I loved it but I also played because I was paid for it. Admittedly, I would have played if no pay packet had been attached, but since there was, I played where I was told.

I sometimes ask myself if I had stayed as a centre-half, would all this fuss and glory have followed? I doubt it because the lifeblood of the game are the goals scored, not the goals saved. Even when I played the charity games, long after hanging up my boots, the fans preferred to see me playing up front. I had to stop playing charity matches when I suffered a heart attack.

Talking of hearts, mine is divided into three – Wales, Leeds and Italy. Maybe the Italians are more nostalgic or romantic but even the kids over there know who I am and can recite my exploits. When I go back I am still the King. I am a bigger hero in Italy than I am in Wales – maybe because Wales is a rugby union nation – but I am immensely proud to be Welsh. When I returned to Leeds, I could have eaten out every night if I had accepted the invitations; as for Italy, I could have had lunch and dinner every day in Turin.

In the last few years, when I should have been putting my feet up, I have had a number of honours bestowed on me, all of which make me very proud, if a little embarrassed.

Perhaps the best was being made a Commander of the British Empire in the Queen's Birthday Honours list in 2001. A friend of ours, Geoff Wine, an accountant in Leeds, instigated the idea. He made his initial suggestion to Glenda who wrote five letters to various people. She forgot all about it until two or three years later when eight English and Welsh Members of Parliament tabled a motion in Westminster calling for my achievements to be recognised. They must have had good memories!

It was a lovely surprise when the letter dropped through my letterbox from the Queen at Buckingham Palace. I was sixty-nine years of age and still getting awards for what I did when I was a fit young man. I feel doubly proud as a Welshman – it is an award for Wales.

Journalist John Lloyd, who worked for the *Daily Express*, was in touch as soon as he heard about the honour and he made the event special by arranging for us to go to London for the weekend; he organised a show and a buffet afterwards. It was a really nice gesture and I am delighted John keeps in touch.

My home town of Swansea granted me the Freedom of the City in 2002. The ceremony took place on Monday, 4 March in Branwn Hall, a massive banqueting hall in the city, hung with famous tapestries. It was a full house for the event; I think some 700 people were present, including my old friends Kenneth Wolstenholme, who sadly died not long after and the brilliant Welsh comedian Stan Stennett, who lived just up the road from me, plus lots of the old players with whom I had played for club and country. My sister came from Spain and all my family were there.

We set off from the Lord Mayor's office, meeting people on the way, and when we got there, I walked down the room to a fanfare. The Welsh Choir was singing at the Variety Club dinner in Cardiff. Glenda and I walked in to a trumpet fanfare. When we reached the table, the choir sang 'Will You Come Home Again to Wales'. It was beautiful, very touching, and I wasn't sure whether it was a request or a demand. It was a super evening, made even better because the current Welsh team were there and came up on stage; they had a game in Cardiff that week. Former Leeds player Gary Speed, whom I had watched regularly at Elland Road, came straight up to me and I appreciated his interest and told him how delighted I was to see him do so well at Newcastle.

Before that, in April 2002, I received a Variety Club award from former Leeds captain and manager Terry Yorath, a fellow Welshman in Leeds. Things like fires and personal illnesses pale in comparison with what Terry has had to come through, losing his son Daniel, a fit, apparently healthy young man in the prime of his life. Terry runs a golf day every year to help raise money for a hospice. I used to go regularly.

For a lad who left school at fourteen, I was honoured to be given an Honorary Doctorate from Leeds Metropolitan University, and also an honorary degree from the University of Wales in Swansea. And I was truly thrilled when I was inducted into the Welsh Sports Hall of Fame in March 2001. There were a lot of really top performers in the running and I never expected to be nominated along with Rush, rugby's Mervyn Davies, swimmer Martyn Woodroffe, Nancy and Roy Evans from table tennis and David Winters from disabled sport.

I was also voted the Greatest Welsh Footballer of All Time, just ahead of another former Juventus player, Ian Rush. The award in Italy was fabulous but it is special when you are recognised at home. It came from my countrymen and I could not have been prouder. It was a massive honour, particularly when I looked at the list from which my name had been selected – Ryan Giggs, Trevor Ford, Mike England, Mark Hughes, Cliff Jones, Jack Kelsey, Roy Paul, John Toshack and Kevin Ratcliffe, to name just a few.

The awards and receptions in London, Swansea, Cardiff, Leeds, Florence and Turin were lovely, made extra special by seeing my old friends there. I feel lucky and happy to have friends in three countries.

I enjoy meeting former players. That's football; it's like a brotherhood. There aren't many who actually make it out of all of those who aspire to a professional career. That's why I enjoy events such as the Wales v. Germany friendly at the Millennium Stadium on Tuesday, 14 May 2002 when, during the interval, the remaining members of the 1958 squad were honoured. There have been similar events in Leeds and Cardiff, while in Turin, the Juventus crowd gave me a standing ovation when I was paraded around the pitch before their game against Atalanta. I, in turn, applaud them and all the fans and the clubs who have given me such a wonderful life. It has been unbelievable.

I have no regrets. I am not a tax exile nor do I have villas on the Amalfi coast, but I have Glenda, our little semi-detached house in Birkenshaw and memories, which will never go away because it seems these days, everyone wants to talk about the past. Much of it was good and only a small portion bad – court, prison, being unemployed when I left Swansea. Now that was not a nice feeling; only someone who has been unemployed after a financially and mentally rewarding career can understand fully how I felt. I tried to keep my problems to myself because people have their own worries and I do not want to burden them with mine.

I still enjoy my visits to Elland Road and the odd trip to Turin, but I have to say I do not see a lot of fun in today's game. There's too much emphasis on money, and players too often hold their clubs to ransom. Players deserve to be well paid, certainly paid properly to reflect the money that comes in from television, but not to the extent that they bankrupt the club that is employing them. The system, I am afraid, has got out of proportion, and one or two big clubs will go bust.

I earned good money in Italy and very little in Merthyr. It did not matter to me – I was playing because I wanted to play. Money can be a big distraction and affect a player's form. That is not guesswork – that is a fact of life. Don't kill the golden goose!

As for me, I will never lose my passion for the game. I will always love it. If I could still play, I would do so . . . for nothing . . . in the park.

Finally, some people despised me for not using my weight, and sometimes I think I would have been a better player with a bit of devil. When I look back on the players who gave me a bashing, I kind of regret not bashing them back; but it is nice to know I have gone through a long career without deliberately hurting anyone.

Career statistics

compiled by Jack Rollin

WILLIAM JOHN CHARLES

Born Swansea 27 December 1931. League debut for Leeds United 23 April 1949 v. Blackburn Rovers. Wales debut 8 March 1950 v. Northern Ireland, aged 18 years 71 days. Second Division runners-up 1956. Transferred to Juventus April 1957 for £65,000. Italy Player of the Year 1958. Italian Serie A champions 1958, 1960 and 1961. Copa Italia winners 1959 and 1960. Transferred to Leeds United August 1962 for £53,000. Transferred to Roma November 1962 for £70,000. Transferred to Cardiff City August 1963 for £20,000. Welsh Cup winners 1964 and 1965. Joined Hereford United July 1966, becoming player-manager December 1967. Appointed player-manager Merthyr Tydfil January 1972. Swansea City youth coach 1974. Technical director Hamilton Steelers March 1987. Awarded CBE 2001.

Season	League Apps	League Goals	FA Cup Apps	FA Cup Goals	League Cup Apps	League Cup Goals	Euro Cups Apps	Euro Cups Goals	Internationals Apps	Internationals Goals
LEEDS UNITED										
1948–49	3	–	–	–	–	–	–	–	–	–
1949–50	42	1	5	–	–	–	–	–	1	–
1950–51	34	3	2	–	–	–	–	–	1	–
1951–52	18	–	5	–	–	–	–	–	–	–
1952–53	40	26	1	1	–	–	–	–	3	2
1953–54	39	42	2	1	–	–	–	–	4	3
1954–55	40	11	2	1	–	–	–	–	4	5
1955–56	41	29	1	0	–	–	–	–	4	–
1956–57	40	38	1	1	–	–	–	–	6	1
JUVENTUS										
1957–58	34	28	–	–	–	–	–	–	6	1
1958–59	29	19	–	–	–	–	2*	–	–	–
1959–60	34	23	–	–	–	–	–	–	1	1
1960–61	32	15	–	–	–	–	2*	–	–	–
1961–62	21	8	–	–	–	–	6*	–	4	1
LEEDS UNITED										
1962–63	11	3	–	–	–	–	–	–	1	1
ROMA										
1962–63	10	4	–	–	–	–	2#	1	–	–
CARDIFF CITY										
1963–64	33	11	1	–	1	–	–	–	1	–
1964–65	28	3	–	–	1	–	5+	–	2	–
1965–66	8	4	–	–	1	–	2+	–	–	–
Totals	537	268	20	4	3	0	19	1	38	15

* European Cup
# Fairs Cup
+ European Cup-Winners' Cup

ITALIAN LEAGUE
1962 v. Scottish League; Football League (2)

REPRESENTATIVE
1955 Great Britain v. Rest of Europe

WALES INTERNATIONALS (AND GOALS)

1950 v. Northern Ireland; 1951 v. Switzerland; 1953 v. Northern Ireland (2), France, Yugoslavia, England, Scotland (2); 1954 v. Northern Ireland (1), Austria, Yugoslavia, Scotland, England (2); 1955 v. Northern Ireland (3), England, Scotland, Austria; 1956 v. Northern Ireland, Scotland, England (1); 1957 v. Northern Ireland, Czechoslovakia, East Germany, Czechoslovakia; 1958 v. Israel, Israel, Hungary (1), Mexico, Sweden, Hungary; 1959 v. Scotland (1); 1961 v. England; 1962 v. Brazil, Brazil, Mexico (1), Scotland (1); 1963 v. Scotland; 1964 v. Scotland; 1965 v. USSR.

Index

Acknowledgements

John Charles and Bob Harris would like to thank Glenda Charles for all the hard work she has put into this book; Benito Boldi, for his enormous hospitality and friendship in Italy, and his son Stefano and his family; Bruno Garzena, Giampiero Boniperti and Umberto Colombo from that great Juve side; Paolo Barazzotto of ABC for his friendship in Biella; John's many friends at Leeds United, in Wales and Italy who helped make his life what it is; our agent Jonathan Harris; Ian Marshall, Lorraine Jerram, Caitlin Raynor and all the staff at Headline.